CONTENTS

WHERE THE SKY TOUCHED THE EARTH

Where the sky touched the earth

The Cosmological Landscapes
of the Southwest | DON LAGO

UNIVERSITY OF NEVADA PRESS | *Reno & Las Vegas*

University of Nevada Press | Reno, Nevada 89557 USA
www.unpress.nevada.edu
Copyright © 2017 by University of Nevada Press
All rights reserved

Cover design by Trudi Gershinov

Frontispiece photos: Kenneth C. Zirkel / istockphoto.com; Veronika By / shutterstock

Credits: *Alaska Quarterly Review*, "Storm Pattern" (Fall and Winter 2010).
Carbon Culture Review, "The Blood of the Martians" (2015).
Confrontation, "The Expanding Mesa" (Fall 2014).
Gettysburg Review, "Tree Rings" (Summer 2013) and "Rooted in the Sun" (Spring 2015).
North American Review, "Tranquility Base Here" (Winter 2015). An earlier, shorter version
    of "Tranquility Base Here" appeared in *Sky and Telescope* in February 2000.
Prairie Schooner, "Sandpaintings" (Fall 2012).
Weber: The Contemporary West, "Unidentified Mountainous Objects" (Spring–Summer 2014).

LIBRARY OF CONGRESS CATALOGING-IN-PUBLICATION DATA
Names: Lago, Don, 1956–
Title: Where the sky touched the Earth : the cosmological landscapes of the Southwest /
    Don Lago.
Description: Reno : University of Nevada Press, 2016. | Includes bibliographical references.
Identifiers: LCCN 2016035737 (print) | LCCN 2016042090 (ebook) |
    ISBN 978-1-943859-34-4 (pbk. : alk. paper) | ISBN 978-0-87417-474-8 (e-book)
Subjects: LCSH: Landscapes—Symbolic aspects—Southwestern States. | Earth analogs. |
    Landforms—Southwestern States. | Nature (Aesthetics) | Cosmology.
Classification: LCC QH76.5.S695 L34 2016 (print) | LCC QH76.5.S695 (ebook) |
    DDC 577.27—dc23 LC record available at https://lccn.loc.gov/2016035737

The paper used in this book meets the requirements of American National Standard
for Information Sciences—Permanence of Paper for Printed Library Materials, ANSI/NISO
Z39.48-1992 (R2002).

FIRST PRINTING

Manufactured in the United States of America

WHERE THE SKY TOUCHED THE EARTH

INTRODUCTION: THE ECLIPSE

OUT OF THE CYCLES OF THE COSMOS, out of the circling circles of fire and rock and gas and ice, out of the steady turnings of light into darkness into light, somewhere between the spinning atoms and the spinning galaxies, somewhere between the beginning and the end, the cosmos was disclosing a secret.

Hidden within the reliable turnings of the solar system and the comings of light through the days and seasons and years, there was a sliver of darkness, waiting for centuries to cut the sun apart. Hidden within "ellipse," requiring only a slight curve, was "eclipse." Out of egg-shaped orbits was hatched a very rare if thoroughly predictable mutation.

The moon crept across the sun, slowly, so slowly that at first nothing seemed to be happening; the sky did not seem to be dimming. Slowly, steadily, the midair sunset became evident. The moon covered a quarter of the sun, and the light and colors and shadows began changing. The moon covered half the sun, and the sky was noticeably darker, the ground no longer familiar ground. I looked at the unearthly tones of the earth, the subdued colors, the peculiar shadows.

I gazed not just at the ground but into it, a mile deep into the ground. I gazed into layers of rock nearly two billion years old, glowing with strange light and colors and shadows.

The eclipse would have been extraordinary anywhere, but it was even more extraordinary here, at a landscape already famous for its extraordinary light, colors, and shadows. I was watching the eclipse from the rim of the Grand Canyon. Every evening for more than a century people had gathered here to watch the eclipse called sunset that threw the canyon's always-unique light into even greater intensity. Now a crowd had come to watch a solar eclipse projected onto one of the most dramatic screens on Earth.

The moon became the ultimate cliff, a deranged horizon blocking the sun, melting the canyon's normally strong light and colors and shapes, absorbing its shadows into a far greater shadow, proclaiming the moon's longevity over the canyon's, for the moon had barely changed during the millions of years that Earth rock a mile deep had cracked apart and melted and flowed away to leave a Grand Canyon.

As the lunar shadow deepened, all the plants around me, the tallest trees and the agave, the sagebrush and the wildflowers, felt a loss, not the excitement humans were feeling but a loss of excitement, a slowing down of their lives, a rising hunger ancient and DNA rooted and undeniable, a hunger for light and for life. The moon was baffling them with a shadow greater than any cloud, stealing the food right out of their mouths, stealing the photo right out of synthesis. In billions of cells the swarming molecules were slowing, slowing, and the biological loom was shutting down. The moon had invaded a living world and clogged with moon dust the flow of energy out of leaves, the flow of air and water into plants, the zipping together of molecules, the dividing of cells, the growth of plants, the urgency of life. The green Earth, already so small in the cosmos, whimpered against the gray dust and the dark cold night, the dead cosmos.

Now the light that had been nurturing the life of Earth was falling onto a world of craters and rubble, lava and dust, seas without water and mountains without forests. The sunlight heated the dust and made its molecules vibrate a bit more, but the dust lacked the talent to do anything with this energy except bleed it back into space. The sunlight set the dust aglow, brilliant gray, but the moon had no botanical paintbrush to turn the light into a brighter and lasting landscape. The light metabolized only shadows behind boulders and craters; the only eyes that saw the sunlight were millions of empty sockets. The lifeblood of Earth spilled futilely onto a dead body.

Earth was once like this, only craters and rubble, lava and dust. The sunlight had only tickled the dust and translated itself into wind and later into ocean currents and rain clouds. The eclipses eclipsed only a rugged blindness and coaxed a few molecules to crystallize into snow.

Yet now the circles of the sun and Earth and moon were intersecting with another circle, from another kind of orbit. Somehow the flowings of sunlight and the circlings of the solar system had woven the exquisite order not only of leaves but of eyes that received the sunlight and gave it deeper order, turning seething into seeing, star into stare. The imperturbable solar-system heartbeat had become animal heartbeats that quickened to the power of the sky.

Over the aeons life became ever more connected with the cycles of the cosmos. With the sunrises life raised its leaves and its eyes; within the seasons life embedded its life cycles, its emergence, nesting, births, growth, and migrations, continental migrations that were, like the wind and surf and the moving continents themselves, another pulse of the wildly energetic Earth.

For a long time life didn't see the place of eclipses within the cosmic order but perceived them as disorder, perceived them with fear, eventually through human eyes perceived them as omens for empires and crises for the cosmos. Yet through human eyes, light-loving eyes saw that darkness, whether the darkness of eclipses or the darkness of a 13.7 billion-year-old expanding universe, was filled with order and creativity. Life raised out of darkness crude oblivious metals and shaped them into telescopes and spacecraft for seeking out the most secret, most distant, most infinitely small yet infinitely important elements of cosmic order.

I looked down into the canyon, its lunar starkness further magnified by the lens of the moon. The canyon too belonged to the cosmic cycles that carried the moon and the solar system. The same gravity that kept the moon spinning around Earth and kept Earth spinning around the sun had kept the Colorado River in orbit for millions of years, kept it dropping toward the center of Earth, kept it moving across the land and toward the sea, kept it digging into the land, kept thunderstorms falling and flash floods sweeping boulders into the river, kept the canyon growing deeper and wider. The canyon was the trackway of the sky itself, a furrow plowed out by the solar system, another ring of Saturn, another crater of the moon.

The moon was just another boulder, cresting white, in the Colorado River.

As the moon was hiding the sun it was bringing other things out of hiding. It was bringing to light the strangeness of the world, and the unity of humans with the world.

As the eclipse proceeded, the light and colors and shadows became steadily odder, less recognizable, less intense but also more intense. The eclipse revealed that even the Grand Canyon was stranger than humans had recognized, and when humans looked at one another they saw that their faces too were stranger than they normally recognized. This was not a trick of the light but a truth of the light, for the eclipse was translating into physical view the reality that had been there all along. Humans and all the life of Earth and cosmos had always been intensely odd, but somehow humans did not recognize this "in the ordinary light of day"; somehow they failed to notice anything odd about their existence, and it took a Grand Canyon or a grand stone rolling across the sun to rock them into a sense of wonder, into glimpsing their true, surrealistic identities.

I watched the changing shadows, both the giant cliff shadows within the canyon and the tiny flower shadows on the ground before me, and I noticed my own shadow fading, fading, blurring into the shadow of the moon, into the darkness of the cosmos. Human shadows usually seem so distinct, just like human identities, with sharp boundaries between people, between people and objects, between people and the cosmos, boundaries that define us as nothing but a boundary, nothing but what makes us different from the rest of the world. In the ordinary light of day humans like to define ourselves by the realm of our own activity, our own power. Yet the distinctness of shadows is only an illusion; shadows are an absence, our own eclipse of the light that gives life, our tiny interference with the omnipotent sun. Now I was watching myself merging into the night, going back into the night from which I had emerged every morning and at my birth and at the beginning of Earth; I was merging back into the night of which I had always been only a detachment all along, less a self than a cell of the cosmos. I watched the shadows draining from the walls of Plato's canyon and from my own mind.

The eclipse reached its maximum darkness, which would not be total, for this time the moon was a bit too far away to completely cover the sun. The moon became a dark circle surrounded by a thin ring of light, an annular eclipse.

The moon continued passing across the sun, reversing the eclipse process, returning the canyon to its normal appearances, returning life to its complacency, returning human faces to their disguises.

Yet there would be many people in the crowd who would not forget what they had witnessed, who would not entirely return to their normal sense of reality. They would remember that they lived on a planet turning in space, that Earth was connected with larger cycles, that the ground was a sliver of the sky. They would not be so likely to take sunlight and Earth life for granted. They would not entirely forget the strangeness of human faces.

Many in the crowd had not come here to see the eclipse, or even known about it. They had come to the Grand Canyon because they were seeking the experience of wonder and the Grand Canyon was one of the world's great natural wonders. Many were seeking something primordial, something deeper than daily lives absorbed in work, chores, worries, egos, arguments, busy streets, television, merely human things. They were hoping to get at least a glimpse of the cosmic. With the eclipse they had found a great bonus. The eclipse seemed a natural fit with the canyon.

Many in the crowd were heading for nearby wonders such as the red rocks of Monument Valley or Sedona, where the earth towered not below you but above you. Many would stop at Meteor Crater, where the sky had struck the earth not with light but far more powerfully and lastingly. For some the pull of the cosmos would pull them up Mars Hill to Lowell Observatory, where the sky had quietly flowed into telescopes and revealed some of its deepest secrets, especially that the universe is expanding. Many people would seek out the Southwest's Native American cultures, the Hopis and Navajos who have belonged to this land for centuries and seem to embody its ancientness, beauty, and power. Some people came to the Southwest mainly for its Native cultures, and they found the Navajos living in Monument Valley more fascinating than the rocks around them.

Many people were visiting the Grand Canyon and the other famous landscapes of northern Arizona as part of their exploration of the larger region, the Colorado Plateau, to which those landscapes belonged. They would roam into Utah, to Zion, Bryce Canyon, Arches, and Canyonlands, and into New Mexico to the ruins of Chaco Canyon, where the cycles of the sky are honored with carefully aligned windows and rock art.

On the Colorado Plateau the tectonic forces that had uplifted the land were now raising human curiosity and uplifting hearts. Here time and erosion had sculpted some of the world's most dramatic and exotic landforms: canyons of every size and shape, mesas, buttes, domes, pillars, arches, natural bridges, and hoodoos, painted with a surrealistic rainbow of colors.

This land is powerful, and different. This land is mainly about itself, not about the life that lives upon it, life so sparse it seldom hides the land. This land is the skeleton of the earth and not the green flesh, empty eye sockets and not the "I." This land is about ancient time and not about trends. Plants and animals are merely a period at the end of a very long geological sentence; birds are merely exclamation marks that emphasize the vastness and energy of the sky. This is a dry land that tries constantly to reduce moist, living bodies to its own definition of reality. This land is deeply wrinkled by time: the past is alive and powerful here, steering the courses of rivers and winds and animals. This land tells humans that this land was not made for them, that they may pass through it only by going far out of their way and far up and down, and that they may live here only if they obey the land's strict rules.

This land is a storyteller, one that tells its own story of deep time, deep forces, deep creativity. The humans who live here for a long time begin to hear the land speaking not just about canyons and arches but about the canyons and arches and pillars of creation within themselves.

This land says more clearly than other lands that life cannot be taken for granted, that life is always precarious and precious. For the Native Americans of the Pacific Northwest the salmon flowed as unstoppably as the rain; on the plains the great rivers compelled the growth of crops and bison herds; in the eastern woodlands the nuts paved the air and ground with protein. Native Americans in these regions might celebrate abundance but they didn't worry that the flow of life might stop abruptly and completely. While Cahokians grew hundreds of miles of crops along the often-flooding Mississippi, the Hopis relied on a handful of small springs and greatly fluctuating rains to grow modest desert corn that was barely enough to get them through the winter. While the Lakota had to keep stampeding bison herds from flattening their villages, the Navajos might wander for miles to catch a couple of rabbits.

If the deepest wellspring of religion is the ancient impulse of life to go on living, then logically the humans for whom survival is most precarious should develop religions with the deepest sense of vulnerability, humility, and appreciation. And indeed, the Hopis have an exceptionally elaborate ceremonial cycle to encourage and celebrate the rains and the crops. The Navajos, from an acute sense of vulnerability to forces antagonistic to life, have exceptionally elaborate healing ceremonies, including making sandpaintings that are matched only by Tibetan mandalas as the most elaborate sandpaintings in the world. Hopi and Navajo ceremonies are essentially the same today as centuries ago, while the spirituality of most other tribes has been heavily diluted, which could mean that Hopi and Navajo religion was more powerful to begin with. Also, the Hopis and Navajos are living on the same lands where they lived centuries ago, while most other American tribes have been uprooted from their original homelands and dumped onto lands with which they had no emotional or spiritual connections. The Hopis and Navajos were also more physically isolated, much less invaded by American Manifest Destiny, Christianity, and the modern world. This isolation was another measure of the stark power of this land; desert plants can't survive without deep and ingenious roots, and neither can desert people.

It was in the desert that humans generated the three great monotheistic religions, and it was into the remotest deserts that their prophets went to seek spiritual wisdom. Yet the monotheistic religions also grew out of the Nile and Tigris and Euphrates, which prompted humans to imagine the world as a Garden of Eden made for human abundance and domination. In the American Southwest, humans would never imagine such a thing; it would be a sign of madness. The Hopi and Navajo creation stories hold far more humility. The southwestern desert generated cosmologies that would turn out to be better metaphors for the astronomical cosmos in which life is a tiny and fragile thing amid vast emptiness.

By the later third of the twentieth century millions of young Americans had become frustrated by the results of their Manifest Destiny history, by social values obsessed with conquest, wealth, and social status, and they began searching for something more nourishing. Smothered by urban life and summoned by the environmental movement, they began seeking a deeper sense of connection with the earth, which drew them to Native American cultures. They also explored eastern religions and esoteric spiritual traditions and tried to devise Space Age religions with UFOs playing the role of angels. It was no coincidence that this spiritual groping attached itself to northern Arizona, to the red rock domes of Sedona. The vague longing to feel the power of the earth mutated into the conviction that the red rocks were emanating a real physical and spiritual force, the vortexes. This spiritual hunger and quest could have attached itself to any landscape in America, but it felt that the Sedona red rocks were the most cosmic of landscapes.

It was a quest of a different kind—but perhaps not so different—that in the 1890s built Lowell Observatory only thirty miles from the Sedona red rocks. The red rocks are red for the same reason Mars is red, iron and oxygen, and Mars held some of the same mythological magnetism as Sedona. Percival Lowell was convinced that Mars held an advanced civilization and a planet-wide network of canals, and he built his own observatory to study the Martians. Lowell spun an elaborate cosmology in which the universe was generous at creating life and full of friendly beings with much to teach us, lessons not just technological but philosophical and moral. Lowell was convinced he was being a good scientist, but his vision of Mars owed much to the same cosmological hunger that had inspired Native Americans before him and that would inspire New Agers after him. He wanted to find a deeper connection between humans and the cosmos, a connection not just with rock and fire but with life, meaning, and guidance.

Lowell's Martians may have been illusory, but he was the first astronomer to see clearly that the best location for astronomical observatories was the desert Southwest, with its high elevations, dry air, and remoteness from city lights. He built his observatory at more than seven thousand feet, giving him a sharper view of the night sky than any observatory for decades to come. The brilliant stars of northern Arizona remain a part of its attraction and culture, and in the 1950s they inspired Flagstaff to pass America's first law to curtail artificial lighting and protect the view of the night sky.

The tectonic forces that had uplifted this part of the Colorado Plateau a mile and a half above sea level had made it—more than metaphorically—far closer to the stars, and this helped Lowell Observatory astronomers discover Pluto and the first solid evidence that the universe is expanding. While this land could not claim credit for this cosmology, the expanding universe did seem a natural fit for a land so ancient, so full of empty spaces and primordial forces, so exotic in shapes, so rich with light, a land with a steadily expanding Grand Canyon.

Lowell Observatory sits atop a volcanic mesa that flowed from a volcano, one of six hundred volcanoes in the area. The volcanoes provided another sort of stepping-stone to the cosmos in the 1960s when the Apollo astronauts came here to learn the geology they would need on the moon. Northern Arizona landscapes were suitably unearthly. The astronauts trained at the volcanoes and lava flows around Flagstaff, at the Grand Canyon, and at Meteor Crater.

The meteorite that created Meteor Crater fifty thousand years ago seemed to have anticipated that this would be the best place to join a richly cosmological landscape. It was all here: a land displaying the same deep time and evolution as the night sky, a land rising and pulsing with primordial power, a land that generated the Big Bang and the expanding universe, a land that reveals the true equation between life and cosmos, a land that generates and protects Native American visions of the cosmos, a land that draws from around the world the endless, messy, and unsolvable human hunger for cosmic meaning. It all added up to inspire humans to more expansive thoughts and lives.

I have been privileged to live on this land for a long time, to explore its places, feel its power, see its magical light, and get to know its peoples. It has stirred me to wonder many times, at telescopes, canyons, and katsina ceremonies, at the rims of Meteor Crater and of long-abandoned kivas, seemingly different experiences that tended to flow together into the same experience of wonder at the cosmos, at this planet and the life it generated, at the presence of humans in the cosmos, lonely and awestruck.

This book reports on what this land has spoken to me and to others who were listening respectfully. This book remains on the southern circle of the Colorado Plateau, the part somewhat artificially defined as northern Arizona, but this part of the plateau is more than rich enough with stories.

This book belongs to the literary nature-writing tradition: personal, poetic, philosophical musings on nature. Yet while most nature writing never leaves the ground, this book only begins there. The nature of Earth is but small cycles of much larger and older cycles, only one part of a much larger story. Rocks are ripples of the galaxy; life pulses with the energy of the Big Bang; the Grand Canyon is a doorway to the labyrinths of the sky. The order-building impulse that was released by the Big Bang and that wove atoms, planets, DNA, cells, and brains has, in human form, continued groping to find order, the largest patterns of the cosmos.

This land is the mother lode of wonder.•✦

·1·

THE EXPANDING MESA

ON THE RIM OF THE VOLCANO I stood, propelled there by the volcano's power.

I was standing on the backside of the volcano and looking down a steep thousand feet to its base. On the opposite, front, side of the volcano, its base was about six hundred feet below the rim, for on its front side, through a V-shaped gap, the volcano had poured out lava that piled up hundreds of feet deep, building a mesa two miles wide and four and a half miles long. At its edges the mesa dropped steeply, as much as four hundred feet.

The mesa left a large imprint upon the landscape, and upon human activities.

The main tracks of the Santa Fe Railway, running from Chicago to Los Angeles, approached the mesa from the east, aiming straight at it, but then veered around it, hugging its contours. The mesa's volcanic layers funneled its underground waters to a spring at the mesa's edge, and in the age of steam trains, when locomotives needed a lot of water, this spring was an essential stop amid hundreds of miles of Arizona deserts. The mesa's waters nourished the westward dreams of a nation, floating the lumber, hardware, grain, minerals, and people that filled the West with towns. The lava's ancient energy was transformed into the energy of iron wheels climbing mountain passes.

Half a century later, in the age of the automobile, Route 66 was built alongside the tracks of the Santa Fe Railway, so Route 66 too aimed straight at the mesa and then veered around it. Every passing car had to expend extra gas and time to pay tribute to the mesa and its volcano. The national dreams that now included California sun and Hollywood glamour and the grapes of wrath were still grounded upon geological sleep.

More decades later, Interstate 40 followed the path of Route 66 and the Santa Fe Railway, and it too bent around the mesa; the big trucks that carried the lifeblood of the world's greatest economy still had to pay tolls to the mesa. Another highway, one of the main routes to the Grand Canyon, curved around the other side of the mesa, teaching a million tourists every year how and why rivers and canyons curve.

Around the base of the mesa was wrapped the city of Flagstaff. Every day thousands of residents curved around the mesa on their way to and from work and school and groceries, but sometimes impatiently, barely even noticing the mesa. From most of town the mesa hid the view of its mother volcano.

From where I lived I could see the volcano, including the V vent from which its lava had become the mesa, but I too was often guilty of barely noticing it. As I drove from my house the road pointed me straight at the volcano, at least for a moment, but soon I was preoccupied with the traffic of a busy highway.

Even as America's traffic and westering dream detoured around the volcano's far more ancient geological reality, America imposed its dreams upon the volcano, turning it into a mere stage prop of the Wild West. For about twenty years starting in the 1880s the volcano was near the center of a large ranch, the Arizona Cattle Company, which branded its cattle with the symbol "A-1". The ranch became known as the A-1 Ranch, and the volcano became known as "A-1 Mountain." A century later, long after the branded cows had been eaten and their leather had worn out and the cowboys had died and their branding irons had been melted down and ranchers had realized that the grasslands at more than seven thousand feet weren't the best for grazing, the volcano was still branded with the name "A-1." The volcano had glowed with vastly more heat than a branding iron, and it had branded the land with a symbol miles long, but the brash and fleeting Wild West had left upon the volcano the incomprehensible human concept of cattle rustling, of the theft of property. Brash indeed was the superintendent of the A-1 Ranch, Captain

B. B. Bullwinkle, who had been a fireman during the great Chicago fire of 1871, who played poker with cows as poker chips, and who always raced his horse into Flagstaff until one day the horse tripped and Bullwinkle flew off and was killed. The volcano was also clouded by the local lore that the A-1 Ranch was the birthplace of A-1 Steak Sauce (it really came from Britain).

Fortunately there are cures, or at least temporary antidotes, for the superficialities of human culture and the human mind. The power of nature can break through the dull surface. The (w)hole reason all those tourists were driving past A-1 Mountain and going to the Grand Canyon was because they wanted to break the dull surface in the grandest way, break it into a ten-mile-wide canyon full of strange shapes and glorious colors. Even tourists who were inclined to see the Grand Canyon as a theater of Wild West adventure and conquest couldn't help noticing that nature was much larger than humans. Humans could also be stirred by Niagara Falls, by Yosemite cliffs, by Old Faithful, by Kilauea. An erupting volcano might be the most reality breaking of geological forces, for it violates our sense of the ordinary, solid, hard earth and reveals the strange powers always beneath us. All over Earth humans saw volcanoes as the work of powerful gods and gave volcanoes elaborate offerings, including human sacrifices. Sometimes volcanoes were seen as the gateway to Hell. Even extinct volcanoes were inhabited by gods.

It seemed wrong, then, that I often barely even noticed the volcano right in front of me. I too would travel far to see a wonder of nature, yet I had failed to fully inhabit my own neighborhood, my own naturehood. I might live here, but here did not live in me. With mere eyes I might touch the volcano, but the volcano did not touch me.

I wanted to be a native to this earth. I decided I would go and welcome the volcano into my world of human experience. I would climb the volcano, then climb back down and hike to the far end of the mesa. I would re-create the journey of lava out of the ground, down the volcano, and across the land. I would take the measure of the volcano and the mesa, not in numbers or concepts but in my own footsteps, in human muscles, in impacted senses, with the red button of human consciousness pressed to *Record*. I would try to translate the vast powers of nature into the language of the human body and mind.

+ + +

I stood at the base of the volcano and looked up. I imagined the volcano erupting, perhaps for years, shooting high a plume of magma, thousands of red-yellow hot blobs spreading out and raining down. The magma that fell onto the back rim of the cone piled up and began cooling off, while the magma that fell back into the caldera remained hot and fluid and turbulent, then overflowed out of the volcano and flowed across the land. Gravity did its best to stop the volcano from rising, but the upward forces of the earth were too powerful.

Gravity now tried to stop me from rising up the volcano. The slope was steep, and the volcanic cinders rolled beneath my boots. But my hard work allowed me to feel the strength of gravity and the strength of the magma that had overpowered gravity. The volcano was registering itself in my muscles and breath, speaking volcanic height and mass and power in the language of flesh. The volcano was growing larger. When I paused to catch my breath, I could imagine the volcano saying: *I didn't stop—you should have felt the roar of my breath—you would have been incinerated into ashes instantly.* When I glanced up to see the route ahead, the volcano laughed: *I never worried.* Because I was scaling the volcano to be a scale to take its measure, the volcano tried to fit into me, but my body was far too small to hold it.

When I reached the rim and felt pleased with myself, the volcano snorted: *Why is it that humans climb mountains because they want to feel big? With every step of the way, we mountains are telling you how small you are, how fragile your bodies, how brief your lives. Yet when humans reach the top their pride swells to absurd Everest size. Maybe it's not really mountains you are feeling superior to; even on remote mountains humans remain obsessively social animals who derive their worth by feeling superior to one another.*

From the rim I gazed onto a horizon filled with volcanoes and lava flows. This volcano was part of a volcanic range that stretched for more than 50 miles and included more than six hundred volcanoes.

The first volcano had erupted about 6 million years ago, and the most recent volcano, Sunset Crater, appeared less than 1,000 years ago, when humans were living around it and had to flee and abandon their fields and houses to the lava. A-1 Mountain appeared about 330,000 years ago. The volcanic range was quiet for the moment, the long geological moment, but not finished.

This volcanic range was an oddity for being far away from the colliding edges of tectonic plates, which produced most of Earth's volcanoes. But it was on the edge of the Colorado Plateau, a 130,000-square-mile region that was uplifted, leaving cracks along its edges, through which volcanoes had erupted. This volcanic range was generated by a "hot spot," a vein of magma welling up from deep in Earth's mantle; as the North American plate crawled 50 miles across this hot spot during 6 million years, the hot spot continued breaking through the crust and left a 50-mile track of volcanoes. About 400,000 years ago the hot spot had built one giant strato-volcano (the same type as Mount Fuji and Mount Kilimanjaro), maybe 15,000 feet high, which today would be the tallest peak in the non-Alaska United States, except that the volcano had collapsed and left a ring of peaks, today called the San Francisco Peaks, the tallest of which is 12,633 feet. The peaks loomed only a few miles from where I stood. Several other volcanoes in the range were taller than 9,000 feet, but since the base elevation here is about 7,000 feet, these volcanoes stand 2,000 or 3,000 feet above the surrounding land. Most of the six hundred volcanoes are cinder cones a few hundred feet high. Very few had produced a lava flow as long as that of A-1 Mountain. The A-1 volcano was probably fed by the same power-ful magma chamber that had built the 15,000-foot San Francisco volcano.

It was my turn to flow down the volcano. I stepped off the back-side rim and headed into the caldera, still a distinct bowl. The cal-dera held a mixture of volcanic cinders, formed when flying blobs of magma congealed before hitting the ground, and thick strands of lava, which flowed out of the ground like toothpaste and acquired lengthwise striations where the lava scraped harder lava. Today the caldera was also full of ponderosa pine trees. From the caldera I flowed downward, following the chute the lava had taken, following gravity. I wasn't moving nearly as fast as the lava had flowed, and I wouldn't be even if I were running, and if I were running I would be tripping and tumbling and breaking my crust and erupting with my own lava, of which I had a far more limited supply than did Earth. Measured by my biological caution, I felt Earth's prodigal power and violence. I saw a river of lava rushing down this slope.

From the volcano's base the lava had formed various lobes and ridges and bumps; I followed the longest lobe to where it dropped down to a smoother plain. It also dropped down to a dirt road, probably an old A-1 Ranch road, now a Forest Service road, which I would follow, through a mixture of meadows and ponderosa forests, to the far edge of the mesa. If I had brought a compass I could have taken a shorter route, straight through the forest, rather than wandering with the road. I could have trusted my course to Earth's giant magma magnet, not to the needs of 1880s cattle ranching, which had bent this road to an artificial pond for watering cattle. The lava had trusted Earth's magnetic field; its tiny mineral compass needles, frozen when the magma cooled, were still loyally pointed to the direction of Earth's magnetic north 330,000 years ago.

Now I was probably walking at about the same pace that the lava had flowed. The pace of lava is determined by the combination of the land's gradient, the push of lava from behind, and the lava's own composition. On this plain the slope was so gradual that I usually didn't notice it, but the lava had. Here and there the lava seemed to have lost momentum and mounded up into modest bulges. Compared with other types of lava—types are defined by their content of minerals, gases, and water—this lava had been moderately fluid. Basalt is the most fluid lava: it forms Hawaii's readily flowing lava rivers and gently sloping shield volcanoes. Rhyolite is the least fluid lava: it gums up a volcano until the volcano explodes, like Mount St. Helens. In between basalt and rhyolite are several other types, including the rare benmoreite, which makes up A-1 volcano. Benmoreite was fluid enough to flow a long way, yet thick enough to pile up into a tall mesa with steep edges.

As I walked I imagined the ground moving, bubbling, swirling.

Liquid rock. If I could look into the hundreds of feet of lava beneath me, I would see layer upon layer of lava, swirling this way and that, fossilized motions, the geological fingerprints the lava had left as it continually rebuilt its channels and gradients and built the mesa.

I tried to imagine the lava's heat, which I guessed was around 1,500 degrees Fahrenheit. Any trees or grasses in the path of the lava would have burst into flame. The lava beneath me probably contained many lenses of burned carbon. If the lava was slow and cool enough, it may have been imprinted by a tree's round trunk or bark texture. I imagined my own 98.6 degrees being subjected to 1,500 degrees: it would evaporate my water, drive crazy my cells, rupture my organs, cook my skin red and black, and then burst me into flame. Human metabolism is so delicate that it can't operate at even 108 degrees. A century ago the forests on this mesa were logged, and the logs, made of volcanic soil, were thrown into fireplaces, where the ancient, imprisoned energy of the volcano flared forth once again to save humans from suffering in a 50°F room. Human bodies are thin, percolating lenses of carbon balanced between volcanoes and glaciers, stars and the coldness of space. Far below me the magma still brewed, searching for its next invasion route into the biological world. Once, volcanoes ruled the earth, and cells were the invaders.

For the moment, the earth seemed solid enough. With every footstep I was feeling the solidity and weight of the lava. It was hammering its strength into my flesh and bones and mind. The lava river had become rock that had strongly resisted the rains that for a third of a million years had tried to set it flowing again.

I tried to feel the age of the lava. I tried to think of 330,000 years in terms of human lifetimes, about five thousand human lifetimes. This didn't seem so hard to grasp. But then, a third of a million years is a long time in the lifetime of a species. When this mesa was forming, humans were still sharing the world with Neanderthals, and indeed humans were still evolving into *Sapiens*. In the time this mesa has been sitting here, modern humans had emerged and migrated all over Earth and developed thousands of languages and learned to stack rocks into houses and cities. The mesa saw climates change and plant and animal species come and go; in the last 5 percent of its history, the mesa held Ice Age snows and its first human footprints. And this mesa was a recent event in the history of its volcanic range, itself a recent event in the history of this continent, only 2 percent as old as the youngest rocks in the Grand Canyon.

At least I was getting a good feel for the mesa's size. I was feeling it with my leg muscles, with about ten thousand footsteps, with little eruptions of thirst and hunger. The mesa was growing larger. And more real. For a while I was following in the footsteps of an elk, craters imprinted in mud and now dried solid. For the elk this mesa was far more real and intricate and tasty than it ever would be for me. Yet the elk would never imagine this mesa as lava flowing from a volcano. The elk wouldn't feel the awe that compelled humans to make sacrifices to volcanoes and that now propelled me on my own little ceremony. I was following the tracks of the volcano, and the six hundred footsteps of the magma hot spot. I was beginning to feel not just the power of this volcano but the greater powers of which this volcano was a small, momentary swirl. I felt the magma sun hidden deep inside Earth, and the upwelling currents that moved continents and raised mountain ranges and triggered earthquakes and generated Earth's magnetic field. I felt a power that had been churning for more than 4 billion years and that was far from tired out. I saw this volcano revealing Earth's deepest secrets.

Ahead of me I focused on one cluster of black volcanic rocks. I focused on it because my motion detectors signaled that one of the black rocks was moving. Yes, it really was moving. The black rock leaped into the air. The black rock spread its wings and flew. The black volcanic rocks, transmuted through leaves and seeds and bugs, had become the black body of a raven, the black wings of flight, the bright fire of life. Perhaps *this* was actually Earth's deepest secret.

✦ ✦ ✦

Ahead of me the woods seemed to be less shady, more filled with light, as if I were soon going to emerge into another meadow. But it was also about time for me to reach the edge of the mesa, the edge of the forest, the edge of the sky.

Through the vertical lines of the trees I began to see another shape, with vertical lines but a much wider body than a tree. I saw that it was made of lava. The mesa's jagged lava rocks had arisen into a pile of rocks about twenty feet high, fitted together like jigsaw pieces. The pile was circular, as circular as a perfect volcanic crater, and like a crater, it held a lot of empty space inside. This empty space was a conduit, an air lock, through which the empty spaces of the universe were vacuumed out of the far sky and brought to Earth. This circle of lava rocks, roofed by a wooden dome, contained a telescope. Like the lava rocks, the metal of the telescope had been squeezed out of the earth by deep, powerful forces. With this telescope Earth became deep and powerful enough to see and meet the deep and powerful forces of the universe. The volcanoes of Earth could crater-eye see the volcanoes of Mars, the wheelings of the planets and moons, the eruptions of stars, the subductions of black holes, the swirls of our galaxy, the swarms of galaxies.

This telescope had become one of the more famous telescopes on Earth. Out of the parade of tens of thousands of lights across the sky, this telescope had sifted one light that behaved differently than the stars, behaved like a planet. This was the telescope that had discovered Pluto.

I walked past the observatory dome and onto a sidewalk and down a hill. Embedded in the cement were a few small metal discs, each representing a planet. Alongside each disc was a sign with a photo and facts about the planet. I had started at Pluto and was heading into the solar system. I passed Neptune, Uranus, Saturn, Jupiter, making a dozen or two dozen footsteps between them—the sidewalk was longer than a football field. I arrived at Mars, where the sign showed a photo of Mars's giant volcano, Olympus Mons, and explained that it was six and a half times as high as the San Francisco Peaks and as large as the state of Arizona. The discs for the rest of the planets were clustered nearby.

The purpose of this "Pluto Walk" was to give people a better sense of the scale of the solar system, to translate the numbers and concepts of astronomy into human experience. The Pluto Walk was doing the same thing I had done on my plutonic walk from A-1 volcano. Now, at the end of my walk, I was being offered a larger map on which to locate the volcano and the mesa and myself.

I stopped at the metal disc of Earth. I bent down and looked at it more closely. In it I imagined I could see, only a speck, the entire mesa I had just walked, big enough to tire me yet only 1/5,000th the circumference of the planet. I looked again at the lava landscape around me, so long and firm and textured and full of tall trees, so real in human experience, yet so invisible in the experience of Pluto, Jupiter, or Mars.

I walked past another, larger, building made of volcanic rocks, with a large silver dome. This was the original headquarters and library of Lowell Observatory, now a museum. It held the photographic plate on which astronomer Clyde Tombaugh had discovered Pluto in 1930 and the instrument, the blink comparator, he had used to study the plate. Another exhibit held a simple-looking instrument, a shiny metal tripod three feet long. This was the spectrograph astronomer Vesto Slipher used around 1910 to study the motions of what were then called spiral nebulae, what we now call galaxies. The spectrograph measured an object's light spectra, shifting toward the blue end of the spectrum if an object was moving toward us and toward the red end of the spectrum if an object was moving away from us. Slipher discovered that the spiral nebulae were racing outward at incredible speeds. A decade later Edwin Hubble used Slipher's spectrographic measurements to prove that the universe is expanding, expanding from some primordial eruption.

I walked onward, toward a large white observatory dome with a base of volcanic rocks. Here Slipher had attached his spectrograph to a large telescope and discovered that the universe is expanding. I walked a few feet past the dome and stopped. I looked out at empty space. I looked down hundreds of feet. I had reached the edge of the mesa, the end of the volcano's energy.

Because of the observatory perched on its edge, the mesa is officially called Observatory Mesa. Informally, the mesa is called Mars Hill, since Percival Lowell had founded his observatory to study Mars. Yet as cosmic as these names might seem, they also showed provinciality, the limited perspective of Flagstaff residents who looked up and saw an observatory dome and let it define the entire mesa, when the observatory was only a dot on the edge of a large mesa, no hill at all. From its origin as a branding iron (or a bottle of steak sauce) to its end as a Martian hill, the mesa was refused recognition of its own volcanic identity. I would guess that most Flagstaff residents didn't even realize that Mars Hill was connected to A-1 Mountain. The name Mars Hill might have been appropriate given that the planet Mars is full of lava flows and holds the largest volcano in the solar system, but in fact Percival Lowell never knew this, and he always insisted that due to aeons of erosion there were no mountains on Mars.

I had done my best to honor the mesa's true identity. Now I felt that I knew it. Even after stopping I was still feeling the volcano's strength—with my tired legs. My mind didn't feel drained by my walk, but felt enriched by it, for now the flowing lava glowed onward in my consciousness.

Yet even as I wished to congratulate myself for taking the human measure of the volcano and the mesa, I was feeling discouraged about the ability of a human to feel like a native in this world. When I had walked down the Pluto Walk and walked past the observatory dome in which humans had discovered the expanding universe, I had walked off the solid Earth and into the realm of space, a dimension far, far vaster than one mesa on one planet. My walk had already left me feeling small, and now I felt far, far smaller. Now I stood on the edge of a sky onto which I could not take even one footstep, or the sky would hurt me.

How could a human "get a feel for" or "grasp" empty space that could not be touched? How could human senses "get a sense of" distances they could never experience? The Pluto Walk was a good try but it was very deceptive. If a human were able to walk to Mars for real, and walk twenty-four hours a day, he would need 1,300 years to reach Mars, at its closest approach to Earth. He would need more than 100,000 years to reach Neptune, nearly two thousand human lifetimes. And this was just our own snug little solar neighborhood. The distance to the nearest star was so vast that it was meaningless expressed in walking years or even in peregrine falcon flying years and had to be measured in light-years, and even this was somewhat deceptive because the "years" half of "light-years" could seem to remain within human grasp but it was the "light" half that did the real measuring, and this half was beyond human comprehension. How could humans experience the 2.5 million light-years to the nearest galaxy? Or the billions of light-years to the farthest galaxies? How could bodies that rarely lived 100 years grasp the time dimensions of a universe 13.7 billion years old? How could a body that strained to take the measure of one volcano grasp a universe with trillions upon trillions of planets full of volcanoes, roaring with volcanoes? I would singe my mind trying to grasp a sun that was a third of a million times more massive than Earth, or stars that were hundreds of times larger than our sun. How could a 98.6°F body grasp the heat of stars, of supernovas, of the Big Bang?

Yet in one respect, my walk had been taking an accurate measurement of the universe, not in distance, but in difference.

If I had been seeing the volcano all along not just in the context of my naturehood or even in the context of the entire Earth but in the context of the expanding universe, I would have seen that it contained a greater power, a greater story. The matter that had erupted here had not begun here. Its elements had been constructed step by step in stars, in supernovas, in the Big Bang. The volcano's eruption was but a continuation of far greater eruptions, of far fiercer heat, of the cascading energies of the universe. The flowing lava had been pushed by 13.7 billion years of momentum. The expanding mesa was an inner ripple of the expanding universe, set flowing by one drop of the energies of the Big Bang. The red glow of the lava was one glimmer of the redshifts of the galaxies.

The universe had expanded not just in space, but in form and ability. The erupting energies of the Big Bang had become the energies of galaxies and stars and planets and moons, the energies of tectonic plates and rising mountain ranges and erupting volcanoes, and then on Earth they erupted as ponderosa pine trees—wooden volcanoes spewing green needles a hundred feet into the air. They erupted as red wildflowers whose redshifts spread life into the future. They erupted as red-tailed hawks whose redshifts traced a far more skillful trajectory than any galaxy. They erupted as cardinals whose voices rippled the morning air with affirmation. They erupted as elk and deer and coyotes in whose brains a dead volcano became a flickering image, the energies of consciousness. And within the human brain the energies of the cosmos learned to ripple backward into time and see a volcano blasting out lava, see a mesa expanding. Farther back into time, humans could see volcanoes creating Earth's atmosphere and brewing organic molecules and perhaps energizing the creation of life; those volcanoes were still glowing inside every life on Earth. And farther back into time, to the beginning of time, in the ferocious fire of the Big Bang, the red glow of consciousness could see the birth of the universe and itself.

Human senses may be dim, the human mind opaque, our sense of wonder jet-drowned-out by animal worries and egos, daydreams and obsessions, but it was through conscious minds like humans that the universe could finally take the measure of itself.

With this mesa the volcano had built a platform that reached to the planets and the stars and the galaxies, an edge that wormholed to the edge of the universe, a black mirror in which the blackness of space could see itself, a fire through which the fire of the Big Bang was reincarnated to finish—after uncountable oblivious volcanoes throughout the universe—the long, void-filling, planet-building, song-rippling soul work of self-recognition.◦◆

·2·

TREE RINGS

I FELT THE STARLIGHT ON MY FACE. Star bathing, my face glowed with the power of distant suns. This wasn't the power of heat, but the power of time.

Gazing out the opening of the observatory dome, I was greeting starlight arriving on Earth after long journeys. For hundreds or thousands of years, this light had been flowing through space, flowing in ripples of light expanding outward from stars.

I watched the waves of starlight rolling onto Earth, folding themselves around me, caressing me with light, setting off ripples in my mind.

When this starlight had left its parent stars, it was ferociously energetic, hot enough to zap comets into gas and to bake the nearest planet into slag; it had been brilliant enough to blind animals on a planet a hundred million miles away. This tsunami of starlight had rolled outward, yet soon it encountered a force far greater than itself and was reduced to a whimper of energy. The starlight encountered the power of mere emptiness, the enormous distances of the universe. A tsunami of light faded into a mere speck of light. Intense daylight was transformed into night. All the daylight pouring out of hundreds of billions of stars was swallowed up by night, becoming the twinkling definition and look and poetry of night.

As the daylight flew into space, it became yesterday light, then yesteryear light, then yestercentury light.

I watched a sky wavering with layer upon layer of time. Some of the light I saw was born in the same year that Albert Einstein was born and had been reciting his equations all this time. I saw light that was created in the same year that the stained-glass windows of Chartres Cathedral were finished and that had been offering a greater prayer to the glory of light. I saw light that first saw the light of day on the same day that the Giza Sphinx first obtained eyes to see the days on Earth. I saw light that had already been deep within the cave of space when sun-charged hands painted sun-charged beasts on Lascaux walls.

At the same time that the light of distant stars was arriving on Earth, the light of our sun was arriving at those stars. It had expanded outward, baking rocks on Mercury, driving the winds of Venus, warming the flesh of Earth, sparkling on the ice of comets. As it flew into interstellar space, it continued diminishing in power. When our sunlight arrived in distant solar systems, it couldn't penetrate a centimeter into a glacier or guide the wanderings of a mouse—but perhaps somewhere it still registered in a telescope, or set off a ripple of wonder in a child. On and on the ripples of our sunlight expanded, blending with the light of all the billions of stars of our galaxy to enter and cross intergalactic space, arriving in other galaxies as but a ghost light.

As I watched the ripples of starlight and time flowing into the observatory dome, as I imagined the ripples of our sunlight flowing outward, I began to feel time itself, feel it bodily, feel it with my hands and feet and back, as if time were as real and solid as a floor and a wall. And it was, for the observatory floor and walls were made of wood, and I was standing on that floor and leaning against that wall, wood that contained the same ripples of sunlight that were now hundreds of light-years away. Those distant ripples could no longer tickle a molecule of dust, but here they had embodied themselves into matter solid and enduring.

The wood I was touching was full of sunlight that had knotted itself together with earth, water, and air. This sunlight was the rocket flame that lifted trees out of the ground and hundreds of feet into the air. This was the sunlight of spring and summer, of renewal and growth and undeniable life. Every spring when a tree began growing again, the new cells in its trunk were large, thin walled, and light colored. As growth slowed in the autumn, new cells were smaller, thicker walled, and darker colored, and then growth stopped for the year. This cycle of growth created a new ring of wood every year, with a dark boundary line defining a ring from the previous year's ring. The *write* of spring. The ring cycle. Each ring was a circling of Earth around the sun. Each ring held not just sunlight but darkness, the space through which Earth journeyed. In this wood I was feeling a layer cake of sunlight and space, sunlight and earth, sunlight and rainfall, centuries thick.

A century ago, an astronomer here at Lowell Observatory had taken a deep interest in tree rings, and he had turned them into a new science: dendrochronology. Tree time.

Andrew E. Douglass was one of the first two astronomers hired by Percival Lowell for his planned observatory, and Lowell assigned Douglass the task of finding the best location for the observatory. After testing five sites in Arizona for their viewing conditions, Douglass selected a mesa above Flagstaff. Lowell Observatory became the first observatory located to take advantage of the superior viewing conditions of the desert Southwest. Most previous observatories had been located near the colleges that operated them, near the East Coast and sea level, shrouded by atmosphere, moisture, and city lights. By chance, Flagstaff was also located amid the world's largest forest of ponderosa pines, the perfect tree for tree rings that could reveal the secrets of the past.

Flagstaff was located on the main line of the Santa Fe Railway, which on its route from Chicago to Los Angeles ran through mostly prairies and deserts. The railway needed wood for bridges, ties, and earthworks; the booming towns along the route needed lumber. The lumber mills of Flagstaff shipped out large quantities of wood. Flagstaff residents knew all about trees. When Percival Lowell needed a dome for his observatory, he hired two Flagstaff master mechanics, the brothers Stanley and Godfrey Sykes, who built an all-wood, cylindrical, forty-foot-diameter, four-ton dome, still sturdy today.

Douglass's first observing project for Percival Lowell was studying and mapping Mars. In his 1895 book, *Mars*, Percival Lowell frequently cited "Mr. Douglass" as the reliable source for Lowell's depiction of Mars as holding a planet-wide grid of canals, built by a great civilization. Douglass became uncomfortable at being identified with

Lowell's confident vision of Martian canals, canals that most astronomers didn't see at all. A few years later Douglass complained privately about Lowell's lack of scientific rigor and caution, and Lowell fired him. Douglass went on to the University of Arizona, where he founded its now famous Astronomy Department.

While still in Flagstaff, surrounded by ponderosa forests, Douglass began his research into tree rings. Douglass considered this a form of astronomical research. Around 1900, astronomers knew little about the sun, including what caused it to burn or whether its energy output was steady or variable—some other stars appeared to be variable. Douglass thought he could get a grip on the variability question by examining ponderosa trees. If the sun's energy varied, perhaps in the rhythm of the twenty-two-year sunspot cycle, it should cause some variations in annual precipitation, and this should show up in the annual growth of ponderosas, which are unusually sensitive to precipitation. As Douglass rode the train climbing toward Flagstaff, he noticed the quick transitions from open grasslands to piñon-juniper forests about 30 feet tall to ponderosa forests 150 feet tall. The rising elevations meant more coolness and more precipitation and created an abrupt boundary at which ponderosas could grow. Even where ponderosa forests grew, a dry year could stop trees from growing for a year. In wetter climates tree growth was seldom limited by precipitation, and annual tree rings—if trees had rings at all—were about the same size from year to year, century to century. But in the desert Southwest, where precipitation was marginal to begin with, normal fluctuations caused large differences in annual growth and in annual tree rings.

Douglass gathered his first tree-ring specimens from the logs of Flagstaff's Riordan lumber mill. With a magnifying lens and a steel ruler, he measured the width of each tree ring. He found patterns of thicker and thinner rings and found that these patterns were consistent from tree to tree, which meant they were caused not by tree personalities but by environmental factors. Douglass proved that trees could be cross-dated, that the same sequence of thick and thin rings could be located in different places in different trees: at the outside of the rings in one tree, twenty rings inside in another tree, and a hundred rings inside in a third tree. By cross-dating trees, Douglass built a tree-ring map that went back five hundred years, the life span of a ponderosa tree. The longevity of ponderosas was another reason they were great for dendrochronology.

Douglass thought he had hit a dead end at five hundred years, but then an archaeologist pointed out that Native American ruins were full of ancient trees. Douglass began examining ruins, including Mesa Verde and Chaco Canyon. Often the best logs were found in kivas, for kivas were the largest spaces in Puebloan villages, requiring the largest logs. Being community and sacred spaces, kivas justified the greatest effort to bring logs from afar.

At first Douglass thought of trees in ruins as mere raw material for his climatological research, but soon, as he began recognizing the same sequences of tree rings in different ruins, he realized that dendrochronology could become the first tool for dating archaeological sites. Douglass extended his tree-ring map back to AD 1260, and he assembled another, older, map more than five hundred years thick, but for a while he was unable to connect this older map with the one that ended at 1260. Because the Hopi village of Oraibi had been inhabited since before 1260, Douglass was hoping that a tree-ring specimen from the kivas at Oraibi would let him extend his map beyond 1260 and perhaps bridge the gap between the two maps, but the Hopis were disinclined to allow some white guy to drill holes in their sacred kivas. At last, at a ruin elsewhere in Arizona, Douglass found a log that spanned the gap, extending his time map back to about AD 700.

Archaeologists had guessed that Mesa Verde, Chaco Canyon, and other great southwestern ruins might be about two thousand years old, and now they were shocked to discover that these ruins were only half that age. Douglass's work allowed archaeologists to build a sophisticated picture of how Puebloan settlements had arisen, spread, and influenced one another and how drought had forced the Puebloans to abandon their villages. It turned out that the reason Douglass had had so much trouble finding the missing tree rings between his two tree-ring maps—missing tree rings that amounted to thirty years—was because these were years of severe drought, so trees weren't building tree rings and humans weren't building new buildings. Douglass had started his research to find evidence of periodic droughts, and in the end he found this evidence not just in tree rings but in entire cities that had been doomed by drought.

A few years ago a favorite ponderosa tree at Lowell Observatory died. The staff hired a chain-saw artist to turn the lower tree into a whimsical sculpture of Percival Lowell, with a pointing hand. The wooden Percival contains two or three centuries of tree rings, of sunlight and rain and seasons and Earth circling the sun. Percival's statue even has fingerprints, tree-ring fingerprints, made by a sun that reached its fiery hand across space and touched this tree and burned its fingerprint into the wood. The real, living Percival Lowell had also contained the fingerprint of the sun, as does every human and every life on Earth, and the fingerprints of all the vast and ancient forces that made us.

Inside the observatory dome I saw on the wooden walls the huge, rich fingerprint of the sun, and the fingerprints of other forces.

I saw the fingerprint of rain, aeons of rain, rain that had made on sand and water tiny impact fingerprints that were soon erased. The shapeless rain flowed down tree trunks, passively following the channels of the bark, yet when the rain later rose back into the trees it would take on form and firmness and become the xylem and bark that shaped the flowing of water. The observatory walls contained subtler traces of the same storms that had carved slot canyons, torn off Grand Canyon cliffs, swept boulders into the Colorado River, and formed rock dams that centuries later were still generating whitewater waves. The walls contained hurricanes, blizzards, summer thunderstorms, flash floods, and rainbows.

I saw the fingerprint of life, the whorl within whorl of order, the rings of DNA and proteins and cells and multicellular structures. I saw the whole Earth full of life-generated ripples: the air ripples of bird wings, the water ripples of fish and whales, the sand ripples of snakes slithering, the leaf ripples of primates swinging and giraffes eating, the green waves moving north in the spring. The whole Earth is full of life rippling with time, observing time with the opening of flowers and eyes every morning or night and enacting time with the annual ceremonies of birds migrating, salmon leaping upstream, bears awakening from hibernation, animals breeding, plants seeding, antlers growing, katsinas dancing, and trees exploding with leaves and secretly adding another ring. Here and there trees built time records that would last millions of years, for in their mineral-ticking burials, they turned into petrified wood. All of life's ripples added up into calcium and carbon piling up on the ocean floor until they were a mile thick and turned into limestone, into rock tree rings that recorded the past for a billion years to come. Like human fingerprints, the fingerprints in the observatory walls disclosed life's identity and longtime secret activities.

I saw the fingerprint of time, not only in the observatory wood but in wood everywhere. The ancient circles of wooden posts that, like Stonehenge, measured the cycles of the sun and moon and seasons already knew the secrets of those patterns. The paintbrushes with which Monet or Bierstadt painted the sunrise had themselves been painted by thousands of sunrises. The baton that conducts *The Four Seasons* was a lightning rod that had been conducted by the four seasons. The tribal drums that pray for the continuation of time were refuting their own insecurity. The sun itself had taught katsina dolls, including Tawa the sun katsina, the lessons they were created to teach. Through totem poles time took on animal faces with which to plea to inhuman powers the case for humans. The Bodhi tree of Buddha's enlightenment had been en-light-ened all along. The coffins with which even pharaohs tried to shut out time would long outlast the bodies within them, for there was nowhere to hide from time.

Douglass's transformation from an astronomer into an archaeologist was fitting, if you consider that astronomy is a form of archaeology, of excavating the past. The sky is a deep, dark ground full of time, full of the artifacts of long-gone, long-buried entities and events. The sky is full of star sherds, supernova projectile points, nebular Lascaux murals, the ruined walls of spiral arms, the curving white bones of galaxies, and black-holed death-stare skulls.

As their telescopes troweled deeper and deeper into space and time, astronomers saw planets hours deep, stars years deep, and galaxies millions of years deep. For a long time astronomers faced the same impasse as did archaeologists, an inability to come up with a reliable scale for measuring how distant and old objects were. Astronomers could gauge the distance to nearby stars with the parallax method devised by the ancient Greeks, but beyond that they were stuck. When astronomers couldn't tell how distant an object was, they often couldn't tell what it was. At the time Lowell Observatory was built, astronomers were debating the nature of spiral nebulae. Most astronomers took spiral nebulae to be gas clouds—perhaps condensing into solar systems—in nearby space. A few astronomers guessed that spiral nebulae were galaxies far outside our Milky Way galaxy, which would mean they had to be huge and incredibly luminous. It was Lowell Observatory astronomer Vesto Slipher who provided the evidence that settled this question and that established the distance scale and the time scale of the universe. Slipher did for astronomy what Douglass did for archaeology, giving it a reliable scale by which to organize objects, events, and changes into larger, more meaningful patterns.

Slipher studied the spiral nebulae with a spectrograph that spread light into its spectra and showed how fast an object was moving, and in which direction. Slipher was astonished to find that spiral nebulae were moving incredibly fast, and almost all of them were redshifted, moving outward. Slipher was seeing the expanding universe. Edwin Hubble soon proved that spiral nebulae really were distant galaxies, and then he used Slipher's spectrographic measurements to map out a universe of galaxies that were spreading outward from a great beginning. Slipher had discovered the luminous fingerprint of the Big Bang, the tree rings of creation.

And Vesto Slipher uncovered the expanding universe right here in this dome, surrounded by tree rings dense with light and time.

As the energy rings of the Big Bang spread outward, they transformed themselves into new rings, into galaxies and spiral arms and nebulae, into stars and star clusters and solar systems, into planets and comets and moons and Saturn-like rings. The energy rings of the Big Bang transformed themselves into DNA, cells, and the rings of trees; the redshifted galaxies became redshifted autumn leaves.

The energy rings of the Big Bang transformed themselves into the paper on which Vesto Slipher and Edwin Hubble calculated the expanding universe, transformed themselves into brains in which they rang with wonder.

In the fertile soil of human wonder, trees often became symbols of the cosmos. Trees gave structure to the cosmos. Many cultures imagined the cosmos as a great World Tree, with a trunk that held up the heavens and connected the heavens and the earth, and with roots that connected the earth and the underworld. For the Norse, the World Tree was Yggdrasill, a mighty ash tree, which would survive even Ragnarok, the collapse of the cosmos, and provide shelter for the man and woman who would emerge to regenerate the human race. To the Babylonians the center of paradise held the Tree of Life, from which the great rivers flowed. In *The Egyptian Book of the Dead*, sycamore trees framed the doorway to heaven, out of which Ra the sun god flew every morning and into which human souls would pass. In Europe evergreen trees became symbols of life enduring through the winter, even through death. Many summer-solstice ceremonies revolved around trees. When humans built churches and temples and kivas in which to worship, the trees and tree images in them became sacred connectors between humans and the cosmos.

I thought of Andrew Douglass kneeling in an ancient kiva, probing trees to find the secrets of time, the connections between the sun and Earth, between the cosmos and humans. Douglass was surrounded by ghosts who also sought the connections between the cosmos and humans. He was surrounded by katsinas past, the katsinas that brought rain and sunlight and fertile earth and abundant corn. Tawa the sun-faced katsina watched Douglass working, and perhaps Tawa smiled. The kiva was filled with the echoes of ancient ceremonies, with tree-stump drums beating out ripples of sound, ripples of time and rainfall and growth, ripples to which the katsinas moved, meshing themselves with the cycles of the cosmos, welcoming the cycles of the cosmos into human lives to give humans the strength and rhythm and balance and abundance of the cosmos.

I looked up at the observatory dome, with its spiderweb of support beams and its reddish wood. I looked at the narrow opening in the roof, with its view of the stars. It was like being inside a kiva and looking out its roof opening.

Observatory and kiva had a lot in common. Both were round, deep chambers, upheld by wood, with a roof opening and with a long object—ladder or telescope—connecting the ground and the opening. Both observatory and kiva were conduits for connecting humans with the cosmos. Both observatory and kiva were tunnels that cut people off from merely personal lives and worries and turned their attention to greater realities. Both observatory and kiva were instruments of awe. Both observatory and kiva were echo chambers that magnified and dislocated human voices into a larger voice, a stranger voice, a voice with a greater ring and identity, a voice deep with time and space, a true voice, the voice with which humans had been speaking all along. Both observatory and kiva were dimly lit, turning human forms into vague shapes, hiding the faces into which humans put so much effort and grooming, faces with which humans tried to create an image to present to others, an identity that depended on the recognition of others. But the night refused to show these faces or honor these identities. The night turned human forms and faces into elementary, undifferentiated, womb-new, primordial human shapes, mysterious shapes, allowing humans to see clearly their primordial selves, their primordial mystery. Both observatory and kiva, in their own ways, were churches for contemplating ultimate things: the cosmos and its gift of life, the ancient and endless struggle between order and chaos, the mysteries of light and darkness. Here the order triumphant in tree rings and in living cells celebrated itself, celebrated how the rings of the Big Bang had become the rings of trees, the rings of kivas, the rings of telescopes, and the rings of eyes fully open with awe.◦✦

·3·

ROOTED IN THE SUN

AHEAD OF US, where the river curved, the river was cutting into the bank, leaving an earthen cliff seven or eight feet high. The cottonwood trees atop the bank were resisting the river's power, their tangled roots holding onto the earth, but it was only a matter of time—the river had aeons of time—before the river carved away the bank and the trees fell. The trees were thick and tall, perhaps eighty or one hundred feet tall, so when they fell they might divert the current for a while, but soon the river would carve away the trees. Fifty miles downstream from here the San Juan River had carved away a thousand feet of rock, carved deep looping canyons.

But instead of appreciating the carving power of water, I was paying too much attention to my own power. I was watching my wooden paddle carving into the water; I was watching my kayak carving through the water; I was watching my boat going exactly where I wanted it to go. Perhaps I was feeling that I was the master of the river.

Until we came around a bend and I saw a man walking down the river. He was halfway out from shore, but the water came only halfway up to his knees. He was walking slowly but having no trouble with the current.

We paddled up to the man, a Native American. I asked him what he was doing. He pointed to the cut bank ahead, with its exposed cottonwood roots. He was searching for cottonwood roots that could be carved into katsina dolls. Only the wood of cottonwood roots was perfect, perfectly soft and strong, for carving katsina dolls. The washes below the Hopi mesas held some cottonwood trees, but not many and not large ones, and the Hopis soon harvested the available roots there. The Hopis had to find sources farther away, sometimes much farther away; we were about a hundred miles from the Hopi villages.

I looked at the maze of cottonwood roots sticking out of the earth, into the river. The power of this river had flowed into the roots. The katsina dolls carved from these roots would hold the river's power. They would hold snowy mountain peaks, roaring rapids, deep canyons, and the lifeblood of mountain lions and coyotes and eagles.

I looked up at the Native American standing in the river and he looked down at me in my life jacket, helmet, and plastic kayak, and I felt a bit silly. He didn't ask us what we were doing, for no doubt he knew our type. We were conquering the river. We were the heroic conquerors who had conquered the frontier, the wild mountains, the wild beasts, the wild Indians. After Hopis and their ancestors had been enjoying the shade of cottonwood trees for thousands of years, one conqueror, John C. Frémont, had shown up and noticed cottonwood trees and gotten them named for himself, the Frémont cottonwood, the subspecies found in the Southwest. John C. Frémont had wandered all over the West, gotten lost, gotten directions from Indians, gotten hungry when surrounded by perfectly good food, killed Indians who hadn't bothered him, named a lot of things, and become the Great Pathfinder, a national hero, nominated for president in 1856. Frémont even got a vanished Native American culture named for him, if indirectly: the Fremont Indians were named for the Fremont River.

We had also conquered the Hopis linguistically, not just calling them "Indians" but more specifically "Moquis," a Spanish word that was a bit insulting and had stuck to the Hopis for centuries. We gave the slightly comical name "Tuba City" to a town that was supposed to honor a Hopi named "Tuuvi." We spelled their spirit messengers, the katsinas, as "kachinas," though the Hopi language has no *ch* sound, and we called carved katsina figures "dolls," which could imply they are toys, when they are serious gifts the katsinas give to Hopi children to teach them Hopi ways.

As we—me and a few archaeology-minded friends—went down the river, we stopped at ruins of the Ancestral Puebloans (the Anasazi), the ancestors of today's Hopis and Zunis and the Pueblo peoples of the Rio Grande Valley in New Mexico. A thousand years ago the San Juan River basin was well populated, for it offered good soil for farming, abundant trees for wood, and endless water for drinking and gardens. Yet the Ancestral Puebloans were still dependent on rain for their corn and other crops, and the rains had failed for many years. People were forced to abandon their villages and migrate to better places, including the Hopi mesas, which were about two thousand feet higher, and thus cooler, which offered reliable springs. The Puebloans couldn't carry all their possessions, so they left much behind, such as pottery. We wandered among the ruins and examined hundreds of potsherds, some of them unusually large—unusual at least at other ruins that had more visitors than these ruins. This section of the San Juan River was seldom used by river runners, who preferred sections downstream with more rapids and canyons. Many of the potsherds were decorated, in different styles that told us their origins in place and time. Some potsherds still held the imprints of the fingers that had made them.

The ruins also contained kivas, which, if excavated, would reveal design features and religious symbolism that are identical to the kivas in Hopi villages today. To archaeologists this suggests a long continuity of religious practices. Of course, say the Hopis. By the 1300s there were abundant katsina images on pottery and rock art (though no katsina dolls), and some images are quite similar to images seen in katsina dolls today.

Amid some of the ruins grew cottonwood trees. They were descended from trees that had been here a thousand years ago when these ruins were proud houses. These trees were loved for their summer shade; for the way their uniquely-shaped leaves fluttered musically in the wind; for the snowstorm of white, cottony parachutes carrying seeds; and for how the leaves turned golden in the fall and glowed with sunlight. They were loved because cottonwoods grow only where there is continuous, reliable water—for a desert people, cottonwoods signified a place where they belonged. They were loved for the fallen branches that became winter fires and well-cooked foods and luminous kiva ceremonies.

As I looked up at one huge cottonwood tree, I saw the power of trees to lift tons of matter high into the air and give it shapes and skills. I looked at the ground and imagined the root system, two or three times the size of the canopy, tunneling in search of water and nutrients.

Next to the trunk I noticed a potsherd. Under this ground were a lot of potsherds, which the roots were embracing and cracking and sucking into themselves. The tree was full of potsherds. Clay had become wood; the shapes and designs of pottery had become the shapes and designs of leaves and bark. The former pottery was still holding water and seeds to carry life into the future.

If a katsina doll was carved from these roots, it too would hold potsherds. Clay given life-affirming shape a thousand years ago would be shaped once again by hands molded by the hands of the ancestor potter. A pot that had given the Hopis physical nourishment would now offer spiritual nourishment. A potsherd that had been left behind eight hundred years ago would finally make its own migration to the Hopi mesas and rise onto a wall to watch over its people.

This ground was also full of wooden tools, bone tools, cotton clothing, yucca baskets, shell jewelry, and corn husks, and they too were being absorbed into the tree. They too might become part of katsina dolls and renew their service to the Hopis.

I looked at the ground far around me. Somewhere, somewhere within the reach of the cottonwood roots, there might be Ancestral Puebloan bodies. The tender hands of the roots were embracing the two hands that had made these potsherds and were summoning her to rise into a new life, to become wooden hands reaching skyward and strewing the air with snowy seeds. She too might be handled lovingly by her thousand-year grandson and shaped into a katsina doll. A katsina in the plaza would hand her lovingly to her thousand-year granddaughter. Rising onto a wall or shelf, she would watch over the baking of bread or the shaping of pottery. After her long burial in darkness she might become a Tawa—the sun—katsina doll and watch the patterns of sunlight flowing across the walls, changing from day to day, season to season. She might become an

Ahölatmana'at katsina doll, a katsina maiden who goes from home to home offering kiva-consecrated seeds as the priest katsina offers blessings for the year to come. She might become a katsina doll responsible for rain or the germination of seeds or a good harvest. She would send her ancient blood into new bodies to give them life. She would whisper ancient secrets into children's ears to inspire them to continue Hopi ways for another thousand years. She would help the Hopis remain rooted.

Considering the importance of cottonwood roots to the Hopis, I wondered if cottonwood trees were, in some way, sacred to them. Yet I am reluctant to ask Hopis about the sacred, since Hopis are often reluctant to talk about it, even among themselves. In many cultures, the sacred involves secrets. And more than other tribes, the Hopis are wary of inquisitive whites, for Hopi beliefs have been distorted and hijacked by a long parade of missionaries, anthropologists, and religious seekers. Thus, I tried to be subtle. I knew that most things important to Hopi life have katsinas dedicated to them, so I asked if there was a cottonwood-tree katsina. But no, there was not. Nor is there a coyote katsina, though coyotes are a prominent part of southwestern life and the Hopis have a lot of coyote stories. One person answered how right it was that cottonwood roots are the perfect and only wood for katsina dolls, since cottonwood trees are just like Hopis, lovers of water in a world with too little water.

Cottonwoods do love water. Their roots are very twisty because they have to twist through rocky ground to find water. Cottonwoods release their seeds to match the timing of annual river floods so that seeds land on wet ground; one tree might produce nearly a million seeds, but only one seed would fall in the right spot to become a new tree.

One time a Hopi led me into her family home where her brother was carving a katsina doll. On his lap was a cloth onto which the cottonwood shavings were falling. I asked him what he did with the shavings. I had heard that Hopis buried their cottonwood scraps, but this wasn't possible here, atop a stone mesa. He said that he took them "outside," back to nature. Perhaps this meant that they joined centuries of broken pottery in flying over the mesa rim. He said that

Hopis would never burn their cottonwood shavings, not even for heat on a cold day.

Cottonwoods were sacred for other tribes. Not surprisingly, these were tribes that lived on the Great Plains where water and trees could be scarce and cottonwood groves stood out as oases. For the Arapaho, cottonwood trees, whose winter sap sparkled with sunlight, were the source of all the stars; the Arapahos undoubtedly knew that if you cut open a knuckled twig, it revealed a center with a five-pointed star. For the Hidatsa, cottonwood trees held spiritual power that could heal. For the Lakota, cottonwoods were—and still are—the center of their most sacred ceremony, the Sun Dance. Warriors of proven worthiness cut down a cottonwood, being careful not to let it fall to the ground, and they carried it to a ceremonial space. They raised it to be the center of a symbolic cosmos, surrounded by twenty-eight posts that represented the sun and the moon and the rest of creation. Tribes in the Pacific Northwest used cottonwood branches and bark for sweat lodges.

In my own experiences cottonwood trees had become a bit sacred. Many times on river trips and backpacking trips I have camped beneath giant cottonwoods. In the summer their shade alone gives them a green aura of benevolence. In the autumn their golden leaves glow magically, creating an aura of light. Their leaves vocalize the wind into a soft whispering music that soothes you to sleep and runs through your mind all night long. Their music harmonizes well with the music of a nearby river or creek. To me cottonwoods have an ancient look: their trunks have exotic, twisting, gnarly shapes; their bark is rough and full of confused angles.

As a species cottonwoods are indeed ancient. Their genus, the poplars, arose in the Eocene Epoch, some fifty million years ago, not so long after the age of the dinosaurs, though today's cottonwood species may be "only" twenty million years old. Cottonwoods still practice ancient strategies that more modern trees abandoned long ago, such as relying on the wind to carry pollen from male trees to female trees. Their leaf shapes are still hearing Eocene winds. In some places in the Southwest the cottonwoods are as ancient as the rocks around them: the hoodoos of Bryce Canyon are made out of Eocene lake sediments. Cottonwoods are also better than other trees at vegetative propagation, in which a living limb that falls to the ground or floats downstream and lands onshore can sprout a new root and become a new tree.

Camping beneath cottonwoods can provoke thoughts of mortality, and not because I am contemplating geological eras. As cottonwoods age, their wood becomes seriously brittle. Without warning a large branch can crack off—with a dagger-sharp point—and fall to the ground. The debris scattered beneath a cottonwood tells you what could happen to you. In some national parks, camping spots beneath elderly cottonwoods have been closed and relocated, or the trees have been cut down. As I drift to sleep, watching the stars constantly eclipsed by leaves, I wonder if I am going to wake up again. When I do wake up, I am grateful to be alive, grateful to the tree.

The brittleness and hardness of cottonwoods made them very poor as lumber. Even tree-starved American pioneers on the Great Plains refused to use cottonwoods. When the builders of the transcontinental railroad were crossing the plains and ran out of other trees and tried using cottonwoods for railroad ties, they discovered that driving a spike into this wood would only crack it. Thus, it is surprising that cottonwood roots are unusually soft and strong, good for carving katsina dolls. I've asked several botanists about this contradiction, and they speculated that the softness comes from the cottonwoods being very thirsty trees, sucking an unusual amount of water through their roots, which keeps the roots porous, unclogged arteries. The porous quality of the roots is why they are very lightweight compared with other woods. For katsina doll carvers, this porosity means the wood sponges up and blurs paint unless it is prepared with a clay-rich base.

You could say that I always camp beneath cottonwood trees. In my cabin I sleep beneath a little shelf of katsina dolls. Two of them are a carving style called sculptures, which follows the natural curve of the root, leaving much of the wood exposed, uncarved and unpainted, though the head is a richly detailed katsina head. The carvers of these two dolls, Wilmer Kaye and Ramson Lomatewama, both came from the village of Hotevela, the village most committed to preserving Hopi traditions, whether in language, religion, or art. The sculpture style, which bloomed in the 1980s, made a break from the trend of katsina doll art, which was drifting ever further away from Hopi traditions. In response to the tastes of white collectors, katsina dolls were imitating the styles of western art, becoming miniature Michelangelo statues full of anatomical realism yet also poses and colors and art styles that were unrealistic for katsinas. In the 1990s some carvers, including Ramson Lomatewama, made a more thorough return to tradition by carving in the more basic, flatter style Hopis had used a century ago when katsina dolls were made strictly for Hopis and not for Santa Fe or Paris art galleries; this style is called simply "traditional." Yet even in my sculpted doll, Ramson's traditional impulses came through: he had left the wood not just unpainted but unvarnished, and he hadn't signed his name on the base. Hopis never used to sign katsina dolls because dolls weren't about the artist. (I knew it was Ramson's work because I had commissioned him to carve it).

Sometimes I would look at these katsina dolls more closely. Sometimes, I admit, this was only because I was dusting the spiderwebs off them and I needed to lift them up. Still, I don't like it when things become so familiar that I never see them at all, so I would try to see their designs anew. Half of their designs had been designed by trees. I looked at the wood grain, the way it formed streaks and curves and peaks, or patches lighter or darker. I was seeing the fingerprint of a tree. I would never know the identities of these trees, whether they had lived at a quiet spring or along a roaring river; how old they were; or if they'd held an eagle's nest. I saw the wood grain as the ripples of the water that had flowed through it; I saw wood canyons shaped by the same river that had carved stone canyons. I saw seasons of rain and seasons of dryness, years of flood and years of drought, decades of growth and decades of old age.

As I held a katsina doll to the window to see its fingerprint more clearly, I was also seeing through the window at the mountains a few miles away. Hopis call them Nuvatukya'ovi. Whites call them the San Francisco Peaks, after Saint Francis. They hold the highest peak in Arizona, snowcapped for about half the year. They are also the home of the katsinas for half the year. A few weeks after the winter solstice, the katsinas travel from the peaks to the Hopi mesas to appear in ceremonies, preside over the growing of crops, and bring rain. A few weeks after the summer solstice, with the summer rainy season started and the crops thriving, the katsinas head home to the Peaks. Many summer mornings, in skies clear for dozens of miles around, the first rain clouds form over the Peaks, then spread eastward toward the Hopi mesas.

I live closer to the Peaks than almost anyone, with nothing but forests, no other buildings, between me and the Peaks. One time when I attended the Niman ceremony, which sends the katsinas home to the Peaks, a Hopi joked to me that since the katsinas were heading to my neighborhood maybe I should offer to give them a ride in the back of my truck.

Traditionally, the timing of Hopi ceremonies was determined by watching the seasonal cycles of the sun and moon.

One winter, a few days before the katsinas were supposed to head for the mesas, I looked out at the mountains and thought that maybe this would be a good time for me to visit the mesas. This was also right after the coldest spell in twenty-two years, with temperatures down to minus eighteen, with ice everywhere, so perhaps I was eager to get outside and escape into the desert. If I saw a katsina doll I liked, I suspected it would be a Tawa katsina, the sun katsina, whose smile and colors and feathered headdress radiated warmth. But I wasn't going to Hopi to go shopping. I wasn't a collector. I had only a few katsina dolls, and I hadn't bought one for more than ten years.

My first stop was Orabi, a village founded about nine hundred years ago, making it the oldest continuously inhabited town in today's United States. It offered a great view of the cloud-shrouded, snow-covered San Francisco Peaks about fifty miles away.

On the edge of the mesa was a Catholic church, in ruins. The Spanish conquistadores and missionaries had arrived here in the 1500s and demanded that the Hopis give up their religion. Hopis who refused were whipped or doused with hot turpentine. To build their church the Spanish forced the Hopis to drag giant timbers from dozens of miles away. After the katsinas had kept the Hopis alive for centuries, the Hopis saw no need to abandon them, especially for saints who were clueless about bringing rain or teaching respectful Hopi behaviors and who inspired arrogance and cruelty. In 1680 the Hopis joined the other Pueblo tribes in driving the Spanish out. The timbers in the Orabi church were removed and used to build better kivas.

I went into the shop of Sandra Hamana. She is famous for making large wall plaques, with a wooden center and woven yarn radiating outward. Most of her plaques hold the face of Tawa, the sun katsina, and the brightly colored yarn radiates solar warmth. I had two of Sandra's plaques on my walls, and one of them was a Tawa. It was on my eastern, sunrise, wall and greeted me every morning.

My cabin deserved some Hopi decor, for it had been built by Hopi hands sixty years ago, and it had always been called "Hopi House." It sat on a hill that a thousand years ago was occupied by the homes of Hopi ancestors. The rocks that made up my foundation had very likely been used in those ancient Hopi houses. Nearby were ruins with rock walls that hadn't been recycled. I lived right next to a midden, a hillside down which people had tossed trash like broken pottery and food scraps. I walked down this hillside to where I parked, and when rain fell hard enough to carve a little gully in my pathway it always revealed more potsherds. I was always delighted to see them. They were like a gift, a gift from the rain, a gift from the people who had once lived here. When I reached down and fingered a potsherd out of the ground, I was touching ancient fingers. Most of the potsherds were undecorated, from utilitarian pots, but some bore black and white or black and red designs. Sometimes I found chunks of obsidian, shiny black volcanic glass, which had been struck to make a projectile point. Sometimes I found bits of bone.

I carried the potsherds into my cabin and placed them in a bowl made by a descendant of the most famous modern Hopi potter, Nampeyo. The designs on the bowl were descended from the designs on the potsherds. The bowl sat on a shelf a few inches beneath my Tawa plaque. When I placed a new potsherd into the bowl, it felt like I was making some sort of offering to the sun. The ancient pot makers would have understood. The sun grew their crops and stirred the clouds to give them rain. They probably saw the sun not just as a sustaining force, but as a creative force.

For the Hopis, Tawa is one of their primary deities, one of the creators of the world. (Tawa is often spelled "Dawa," for in the Hopi language the pronunciation is somewhere between the English *T* and *D*). Out of primordial chaos and his own being, Tawa created the First World, a cave within the earth, inhabited by insect-like creatures. Tawa wasn't satisfied with this creation, for its creatures fought among themselves and didn't appreciate being alive. Tawa sent Spider Grandmother to lead the insect creatures to the Second World, another underground world, where they became animals. But still they fought among themselves and didn't appreciate being alive. So Tawa created the Third World, with better water and air, and here the animals became humans. At first this world was good, but then sorcerers unleashed chaos and conflict. Once again Spider Grandmother led Tawa's creatures to a higher world, this time the surface of the earth, where the Hopis try to remember Tawa's gifts.

In spite of Tawa's importance in Hopi creation and his frequent appearance in Hopi art, including katsina dolls, I have never seen Tawa appear in a katsina ceremony. When I asked about this, the answers were a bit evasive. As far as I could tell, the Tawa katsina appeared rarely, inside kivas, at the beginning of the katsina ceremonial season, to give a blessing to the season ahead.

Sandra Hamana had a whole batch of miniature Tawa plaques, a few inches across, made with thread instead of yarn. They were ornaments hanging from a Christmas tree. Considering how the Spanish priests had tried to banish Tawa and the other katsinas, I found it ironic that Tawa was now decorating a symbol of Christmas. Then again, the Christmas tree had been around long before Christmas. It was an ancient pagan symbol of the endurance of life through winter, of the return of sunlight and growth. Christmas trees and cottonwood katsina dolls both spoke from the primordial need of life to continue.

In other villages I went into some other shops. I saw some nice Tawa katsina dolls, but all of them were Michelangelos or traditionals, with the wood completely painted over, which to me seemed to waste wood's natural beauty.

I went into Tsakurshovi, a shop owned by Joseph and Janice Day, famous for their T-shirts that say "Don't Worry, Be Hopi." Yet they were quite serious about promoting traditional-style katsina dolls. Their walls and shelves held maybe two hundred dolls, almost all traditional.

Among the small batch of nontraditional dolls was a sculpted Tawa doll, half of it pure wood. It was gorgeous. River gorge-ous. Its face was painted with softer colors than usual—green, red, and yellow. Its smile was a bit more human and friendly than the usual abstract triangle. Surrounding the face was a huge feathered headdress, also in softer colors than usual. The more natural colors fitted the natural wood. Unlike the traditional dolls, it had not even a suggestion of arms or legs; it was a tree root that had sprouted a human face. I picked it up and admired it.

Joseph was watching me, no doubt disappointed that I had zeroed in on the one little section allotted to dumb tourists. He started educating me about the virtues of traditional katsina dolls. He talked about authenticity, what katsina dolls meant to Hopis, and how traditions had been corrupted by *bahana* (white) tastes and money. Joseph seemed a bit conflicted, for he didn't really want to talk me out of buying something I liked. He took down a traditional doll and pointed out all its authentic features. Look, this carver wouldn't even use glue on his dolls, only old-style wooden pegs, and he mixed his own paints from traditional pigments. I guessed that the sculpted Tawa doll had used glue, *bahana*-white Elmer's Glue, to affix the face. Joseph said that the carver of this traditional doll was well respected for his commitment to Hopi traditions; his name was Ramsom Lomatewama. Hmmm, I said, Ramson's doll was fine work, but I would guess that even Ramson appreciated the beauty of pure wood, like I did.

An hour later we were still talking. I didn't want to corrupt the Hopis, but in the end I bought the Tawa doll.

I stayed on the mesa that night, and I watched the sunset setting aglow the mesas and the San Francisco Peaks.

That evening I took a closer look at "my" Tawa doll. I looked at its almost whimsical smile. In the Renaissance, Italian painters had strongly preferred to paint not on canvas but on planks of poplar wood, the genus that includes cottonwoods. Leonardo painted *Mona Lisa* on poplar wood. It was wood that was smiling so enigmatically, hinting at the secret life of wood. The Latin word for poplar is *populous*, and from this root comes the word *people*. People were rooted in trees, so it was only correct that poplar trees had branched out into Mona Lisa and a Tawa katsina doll. Like Mona Lisa, this Tawa wasn't telling me all the secrets he knew.

I looked at the wood grain, and how it showed through the painted designs of clouds and rain on the doll's base. In the face I saw the sun, of course, but I also saw the sun in its body, its wood. The sun had flowed into the tree and materialized itself into wood. Sunlight had energized the drawing of water and soil into the roots and up the tree. Sunlight had energized the absorption of the sky. Sunlight had twirled molecules into DNA and leaves. Sunlight had pushed the tree higher and wider. Sunlight had become golden leaves aglow with sunlight, and cotton puffs floating through the air like stars floating through the galaxy. In the shapes in the wood grain I saw solar prominences, convection cells, and sunspots. In the solidity of the wood I felt sunlight itself, sunlight that had arrived on Earth long ago. I was touching the sun's earthen fingerprint.

That night I placed Tawa in a window that faced east, so he could greet the rising sun.

In the eastern window of Joseph and Janice's shop there were several glass figures, about six inches tall. They had a head, a sinuous body, various colors, and swirling shapes and colors within the glass. They lived in the window so they could glow with the rising and morning sun.

I had one of these glass figures at home. It was full of orange energy. From its base arose orange swirls that tapered into a thick, curling spine, leaving much of the torso and shoulders as clear glass. When the orange spine reached the head it roiled outward, filling most of the head. The orange swirls were like a flame. They were like the towering nebula, "the Pillars of Creation," made famous by the Hubble Space Telescope.

The glass figures were meant to invoke katsina dolls. Their colors were meant to invoke the elements. Brown was the earth; blue was water or rain; green was plants and life in general; red and orange were fire and sunlight.

I had selected an orange figure after staring into the red-hot glass furnace of the glassblower. I had watched the molten glass glowing like fire, changing shape like fire. Clearly, the glass figures were creatures of fire before they calmed down into creatures of earth, water, or life.

The glassblower was Ramson Lomatewama. Ramson might be traditional at carving katsina dolls, but he had become quite an innovator at working with glass, an art form never tried by Hopis. Ramson started out making stained-glass windows with Hopi motifs, and then he was fired up by the idea of making glass figures. He was careful not to call them "katsinas," for they didn't qualify by any traditional definition. He called them "spirit beings" or "spirit figures." He built a glass furnace at his home at Hotevela and began mentoring younger Hopi artists, several of whom began working with glass in various forms. Ramson's glass figures combined cutting-edge artistic styles and Hopi traditions in a way that wasn't new for him. He had also published several books of poetry about Hopi life. He was often invited to colleges to give talks, for he was one of relatively few Native Americans who could talk about Native traditions in the conceptual frameworks of educated whites, in the language of Joseph Campbell or Carl Jung. Ramson also enjoyed poking holes in white stereotypes about Native Americans, including the positive, romanticized stereotypes widespread on college campuses.

Sometimes I picked up my orange spirit being and held it up to the sunlight. It glowed with flame. It became a prism that brought out the colors hidden within the sunlight. It was quartz that had laid dark inside mountains for millions of years and laid sparkling as sandy seashores, so it contained aeons and the pillars of Earth's creation, and now those aeons and forces were wearing a human shape and glowing.

Two weeks after buying my spirit being, I went to Hotevela for the Niman ceremony, and it was through an orange fiery lens that I saw the katsinas dancing.

The Niman ceremony not only sends the katsinas home to the mountains, but also brings Hopis home from all the places they live, sometimes far from the mesas. For several nights before the Niman ceremony I was hearing construction sounds from near my cabin. Two neighboring cabins had Hopi residents, and one, Vernon, was from Hotevela, so he was making gifts for the katsinas to give to children, katsina dolls for the girls, bows and arrows for the boys. Vernon invited me into his family home at Hotevela, and I took bread and pies as gifts for his parents, though my Safeway deli bread tended to get ignored in favor of the fresh, outdoor-baked Hopi bread.

Vernon's carving of katsina dolls was amazing, for Vernon had only one arm. As a youth he had gone to work at the local *bahana*-owned trading post, which had a butcher shop. The meat-cutting machine was old, and Vernon was given little training for it. One of the first times he used it, it caught his arm and cut it deeply, too deeply. Most people would be left permanently embittered by such a loss, but Vernon had remained a basically joyful person. The accident wouldn't stop him from carving katsina dolls.

Even with two arms, carving katsina dolls with a sharp knife could extract a bit of blood. It could leave hands callused. But the carving went on. The portrayal styles might change, but the katsinas went on. The ceremonies went on because the seasons went on, the cycles of Earth and sun and moon went on, the cycles of plants and animals went on, and human life had to go on. Hopi ceremonies were rooted in the deepest Mona Lisa secrets of the solar system and cells. Carving katsina dolls was rooted in a creativity that went deeper than just human creativity. Making a shape emerge from wood brought some of the same satisfaction as helping corn grow from a seed, but it also contained the creativity of the corn itself, the creativity of cottonwood trees launching their blizzard of seeds, the creativity of stars creating carbon atoms, the creativity of the Big Bang launching the universe of puffy white galaxies.

At Hotevela I climbed a wooden ladder onto a house rooftop— the proper place for *bahanas*—overlooking the plaza.

The katsinas filed into the plaza. Drums began beating. Rattles began shaking. The katsinas began singing. It was all a prayer, an elaborate, performed prayer.

At first I was distracted by the spectacle of it, the colors and motions and sounds, but soon I saw the spectrum of it. I saw it through the prism of my orange spirit being. The spirit beings before me were also filled with fire, with luminous, swirling pillar-of-creation flames. They were filled with sunlight. Through golden corn the golden sun had flowed into these forms. I saw prominences, convection cells, and sunspots. I saw solar energy flowing in strange new ways. The sunlight upheld their forms, energized their motions, and articulated their songs. Sunlight glowed from their eyes. Sunlight glowed as consciousness. The light of the sun had become the light of the sacred.

The katsina dance was one prominence of a much larger dance. The sun too was a dance, a dance far more crowded and intense. The particles of the sun were swarming with fierce speed, spinning and swerving and spiraling, colliding intensely enough to fuse—with a burst of light—into heavier particles. Gravity pulled the particles inward, the outward flow of light pushed the particles outward, electromagnetic fields steered the particles this way and that, and the meshing of these forces carved from the chaos of particles larger currents and shapes, in total the shape of a sphere. The trillions of tiny bursts of light every second combined into a flood of light and heat pouring into space.

Long ago, in other suns, suns long vanished from the sky, the katsina dancers had danced in stars. They had spun and swerved and spiraled at intense speeds. They had ridden currents into the heart of a star and back out to the surface. They had contributed to the gravity that pulled inward, to the energy that pushed outward, and to the electromagnetic fields twisting this way and that. They had helped energize the fusing of atoms, and they themselves had smashed together and by the magic of physics become heavier atoms. They had danced hydrogen into carbon and oxygen and dozens of elements. They had also generated bursts of light, some of which were still out there, still moving through space, billions of light-years away.

The katsina dancers had helped dance into being the atoms that became Earth. They had helped create the rock of continents and the falling rain and the rivers that carved canyons. They had helped create the carbon of life, of cottonwood trees and corn stalks. They had helped create reptiles sponging up the sun, rivers of birds flowing over the continents, insects turning the green wings of plants into their own, and mammals harvesting it all for both stomach and brain. From the solar fire that put atoms together they had helped light the biological fire that put cells together and the consciousness fire that put meanings together.

The katsina dance was the culmination of a dance that had been seeking order and solidity and life and fertility for 13.7 billion years. This dance had exploded into action with the swarming light and particles of the Big Bang, and it had steadily flowed into new movements, small and large, fast and slow, graceful and savage, instant and evolving. Choreographed by the secret yet unfolding laws of matter, the cosmic dance was performed by eternally pirouetting atoms, by spinning galaxies, by nebulae contracting or dispersing, by stars circling the galaxy and planets circling the stars and moons and comets circling the planets, by tectonic plates creeping along, by mountains and lava rising, by water flowing in a thousand forms, by the dance of the snowflakes writing Tchaikovsky, by pebbles rolling mountains into the ocean surf, by lightning and rainbows and sunsets, by the sounds of thunder and wind and rivers chanting the planet into life. Earth's circling of the sun was a ceremony that needed to be repeated four and a half billion times, and the sunrise was a ceremony necessary one and a half trillion times, to create beings who could turn that oblivious ceremony into a celebration.

And here it had arrived, in the plaza canyon of ancient stones. The cosmic dance had become beings who recognized that the cycles of their lives were but epicycles of the rolling sky, that a beating human heart was a gear turned by the ancient intermeshing gears of the universe. Through human eyes the cosmic dance saw the cottonwood roots and the suns it had swirled into. Through human feet the cosmic dance now flowed into the new patterns of a katsina ceremony. Through the human mouth spoke the voice the thunder had been seeking to become. The long journey into life had arrived and proclaimed itself to have been worthwhile. The universe had become a celebrant of itself.

The drums began beating, beating, beating like human hearts. They echoed off the plaza walls. I felt their sonic hypnotism and summons.

The drumheads were made of deerskins, pulled taut, as taut as the senses and attention of a deer at their highest intensity.

A deer was grazing in the woods, enjoying the sunlight and the taste of leaves and the cool energy of a stream, when she became aware that something was wrong. She raised her head and looked around. She searched with eyes and ears and nose and mind, all at full intensity. She looked from the boundary between life and death. She threw her embrace to life. Her heart raced. Her muscles tensed to race. In her alertness, she saw the trees as vividly as she had ever seen them.

And with a whoosh an arrow struck her, or perhaps a bullet, and her heart burst. She grasped at one final vision of life.

And now her skin was here, the boundary between life and death. Her hoofs were here, rattling inside turtle-shell rattles, summoning humans into motion. Her final heartbeats were here, beating, beating, beating, summoning humans to pay attention, to see with full intensity the universe and their presence in it.

The drums were made of hollowed-out cottonwood logs. The wood vibrated with energy, as it had once vibrated with the energy of the wind. The river within the wood pulsed as it had once pulsed with waves. The earth within the wood pulsed as it had once pulsed to raise mountains. The sunlight within the drums was reminded of its ancient solar heartbeat and echoed with it again, summoning humans to recognize and celebrate their own luminous heartbeats.◦✦

·4·

METEOR RITES

THE CIRCLES OF LIFE WERE SO SMALL.

Walking away from the mesa, walking away from the city, leaving her home forever, she stopped and turned and looked back. The black cliffs, the rim of the mesa, already seemed so small. The large black boulders looked like little rocks. She gazed back and forth over the boulders, trying to see upon them a lot of lighter shapes, hundreds of spirals, faces, rain clouds, cornstalks, and snakes, but already they had become invisible. She thought of all the years and all the work people had put into carving those figures—already invisible. The whole city was invisible. She would never see it again.

She thought of all the years, all the lifetimes, all the labor people had put into building the city. Rock by rock, tree by tree, handful of mud by handful of mud, room by room, kiva by kiva, garden by garden, they had built the city. Her parents had migrated here with so much hope. They had chosen big rocks to make rooms that would last a long time. They had smoothed the plaster with care, and painted it with pride. They had migrated here from the north, from near the great mountain, from a village that was dying, its springs drying up, its rains failing, its crops withering. Her parents had come here like so many others, from so many other dying villages. And now their city too was dying. It was full of abandoned dwellings, abandoned kivas, abandoned tools and pottery, abandoned graves. She thought of her parents' graves atop the mesa, and how she would never see them again. She gasped with sadness and worry.

She looked at the desert in front of her, hard and dry and empty. The grasses were brown and shriveled. Even the juniper trees were dying. The horizon was far, far away, several days of walking.

There might be no water along the way. When she had slung her water supply over her shoulder it had seemed so heavy, but now it seemed so light. She loved this water like she had never loved water before. She hated this water because its weight had forced her to leave behind things she loved and would have kept for years— pottery, clothes, her mother's bracelet. People were such small and weak things in the desert. With every footstep, the dust puffed into a little cloud.

She had never been north of the mesa before, not far. Only one person in her group of two dozen had ever before been to the Hopi villages, which now would become their new home. The traveling traders had talked about the Hopi villages having reliable springs and good corn and gardens. When the Hopis looked to the south they could see her mesa, which they called Nuvakwewtaqa, or "Snow Belt," because its north-facing slopes shaded the snow. But this year there had been almost no snow.

They walked all day. They came to a water hole, but it was dry, long dry and cracked. Deer skeletons, four of them. They walked toward a low mesa and camped near it that night.

In the morning the medicine man said that he was going to climb the mesa and make an offering. He said that ordinarily this ceremony was only for the initiated, but this was no ordinary time, no ordinary journey, and they might never see this mesa again. It was no ordinary mesa. She would go along.

The mesa wasn't steep until near the top. She wondered what was unusual about it. Was it the large, scattered, jagged white boulders? Was it the white powdery soil? Was it the numerous strange, distorted, pockmarked black rocks that were—she paused to pick up a small one—much heavier than any rock she'd ever touched?

She reached the top of the mesa—but the mesa had no top! It was a giant hole in the ground. It was far across and deep and entirely empty. It appeared to be deeper than the land all around it. Yes, it was. It had an irregular rim, littered with boulders. Its inside walls were cliffs at the top and slopes farther down. A flat bottom.

It was like a bowl for holding food.

It was like a kiva, an old abandoned kiva with no roof.

She watched the medicine man standing on the rim of the giant hole and tossing corn pollen into it. Was this the kiva of one of the gods? A god who was so displeased with his people that he had taken away the rains and dried up the springs and killed the corn and ruined the villages and her city? She watched the corn pollen being swept away by the powerful, dry wind. She felt the water bleeding from her body into the wind. She felt so small.

✦ ✦ ✦

The circles of life were so small; they were invisible to almost all of the universe.

They were invisible in the asteroid belt. To the asteroids, the universe consisted mostly of gravity and darkness. The sun was so far away that its light was surrendering to the darkness of space. But the asteroids still felt the sun's gravity. It had ruled them for billions of years. The asteroid's only thoughts were: *gravity, gravity, gravity, falling, falling, falling, orbit, orbit, orbit.* Every few years the asteroids passed Jupiter and felt its gravity, felt a conflict of loyalties: *Sun's gravity, Jupiter's gravity, Sun's gravity, Jupiter's gravity.* Occasionally, Jupiter's gravity tugged an asteroid out of its ancient orbit and sent it wandering into the path of another asteroid: they collided, cracked off pieces, gained new spins, even drifted out of the solar system or toward the sun.

Long ago, perhaps hundreds of millions of years ago, one asteroid was forced out of its home orbit and sent wandering toward the sun. The asteroid was about 150 feet across, made of nickel-iron, and weighed about three hundred thousand tons. The asteroid drifted toward Mars and felt its gravity but was not inclined to follow the millions of asteroids that had crashed into Mars and left craters there, craters that might last billions of years. The asteroid passed Mars and headed farther into the solar system, accelerating steadily. The asteroid swept around the sun and away from it, passing Mercury, a Mercury saturated with craters. The asteroid flew out of the inner solar system, back toward the asteroid belt, slowing steadily, and then it curved back and headed toward the sun again, accelerating steadily. The asteroid performed this new orbit for hundreds of millions of years.

Then, about fifty thousand years ago, the asteroid was heading toward the sun when a planet moved into its path. This planet was not like Mars and Mercury but was blue and white and green. At a speed of about twenty-six thousand miles per hour the asteroid flew toward the planet. Miles above the surface the asteroid began encountering a strange resistance, an invisible substance. The asteroid began heating up, then glowing.

A dot of life was about to be reminded—yet again—that it was a tiny rare exception in a universe of death. The planets, moons, and asteroids were dead rock, dead craters, dead volcanoes, dead ice, dead gas. The stars were oblivious fires. The universe was so full of death that Earth couldn't hide from death for long. Even if Earth avoided supernovas and black holes and colliding stars and X-ray blasts, it couldn't escape from the asteroids that were always searching it out. An asteroid was the finger of the dead universe Sistine-reaching into Earth and touching Earth with the fingerprint of death, ripples of death, tsunamis of death that could reach around the entire planet and extinguish a large portion of its life.

◆ ◆ ◆

The circles of life were so huge.

His own footprints were huge, in the mud beside the river.

His tusks were huge, fifteen feet long and curving, strong enough to rip out bushes and to chase off saber-toothed cats, whose sabers were merely one foot long. He was ten feet tall, ten feet wide at his shoulders, and weighed seven tons. His woolly hairs were nearly two feet long.

As the woolly mammoth approached the river he scared away the pack of dire wolves lurking in the grasses and eyeing the giant ground sloths and the musk oxen drinking there. In the distance he saw camels and horses and bison grazing on the grasses, grasses so lush and inexhaustible they couldn't be eaten up by all the types of herds that lived upon them. The river was so abundant and inexhaustible that a million woolly mammoths drinking from it at the same time couldn't dry it out. The earth was an endless stampede of life.

In the mud beside the river he saw hundreds of footprints of dozens of shapes, craters small and large, shallow and deep.

Far in the distance he saw the white gleam of the glaciers atop the great mountain.

Suddenly, he saw another gleam, far up in the sky. It was a lightning bolt—but there were no clouds. It was another sun. A speck of light flashed into a ball of fire with a long fiery tail. It raced across the sky—it raced downward—it hit the ground—the ground exploded into fire—outrageous fire—blinding fire—fire rising high—fire streaming outward—the ground shook violently—then the thunder—outrageous thunder—a rising, growing dark cloud swept closer and closer. Terrified, he turned to flee. All the animals were running, except for the ones too terrified to run and the ones knocked over by the earthquake. The teratorn spread her giant wings and took off, but the terrible dark cloud raced in and swatted her down. The terrible dark cloud raced in, roaring with violence, and knocked over the woolly mammoth and rolled him along the ground, rolled him over and over, snapping off his tusks, tearing off his hair, pounding him with turbulent and hot debris.

✦ ✦ ✦

As the asteroid entered Earth's atmosphere it began heating up and ablating, yet it was moving so fast that it took only seconds to reach the ground, and it lost little of its speed and only about 1 percent of its mass. As the falling asteroid heated up, chunks of iron peeled off and flew alongside it, and these chunks would be the only sizable solid parts of the asteroid to survive. The asteroid and its kinetic energy and its atmospheric shock wave hit the ground; the asteroid blew apart and melted and vaporized, an explosion equal to hundreds of atomic bombs. Melted iron flew upward and outward and cooled and formed tiny iron droplets that rained down for miles around and iron dust that flew miles farther. The explosion blasted the ground apart, digging a hole seven hundred feet deep and four thousand feet across, throwing 175 million tons of solid rock into the air, including massive boulders. Rocks flew for a mile around the crater, dust much farther. The impact shocked the rocks into new minerals and into tiny black diamonds. The blast wave swept outward across the land and incinerated all plants and animals for miles around and killed and injured animals far beyond that. A huge dark, boiling cloud spread high above and far around the crater. Slowly, the cloud yielded to gravity and wind, settling to the ground and blowing away.

Earth now held a lunar landscape, miles wide, totally dead. Even seeds had been incinerated. It was a wound from the dead universe.

Yet Earth refused to surrender. Within days Earth was dropping seed-asteroids onto the black dust and creating tiny craters, then dropping raindrop-asteroids and creating rain craters. Small green plumes arose. Within a few years the grasses had returned. Woolly mammoths walked past the burned mammoth bones and walked the grassy outside slopes of the crater, to draw their lives from it.

Thousands of years later a new footprint appeared on the crater's slopes. A new animal arrived and threw asteroids at the mammoths and gouged bloody craters in them, and lit fires to feast on mammoth meat and to celebrate the abundance of the earth.

More thousands of years later, in a time of faltering abundance, humans migrated from failing villages to a volcanic mesa, from which they could see the little bulge of the meteorite crater miles in the distance. With them they carried corn seeds. They planted the seeds into soil that still contained the meteor's blast and wind and fire and terror and ashes and iron dust. The seeds sprouted and sent up sturdy green plumes and yellow ears of corn, full of meteorite dust. Humans gave thanks and lifted the corn to their mouths and inducted meteorite dust into their bodies. The random raw drifting iron of the universe flowed into their veins and became hemoglobin and flowed into elaborate cellular orbits, flowed to the gravity of brains, flowed into eyes that saw the meteorite crater miles in the distance.

With hands now made of meteorite dust, a human raised a sharp stone tool against a black boulder on the black cliffs and struck it with a stone hammer, leaving a small, lighter-colored impact crater. He continued moving the tool and striking it, creating a line of craters, a curving line, a face. The sound of the striking was the echo of an ancient roar. The skill of the striking was the acceleration of an ancient trajectory. From formlessness, from night-blackness, the face emerged. The face opened its eyes. The face looked out upon the distant meteorite crater. The face looked out upon the sun and the moon and the stars and the secret powers hidden in the blackness of space.

+ + +

With hands made of meteorite dust, a human raised a stone ax high and swung it down into the dirt—thud! Again and again he swung the ax and broke the earth and made this crater deeper. For days he and other men continued digging. When the hole was deep enough and wide enough, they handed hundreds of rocks into the hole and stacked and fit them against the earthen wall, creating a stone wall. They mortared it tight. They stood inside the earth and looked up at the sky. They placed logs across the top of the hole, then branches, then dirt, all except for a hole in the center of the roof. In the floor of this kiva they dug a small hole, a sipapuni, symbolic of the hole from which humans had first emerged into this world. They plastered the stone walls smooth and painted murals upon them, images of life and the powers that support life. The paint was made from hematite—iron—mixed with animal fats or blood (it was the iron that might allow the paint to endure for centuries).

With hands in which it merged with earth dust, the meteorite had gouged out another crater in the earth. Its first crater had been an act of chaos, but this crater was an argument against chaos. Its first crater had been an act of gravity, but this crater was an act of uplift. Its first crater had been an act of raw, mindless physical force, but this crater was a stone organism raised by the dance inside cells, with a purpose, a symbolism, an energy for consciousness. With its first crater the meteorite had spoken for the universe of death, but with this crater it was saying that even an asteroid could emerge into the shapes and intensity of life.

+ + +

She watched the medicine man dropping corn pollen into the crater and offering a prayer.

The corn pollen contained tiny specks of meteorite dust. After fifty thousand years, the meteorite had returned to its crater and was falling into it once again.

Now the meteorite was pleading the cause of life. Against the deepness and endurance of this grave, against the relentless power of the desert, against the hidden powers of the night sky, the meteorite called out to the universe.

The corn pollen fell, once again in the grip of gravity, so tiny compared with the power that had made this crater. And yet so strong.

She looked at the horizon. She looked for the mesas where they were headed. She saw the long walk ahead through the desert. Beyond that, she saw springs flowing and corn growing and katsinas dancing. She saw kivas where the stones would amplify the strangeness of the universe and the strange, relentless longings of life.•✦

·5·

STORM PATTERN

THE SKY WAS GOING TO EXPLODE. The night sky was going to burst out in light, streamers of light. There was going to be a loud noise, a big bang.

The *bilagaana*, the white man, was going to set off his cannon and light up the sky. They watched him aiming and fiddling with the cannon. Yazzie had seen fireworks in July, when his parents took him to Gallup. Yazzie told the other kids that fireworks were how the white men celebrated the beginning of their tribe. Yazzie was always trying to show off how much he knew about the white man's ways. He had even seen a railroad train. In Gallup Yazzie hadn't seen the cannons that shot off the fireworks, but he supposed that this was how it was done. But now the white man only continued staring at one end of the cannon. Was something wrong with it? Perhaps Father Sky was annoyed with the white man. Perhaps an explosion among the stars would be harmful to Father Sky and the harmony of the cosmos. White men didn't know about the harmony of the cosmos.

They watched the white man's pipe glowing in the dark. Then after a long time of nothing happening, the white man spoke to them in white men's words. Yazzie translated: He says we can look through his telegraph. They stood there, perplexed. They had seen the white man arrive by daylight, and he had appeared to be a stern man, and now he was speaking nonsense. He spoke again, and Yazzie translated: He says his telephone lets you see the stars. They had heard of telephones and voices in metal wires. "No," said the man, "telly-scope." Through the metal tube you could hear the stars telling stories. Even in the dark they could see the man pointing to the end of the telly-story. And of course it was Yazzie who had to prove how smart and brave he was by being the first to step up to the tube. He leaned down at the end of the tube the way the white man had, and continued moving his head about. Then he gasped. He saw lights, crowds of little lights. Were these the stars? Were there really so many stars?

Each kid took his or her turn looking through the telescope, puzzling over it, exclaiming over it. Then they looked up at the sky as if they had never seen it before. They had never imagined it held so many stars. They looked up at the white man and wondered about him. It was October, the time of year to begin telling stories of the night sky. Had the white man come with his telly-scope to help tell stories of the night sky?

When the kids were done looking through the telescope, the man took it apart and placed it into a long suitcase and put it back into the trunk of his car. Then he walked to his cabin next to the trading post, struck a match and lit the lamp, and closed the door. As the kids headed up the hill to home, they gazed at the sky again.

The white man noticed the rug on the wooden floor mostly for how it saved his now bare feet from splinters and dust and chill. But the pattern on the rug looked slightly familiar. It was full of geometric patterns. In each of the four corners there were boxes with geometric patterns, and from each box a zigzag line reached toward the center. Zigzags like lightning bolts. The lightning bolts hit another pattern in the center.

The rug felt warm but his feet were cold; the room was cold. This might be the Arizona desert, but it was high desert, and it was October. He glanced at the woodstove, but he didn't want to bother with it. He picked the rug off the floor and tossed it over his bed. The lightning bolts would keep him warm all night.

As he blew out the lantern and lay there in the dark, he mused on his circumstances. Here he was in a bare, crude wooden cabin, next to a stone trading post in the middle of nowhere, far down a terrible dirt road, a cabin without electricity or running water, the only bathroom an outhouse perched above the Little Colorado River. He was surrounded by horses and beat-up wagons, by people who couldn't speak English, people who lived in ancient ways. Yet he had just conducted tests for locating the world's most sophisticated astronomical observatory. Right now he wasn't sure why his boss, George Hale, who had already built the three greatest telescopes in the world, had included Cameron as a potential observatory site. The rim of the Grand Canyon, where he had conducted tests the last few nights, seemed more plausible.

When he had signed his name to the trading-post guest register, perhaps the trader asked him if he was related to the famous Hubbells, the family that ran the Hubbell Trading Post and a constellation of other trading posts on Navajo lands. Navajos trusted the Hubbell name more than that of any other trader. Edwin would have said yes; he didn't know those Hubbells personally, but he was related to them way back in the Hubbell family tree, back in New England. Edwin's branch of the tree had changed their spelling to "Hubble," for reasons no longer clear. But Edwin was accustomed to seeing his name spelled in the old way. When George Hale hired him, Hale spelled his name "Hubbell," and when the *New York Times* announced that Edwin had proven the existence of other galaxies, his name was "Hubbell." Even living in Los Angeles, Edwin couldn't help knowing about the trading-post Hubbells, for two years ago the Hubbells had opened an Indian arts store on Hollywood Boulevard, in Hollywood's trendiest block, right across the street from Grauman's Egyptian Theater, and across from the Pig 'N Whistle restaurant where the movie stars hung out.

How curious that a Hubble had come to the land of the Hubbells to locate the world's greatest observatory.

Edwin Hubble had also crossed over into a parallel universe, the Navajo universe. The rug under which he slept portrayed the Navajo creation story. The design at the center of the rug was the Navajos' place of emergence. The designs in the four corners were the four sacred mountains that bordered the Navajo world. The lightning bolts between the mountains and the place of emergence conveyed blessings. This rug design is called the Storm Pattern.

At least, since the details of Edwin Hubble's two nights at the Cameron Trading Post in 1928 are vague, we are indulging in a bit of imagination to flesh out the beginning of this story. The most common rug design in the Cameron area was the Storm Pattern, so chances are that the rugs in his room included a Storm Pattern.

As Edwin Hubble drifted off to sleep, chances are he thought about the discovery he was making, research he had interrupted to come to the Grand Canyon and Cameron. He was right in the middle of discovering that the universe was expanding. He couldn't stop thinking about it, even in his sleep. The Magritte cloud galaxies that raced through his dreams were not as surrealistic as the racing galaxies he awoke to and saw through his telescope.

As Edwin Hubble lay sleeping, as galaxies raced through his dreams, the Navajo creation story pulsed all around him, dreaming of emergence, sending out its lightning energies of affirmation.

If Hubble had slept within a Navajo hogan, he would have opened a door that faced the rising sun. The design of the hogan is full of symbolism that aligns humans with the life-giving forces and patterns of the universe. Every hogan is a re-creation of the first hogan, built by First Man when humans first emerged into this world. The first hogan, and every hogan since, was carefully aligned with the four cardinal directions. The building of the first hogan plays a large role in the Blessingway ceremony, the most import-ant Navajo ceremony for maintaining harmony between humans and the universe. Of course, a doorway facing the sunrise also has a practical advantage, for in a high-desert climate, where nights can be chilly even in summer, a hogan receives the first morning warmth and minimizes the afternoon heat. The sacred often begins with what nourishes life. The design in the center of the Storm Pattern rug is—by some accounts—the first hogan.

On the day between the two nights Edwin Hubble spent at the Cameron Trading Post, it's likely that he observed the daily life of a remote 1920s trading post, with Navajos coming and going by horse and wagon. Though Cameron was thirty miles from the Grand Canyon, the dirt road between them was steep, narrow, twist-ing, and dangerous, and most Grand Canyon tourists avoided that route. Most of the visitors at Cameron were Navajos bringing things to trade for food or utensils or supplies—few Navajos had cash for buying anything. Edwin would have seen Navajo women in velvet blouses unloading from their wagons bundles of wool or newly finished rugs. He would have seen a weaver unroll her rug on the countertop and discuss it with the trader. Since most Navajos lived widely scattered on a lonely landscape, coming to a trading post was an important social event, and many Navajos remained all day and visited with friends. Like many trading posts, Cameron included guest hogans where customers could stay overnight. Edwin would have heard the Navajo language, full of words for the beauty and emptiness of sandstone space, coloring his nighttime view of astronomical space.

◆ ◆ ◆

The wool being carried into the trading post was the sandstone landscape translated into the language of life, whirls of sand translated through sheep stomachs and sheep genes into whirls of wool.

The sandstone on which the Navajos live is the geofossil of Jurassic sand dunes of nearly two hundred million years ago. Those dunes were part of the largest aeolian sand deposits on Earth, stretching from present-day southern Arizona into Wyoming and Idaho, dunes as deep as twenty-five hundred feet (visible today in the cliffs of Zion Canyon). The dunes were formed in a time of severe drought, which dried up the rivers that had been flowing in from the east and burned the green land into brown. Relentless winds piled up sand into long, tall, gracefully curving and arching dunes. Occasionally old rivers flooded back through, followed by old forests, followed by dinosaurs that left in the mud the footprints that would one day provide a sip of water to Navajos herding their sheep. The sand dunes turned into rock, and after other periods of rivers and forests, the land reverted to desert and eroded into orange-red cliffs, releasing its ancient sand to wander in the wind again. Then arrived a people whose faces matched the color and deep lines of the sandstone cliffs; then arrived animals whose wanderings matched the wanderings of sand.

Like surveyors, like geologists, Navajo sheep map out the ghost landscapes of the Jurassic. They follow canyons that follow old weaknesses in the rock. They find the best grasses where old rivers left the richest soils. They know the location of every spring and seep, the pores of hidden sandstone waves, of ancient wind energies. They are summoning the minerals of dinosaurs into a renewed frustration over the scarcity of food in a desert.

The sheep scramble up the sandstone slopes and ledges, stopping at each patch of grass, obeying where the stone traffic light has turned from red to green, turned from geology into biology, turned from a long stasis into the quick, intricate sedimentation inside cells. The sheep eat the revived sandstone and feel it reinforcing their own energies. The sandstone becomes red blood flowing through their bodies, becomes a red heart beating, becomes red flesh full of curves and cliffs. The sandstone swirls itself into DNA, into cells, into O'Keeffe bones, into a face, into eyes in which sandstone sunsets glow with a living twilight zone. The sandstone swirls itself into a cross-bedded brain that pulses with images of sandstone cliffs. The sandstone swirls itself into horns that deceive sheep into imagining they are strong and dominant, when the sandstone knows otherwise. The sandstone swirls itself into a thick, swirling wool coat, perfect for guarding life's warmth against the cold of winter, the cold of night. The sheep huddle together in the winter and in the night. The wool understands that the starry night is not an easy place for life. In Navajo cosmology the gods were trying to place the stars carefully in the sky, place them in patterns that would sustain and guide human life, when Coyote the trickster grabbed their fawn-skin pouch full of stars and tossed it into the sky, spraying the stars chaotically. But coyote placed one star deliberately and named it for himself, Ma'ii Bizq', Coyote Star, and under Coyote Star the sheep huddle, wide awake, eyes full of fear, as coyotes howl and circle not far away in the night.

The weaver unrolled her rug on the counter. It was a Storm Pattern design. It was a map of the life of sheep. It contained years of wandering through sandstone mazes. It contained thunderstorms that set arroyos flooding and set plants growing; it contained lightning that couldn't find a tree to strike and so left a boulder scarred by the sky, and left brains with long memories of lightning. It contained blizzards and scorching summer days, wind and deep silence.

It contained the pleasures of sheep companionship and the miserable bleating of lost lambs. It contained endless puzzlement at the doings of humans. It contained the dismay of realizing that their proud horns made perfect handles for humans to drag them off to be sheared.

As the weaver unrolled the Storm Pattern rug on the counter, Edwin Hubble looked on. At least, it's plausible that Hubble, knowing the fame of the name Hubbell in Navajo country and now seeing a Navajo trading post for the first time, took an interest in what went on there. Hubble saw the Navajo creation story on the countertop. He saw its order, and its intense energy.

The Storm Pattern rug was sandstone that had now swirled itself into patterns far beyond cells and wool, patterns by which life sought to recognize itself and its origins. It was a map of the universe. It was sand that after aeons of falling into canyon-deep hourglasses had finally begun to hear the echoes of mysterious time. It was Jurassic lightning trying to shed some light on the pathways of energy. It was an ancient wind that had focused itself into a search for meaning. It was a universe of stone that had been transformed into a story of creation.

Ten days ago Edwin Hubble had no idea he would be staying at a Navajo trading post in the Arizona desert. He had been in the middle of the most important work of his life, the most important work in the history of astronomy, when his boss at Mount Wilson Observatory, George Hale, directed him to drop everything and head for Arizona.

Four years before, Hubble had expanded the universe in another way, by proving that our Milky Way galaxy was not the entire universe but one galaxy in a very large universe full of galaxies, millions of galaxies, maybe billions of galaxies. Astronomers had long supposed that nebulae—little fuzzy patches of light, often spiral shaped—were just clouds of gas within our own galaxy, but a few astronomers wondered if spiral nebulae might be other galaxies, making the universe to be unbelievably large. There was no way to settle this question, for astronomers had never had any reliable way to gauge cosmic distances. Hubble found a way. He used the world's

most powerful telescope, at Mount Wilson Observatory, to identify one particular type of star, a Cepheid variable, in the Andromeda nebula, and then he used a new method for determining the
distances of Cepheid variables. It turned out that the Andromeda
nebula lay far outside our own galaxy. Hubble determined the distances to more nebulae, and they too turned out to be other galaxies.

About three months ago Hubble had begun intense research
into the motions of galaxies. By now he had accumulated many measurements of the distances to galaxies, and he began comparing these
with V. M. Slipher's spectrographic studies that revealed the motions
of objects. Stars moved with a great variety of directions and speeds,
yet Slipher found that most spiral nebulae were redshifted—moving
away from us, and at fantastic speeds. When Hubble began comparing Slipher's galactic redshifts with his own measurements of galactic distances, he soon found a pattern. The farther away a galaxy was,
the faster it was moving, moving outward. The galaxies were spreading outward from a common origin. The universe appeared to have
had some sort of beginning.

Three months after his Cameron visit, Hubble would submit
his findings to the *Proceedings of the National Academy of Sciences*. Yet
when he set out for Arizona, Hubble must have already known that
his findings were going to transform the universe. Not only was the
universe much vaster and emptier than humans had ever imagined,
but it also held far more matter; it was full of motion and change
and chaos yet also full of order. All this motion and energy showed
incredible patterns. As Edwin Hubble wandered around the Cameron Trading Post, his mind must have been charged with images
of galaxies flying through space, charged with massive energies and
massive patterns, charged with the outrageous mystery of it.

Edwin watched the weaver showing her Storm Pattern rug to
the trader, pointing out its good workmanship. She pointed to its
central motif, the place of emergence.

Sometimes this central pattern is described as the first hogan,
sometimes as a lake. In Navajo cosmology our world is the fourth—
often the fifth—world humans have inhabited. Humans have
emerged from a series of underworlds.

The first world was dark and small and plagued with evil insects. Two clouds came together, a white cloud and a black cloud, a male cloud and a female cloud, and produced First Man, a supernatural man. Further holy people appeared, though they were Mist People, with no definite form. When the first world became too crowded and the insects too troublesome, the people—including Coyote—climbed into the second world. The second world was already inhabited by various species of blue birds, who didn't appreciate the new arrivals. The people saw an opening in the sky and climbed through it. The third world held two great rivers and six mountains, but no sun. Things started off well, but then the people quarreled and got into troubles. Coyote the trickster went and stole the two children of Water Buffalo; by some accounts, First Woman sent Coyote as an act of mischief. Water Buffalo was enraged and sent a great flood to drown the world. The people fled, climbing a mountain to stay above the rising floodwaters. At the top of the mountain, First Man planted a reed and used his medicine to make it grow. The people climbed the reed into the sky and emerged into the fourth world. Water Buffalo started to emerge too, bringing his flood, so Coyote finally returned one of his stolen children, keeping the other to bring rain.

On the Storm Pattern rug, the flood is represented by logs whirling and by water beetles.

In the fourth world First Man built the first hogan, and here the holy people met and planned an orderly cosmos. They created the sun and the moon and the seasons. They summoned Black God, the god of fire, and he began placing stars in the sky, giving them patterns full of meaning, patterns to support and guide human life. In the North, Black God created *náhookqs bikq'*, or Central Fire, the fire at the center of a hogan, around which all the other stars would rotate. Black God created two constellations, one male and one female, to revolve around Central Fire and remind humans of the importance of family, of protection and nurturing. Black God created constellations that signaled when it was time to start planting or hunting or to hold ceremonies, constellations with stories that told humans what to honor and how to behave, and constellations that reminded humans to remain in harmony with the universe. Black God wasn't finished when Coyote stole his pouch and tossed the rest of the stars into the sky, ruining Black God's patterns.

The Storm Pattern rug acknowledged the chaos of creation with its image of the flood, yet ultimately it portrayed the creation as a blessing. The lightning bolts were not the lightning of the storm that brought the flood, nor were they the evil omens that lightning often is for Navajos. The lightning conveyed blessings. For a billion years the cells of Earth had defined the universe, its good and evil, as mere patches of light and dark, but now life was weaving creation stories with light as symbols, stories full of images and ideas and judgments. Edwin Hubble was carrying on life's primordial quest for order in a still more elaborate form.

The Navajo creation story is unusual in its combination of motifs. Emergence stories, in which humans emerge from a series of underworlds, are almost always associated with agricultural peoples. For farmers life is something that emerges out of the ground, emerges from seeds that are rich and reliable in order and potential. Humans emerged from the nurturing womb of Mother Earth, just as crops do every spring. Father Sky too is full of order that nurtures life, reliable cycles of seasons and rain and sunlight. Plants too offer reliable cycles of planting and sprouting and growth and harvest, harvests of seeds that carry through the winter the reliable secret of a further cycle of life. For agricultural peoples the universe is full of predictable order. This order can be disrupted too easily, but these disruptions are an unnatural invasion of cosmic order. The goal of religious ceremonies is to honor and encourage cosmic order, to make sure that humans are in harmony with it.

Yet the Navajos are not an agricultural people. For most of their history they were nomadic hunter-gatherers, and then they became pastoralists. Their encounter with agriculture was fairly recent and limited.

For hunter-gatherers the universe is usually far more unstable and dangerous than it is for agriculturalists. Wild animals don't behave as predictably as corn; corn doesn't appear randomly, run away, get angry, or turn and attack and kill people. A hoe is much easier to aim than an arrow. Corn lasts all winter, while meat spoils in days. Most wild plants are less nutritious than corn, and take a lot of effort to find and carry for miles. Hunter-gatherers have to keep moving, instead of returning every night to the same stone house where your family has lived for five hundred years. For hunter-gatherers the universe is full of uncertainty, full of tricks being played on you—the universe is a Coyote. For hunter-gatherers the creator god is often a trickster, a Coyote or Raven, and the cosmos was full of chaos from the beginning. Nature is full of evil spirits that constantly have to be warded off with magic.

The Navajo creation story combines emergence and Coyote, order and chaos, pattern and storm. These elements do not fit together easily. The Navajo creation story is full of tension and uncertainty. The reliability of order and the sources and powers of evil are unclear. In some versions it is Coyote who ruins an orderly world by triggering the flood; in other versions it is First Woman, who is supposed to be benevolent but who secretly sends Coyote on his disastrous mission. To the Navajos' Puebloan agriculturalist neighbors, the mere presence of Coyote in the creation story is bizarre; for them Coyote is merely a clown whose bumbling ways make good jokes. For Puebloans coyotes do not represent competition for food, but for Navajos coyotes are always scheming to take rabbits or sheep. Scholars believe that the Navajo creation story emerged from the Navajos' encounter with Puebloan culture, which greatly impressed them. The Navajos adopted Puebloan farming and the Puebloan emergence story, but this could not supplant their own deep experience as hunter-gatherers, so elements of both got mixed together. This mixture seems to include the symbolism of lightning. For Puebloans there is no greater blessing than rain, and Puebloan culture is full of symbols of clouds, rain, and lightning. For Navajos lightning is often evil; a hogan struck by lightning must be abandoned permanently. Yet the lightning in the Storm Pattern design is a blessing.

Whatever the historical and cultural influences on the Navajo creation story, it expresses the universal human longing to find meaning in creation. Every creation story mixes order and chaos, good and evil, if in varying proportions. This mixing reflects a mixed-up universe, a universe that gives us life but does not make it easy and then takes life away. No culture has been able to resolve this mystery, to write out an outright equation that proves the exact value of human life.

The weaver pointed out the strengths of her rug. Normally, she, like many Navajos, was a very quiet and modest woman, but now she was playing a game with the trader, a game whose rules they both understood. The trader recognized the rug's quality, but he pointed to a line that was a bit crooked, a weave that was too rough. The creation of the universe was flawed, he was saying. The creation of the universe was almost perfect, she replied. They were negotiating the value of creation. Edwin Hubble looked on.

At some point Hubble would have taken a look at the canyon of the Little Colorado River, atop which the Cameron Trading Post was perched. Here the canyon was still modest, about two hundred feet deep, and the walls were tiered and broken, allowing a person to scramble down to the riverbed. The riverbed was usually dry, except in the spring when snow was melting in the White Mountains a hundred miles away, or in the summer thunderstorm season; then the river was dark brown with desert sand. Edwin may have walked across the steel bridge across the canyon, the reason the trading post was located here.

As Edwin looked downstream he saw the canyon walls rising and the river dropping. Over the next forty miles the Little Colorado River dropped more than a thousand feet, running through a deep, narrow gorge, then emptying into the Colorado River deep inside the Grand Canyon. A few miles before it reached the Colorado River, the Little Colorado River flowed past an odd mineral dome, hollow, with a spring within. This was the Sipapuni, the place of emergence in the creation story of the Hopis. A thousand years ago the ancestors of the Hopis had lived and farmed within the Grand Canyon, and the Hopis still made a sacred pilgrimage into the canyon to make offerings at the Sipapuni. The Zunis too believe that their place of emergence was at the bottom of the Grand Canyon, though a different mineral dome, Ribbon Falls.

As Edwin looked west he saw the land rising, rising more than three thousand feet to form the Kaibab Plateau and the rim of the Grand Canyon. It was this canyon rim that Edwin was testing for the site of the world's greatest observatory.

The observatory was the dream of George Hale, who twice now had built the world's greatest observatory, first Yerkes Observatory in Wisconsin, then Mount Wilson Observatory near Los Angeles. At Mount Wilson Hale had built the world's two most powerful telescopes, first a sixty-inch-mirror telescope, then a one-hundred-inch mirror. Now Hale was planning a telescope with a two-hundred-inch mirror. But he needed a new location, for viewing conditions at Mount Wilson were being degraded by light pollution from rapidly growing Los Angeles. Hale was strongly inclined toward Palomar Mountain, which was a safe distance from city lights yet still reasonably close to the labs, workshops, and offices Hale had built in Pasadena at the base of Mount Wilson. Hale was ready to announce his plans to build the telescope, though without a designated site, when he was shocked to hear that another astronomer was planning to build an even greater observatory, build it on the rim of the Grand Canyon.

The other astronomer was George Ritchey, an old friend who became a bitter rival. Hale and Ritchey had met in their twenties and collaborated for nearly thirty years. Ritchey was the master telescope designer who had designed and built the Mount Wilson telescopes. But Ritchey's ideas for future telescopes were too outlandish for Hale, and their big egos had clashed for years, so Hale fired Ritchey. In June 1928 Ritchey, now working for the Paris Observatory, announced his plans for a telescope far more ambitious than Hale's. Ritchey would locate it on the rim of the Grand Canyon, which he declared to be the best possible site for a great observatory. Ritchey released a canyon photograph he had taken from the rim at Desert View, onto which was imposed a drawing of his twenty-five-story observatory. Below the observatory was the Colorado River curving for miles, and vague in the distance was the gorge of the Little Colorado River. The *New York Times* covered Ritchey's plan three times in the next few weeks, culminating in a nearly full-page, well-illustrated article lauding Ritchey's genius. This must have been too much for George Hale to bear. A few days later Hale ordered Edwin Hubble to drop everything and rush to the Grand Canyon.

Hale had organized a process for selecting a site for his observatory and designed a special telescope for making tests, but his site list hadn't included the Grand Canyon. How bitter it would be if Palomar was inferior and George Ritchey was right. That Hale would send Edwin Hubble, now the world's most famous astronomer, to the Grand Canyon was a measure of how seriously he took Ritchey.

Hubble already knew that he was reaching the limits of Mount Wilson's one-hundred-inch telescope and that further progress in astronomy required Hale's new telescope. Now Hubble probably realized that astronomy's most important future question was how the galaxies could be streaming outward from some time and place of emergence. Perhaps the riddle of this emergence would be answered from the rim of the Grand Canyon.

Edwin Hubble placed the test telescope into the trunk of his car and headed east on the new Route 66, some of it still unpaved, and into the Mojave Desert.

✦ ✦ ✦

As I turned into the narrow driveway of the Hubbell Trading Post, I glanced over at the Pueblo Colorado Wash to see if it had water in it. The Pueblo Colorado Wash ran for—I guessed—a hundred miles across eastern Arizona. Summer thunderstorms turned the wash into rampaging brown floods, floods that had repeatedly ripped apart the dams and irrigation works the Hubbells had tried to build. The wash flowed only a hundred feet from the old Hubbell house, then flowed past many Puebloan ruins, including the "red house" ruin for which the wash was named. It flowed past abandoned kivas that symbolized the underworld and the place of emergence. It flowed into the Little Colorado River, past Cameron, into the gorge, past the Hopis' Sipapuni, and into the Grand Canyon and the Colorado River. The water flowed in jagged, curving patterns that resembled the lightning bolts that had generated it, lightning bolts now engraved deeply into the earth.

I had arrived early in a flood of hundreds of vehicles. Navajo youths directed us to park in what was usually a green pasture, which over the centuries had been digested into hundreds of Navajo rugs. The big tent next to the trading post gave the day a carnival air. Navajo kids were running and playing. From food booths came the scents of fry bread, Navajo tacos, mutton stew, and roast corn. Inside the tent nearly five hundred Navajo rugs were being examined by collectors who had come from all over the country. Auctions like this eliminated the middle man, the Santa Fe galleries that pocketed half the price of a rug, and gave 90 percent of the price to the weavers, today more than $120,000. Dozens of weavers were present today, so you could meet them and talk with them about their work.

The Hubbell Trading Post was started in 1878 by John Lorenzo Hubbell, whose father had migrated west from Connecticut, where the Hubbell family had arrived from England in the 1640s. John Lorenzo Hubbell started his trading post a decade after the US Army had tried to destroy Navajo society, if not the Navajo people themselves, by herding them off on the Long Walk to a long imprisonment at Basque Redondo in New Mexico. When the Navajos went home they had lost their houses, horses, sheep, tools, and housewares, and they were heavily dependent on the new trading-post system.

Navajo society strongly emphasizes reciprocity, people helping one another, and it's wrong for anyone to consistently extract an advantage over others. Yet this was what the Navajos encountered at trading posts. Trading posts were disturbingly un-Navajo. Some traders saw their trading posts as just another shovel for exploiting the West, just another gun for conquering the Indians. Navajos did their best to avoid predatory traders, and occasionally they put traders out of business, but in a horse-and-wagon and bad-road world where the nearest trading post was twenty miles away and the nearest honest trader might be many more miles away, Navajos were often at the mercy of traders. Fortunately there were traders who had plenty of mercy, who genuinely admired Navajos (sometimes marrying them) and Navajo culture, and who would make considerable efforts to help Navajos, such as by representing them in the baffling world of the white man's law and bureaucracy. The Navajos soon decided that J. L. Hubbell, while a shrewd businessman, was also a reliable friend. This trust helped Hubbell build the largest trading business on the Navajo reservation. While many traders lived in the back rooms of a crudely built store, the Hubbell Trading Post became a large complex of buildings, including a warehouse for shipping rugs and other goods to distant places, such as Hollywood. At one time or another the Hubbell empire included more than thirty trading posts. Partly from stones from nearby Puebloan ruins, J. L. Hubbell built a plain-outside, elegant-inside house where he hosted many southwestern artists, writers, and scientists. In exchange for Hubbell's generous hospitality, famous artists such as Maynard Dixon left Hubbell's walls full of paintings; when the San Francisco earthquake of 1906 sent Dixon fleeing his studio with only one handful of possessions, he abandoned his own paintings and carried away mainly the Navajo rugs he had acquired from J. L. Hubbell. In 1913 former president Teddy Roosevelt visited, and Hubbell took him to the Hopi villages to watch the snake dance, through which the Hopis honor and encourage the rain.

It was the size, historical importance, and relative benevolence of the Hubbell Trading Post that prompted the National Park Service to acquire it as a national historic site in 1967. While dozens of historic southwestern trading posts have been abandoned and fallen into ruin, the Hubbell Trading Post is still functioning, buying rugs from Navajo weavers and selling them weaving supplies or canned fruit.

The Hubbell rug auction seemed a good place for me to pursue a mystery I had been pursuing for two years now. This mystery had led me into rundown, century-old trading posts in remote parts of the Navajo reservation and into the fanciest galleries in Santa Fe. It had led me to talk with ninety-year-old Navajo grandmothers who barely spoke English, with professors of art history, with the fourth generation of famous trading-post families, and with Navajo teenagers in rock-and-roll T-shirts. It had led me to search through a century's worth of books. It was still a mystery. There were people who thought they knew the answer, who didn't even realize there was a mystery, but the more I inquired, the more puzzling it became. The mystery was the origin of the Storm Pattern design. Many other rug designs had a well-documented origin, a place and time and person and idea behind them. But the origins of the Storm Pattern design seemed lost in confusion, in wildly contradictory accounts. For some reason, this bothered me. I had never taken much interest in Navajo rugs, but the Storm Pattern wasn't just another rug design: it was the creation of the universe. Surely, the origins of such an important design couldn't have been forgotten. The creation of the universe couldn't be left a mystery. I set out to find the source of the creation of the universe.

◆ ◆ ◆

Edwin Hubble drove across the Mojave Desert basin and range, where Earth's crust had expanded, and climbed onto the Colorado Plateau, where Earth's crust had risen, and into the ponderosa forest, where Earth's crust had risen into green telescopes for tracking the sun. Hubble drove into Flagstaff and drove up Mars Hill to Lowell Observatory.

A week before, Hubble had written to Vesto Slipher, the director of Lowell Observatory, whose redshift studies Hubble was now using to discover an expanding universe. Yet Hubble's letter made no mention at all that he was right in the middle of using Slipher's data to transform the universe. Nor did Hubble mention it when he saw Slipher in person, judging from letters in which Slipher mentioned Hubble's visit. Hubble's secretiveness represented a personality whose outer brashness masked deep insecurities; as an astronomer Hubble was very cautious, downright frightened of attaching his name to a mistake. The idea of an expanding universe was so outlandish that Hubble must have feared it was all a mistake.

On October 5, 1928, only days after the *New York Times* article lauding Ritchey, Hubble wrote to Slipher to announce his visit: "Mr. Hale is rather anxious for me to start as soon as possible—I am writing within a few hours of his communication—so I shall take the liberty of asking you to wire me as to whether the visit will be convenient and agreeable to you."[1] Yet Hubble remained secretive about the real purpose of his visit, about locating a great observatory in northern Arizona, saying only he was coming to test viewing conditions.

It's likely that Slipher showed Hubble around Lowell Observatory and took special pride in showing Hubble his spectrograph. Hubble must have looked at it with wonder. It was not terribly impressive to look at, just a metal tripod less than three feet long, not very complicated. Yet this little gadget had transformed the universe. Perhaps Slipher noticed Hubble looking at him with an odd smile. *If only Slipher knew...*

◆ ◆ ◆

I became curious about the origins of the Storm Pattern design only because of curiosity about Edwin Hubble's 1928 scouting trip to Arizona. When I realized that Hubble had spent two nights at the Cameron Trading Post, I wondered what it had been like in 1928. I had stopped at the trading post hundreds of times, eaten there dozens of times, hiked far down the riverbed, and stayed overnight. Over twenty years I had watched the trading post adding new wings to its store, dining room, and lodges, in a big contrast with all the other old-time trading posts that were closing. The Cameron Trading Post owed its prosperity to being the eastern gateway to the Grand Canyon; increasingly, it was run for tourists, not Navajos, with little selection of food, kitchenware, or hardware.

Over several visits I asked several Cameron employees about the trading post in 1928 and I got contradictory answers. One person was sure that in 1928 the only place to stay was in primitive cabins; he showed me photos of cabins with uneven logs patched with mud, but they did have glass windows. Another person said that by the end of 1928, the first stone lodge had opened—it was now the two-story Native American fine-arts gallery in front of the main trading post; he showed me a walled-up doorway that had been the original entrance. It seemed that the past of the Cameron Trading Post had become as vague as the origin of the Storm Pattern rug.

I asked what a 1928 visitor would have found inside the trading post. I knew that many trading posts were famous for their own design of rug, designs often named for a trading post. Perhaps the most famous of all Navajo rug designs is the Ganado Red, named for the town of Ganado, the location of the Hubbell Trading Post. Was there a Cameron Trading Post rug design? No, said the Navajo who presided over the gallery, Cameron never had its own rug design. The Cameron Trading Post wasn't founded until 1916, a bit late in trading-post history, and a stagnant time for Navajo weaving. The closest thing Cameron had to its own design was the Storm Pattern design. He took me over to a display of rugs and pointed out a Storm Pattern. I asked him where it originated, and he said that the answer depended on whom you asked. The books on Navajo weaving gave a specific place of origin for most rugs, but for the Storm Pattern the books said only "the western reservation." This was a huge area. Some writers narrowed it down a bit to "the Tuba City–Kayenta area," still an eighty-mile spread. I asked him what he thought, and he said he wasn't sure, but he thought the Storm Pattern design came from Coal Mine Mesa, about thirty miles east of here.

Then I asked him the meaning of the Storm Pattern design. This too, I was to discover over the next two years, depended on whom you asked.

◆ ◆ ◆

Edwin Hubble walked up to the rim of the Grand Canyon. He stood there looking down, looking back and forth, looking across. Everywhere, he saw redshifts. The canyon cliffs were redshifted. The spires and mesas and boulders and talus slopes were redshifted. The sandstone was redshifted; the Hermit shale was redshifted; the Redwall Limestone was so boldly redshifted that it was named for its redshift. The canyon walls were receding, moving ever farther apart. The canyon redshifts revealed depths of time, layer upon layer of time. The canyon redshifts revealed that the rocks were not nearly as stable as they might seem; they were actually the face of endless motion, of dynamic forces, of an evolving universe.

For weeks Hubble had been prompting himself to start seeing an expanding universe. He looked at galaxies he had seen for years and tried to see them racing through space, racing through time. He tried to imagine Earth flying amid millions of flying galaxies. So perhaps when Hubble looked into the Grand Canyon, he saw astronomical depths there. Here was the one landscape on Earth that best personified the same immensities as the sky. The Grand Canyon was already a famous map of deep time, dynamic forces, and great masses moving and evolving. The canyon was its own expanding universe, starting from some primordial crack and growing steadily larger, adding more and more complexity of shapes. The rock strata were the earthly materialization of the same-era light strata in the sky.

As Hubble walked on the canyon's limestone rim he was walking over spiral-shaped fossils, spirals that had once flowed densely through an ancient sea, flowed as a continuation of the flowing of spiral galaxies through space. The canyon rocks recorded the growing complexity of life through the aeons, an evolution that—it would soon be clear—was a continuation of the evolution of the universe itself. The spiral fossils contained a universe of time and power and creativity and changes. The spiral galaxies had become the spiral fingerprints with which Edwin Hubble steered a telescope.

The day lengthened; the shadows in the canyon lengthened; the colors of the rocks lengthened into deeper reds. Hubble was seeing October light, often the most vivid and beautiful canyon light of the year. At sunset the rocks glowed intensely red. Then the stars came out, then the galaxies. A sky full of galaxies swarmed over the darkness of the canyon. A few years ago the nebulae had seemed to be randomly placed, but now Hubble was seeing a deep pattern, a haunting October-light red glow. He saw all the galaxies, including the galaxy on which he was riding, emerging from some cosmic Sipapuni and journeying to become canyons of fossil spirals and of Sipapuni creation stories.

✦ ✦ ✦

Depending on whom you ask, the Storm Pattern design is so sacred that most Navajos are forbidden from weaving it, or it's just a gimmick to sell rugs. It's a picture of creation, a picture of Navajo lands, or simply a pretty picture.

Most of the people I asked, and most of the books, say that the Storm Pattern design portrays the Navajo creation story, with its flood and the emergence of humans into this world. This makes the Storm Pattern one of the few designs that portray Navajo religious ideas. Most Navajo rugs offer simply geometric patterns, although in a southwestern landscape where the mesas and canyons are strongly geometric, these rug motifs can easily invoke images of landscapes.

There are two other rug designs with religious images, one of *yeis*, or spirits, and the other of Mother Earth and Father Sky, an image taken from sandpaintings used in healing ceremonies, though many weavers avoid these images because sandpaintings contain powerful magic.

Most sources agreed that the squares in the four corners of the Storm Pattern are the four sacred mountains that border Dinetah, the Navajo world. Most people agreed that the lightning bolts are indeed lightning bolts, although a few said they are sacred arrows. Most said that the lightning bolts are conveying blessings, although some said that they are simply the lightning bolts of the storm that caused the flood. The whirling logs are sometimes just logs, sometimes a raft used to escape the flood. The central square is usually the place of emergence, which could be a hole in the sky, a lake, an island, or the first hogan. But a few Navajo weavers told me that the central square is simply the weaver's own hogan, or a symbolic hogan for the whole Navajo people, and they refrained from saying that the Storm Pattern represents the Navajo creation story. When I inquired further about this, trying to be subtle by saying, "Some people say that the Storm Pattern is the Navajo creation story," the weavers would be subtle in reply: "Yes, some people say that."

It's a problematic thing for a white person to ask Native Americans about their spiritual life. A century ago such inquiries were usually hostile interrogations by Christian missionaries trying to cure Natives of their pagan errors. Navajos learned to be evasive about their spirituality. Yet even among themselves, there are secrets Navajos don't talk about. Navajos also have an opposite problem: spiritually hungry whites who are overeager to find meanings in Native ways, or impose meanings borrowed from Rousseau or Tibet or theosophy. This syndrome was well known to some of the white scholars, museum officials, and old-time traders I asked about the Storm Pattern design, and it made them hesitant to ascribe spiritual origins to it. They'd heard all sorts of nonsense ascribed to Navajo rugs, such as old horse blankets being advertised on eBay as sacred prayer rugs. They said that while today the Storm Pattern might represent the creation story, perhaps this meaning was encouraged by traders who knew that whites wanted religious symbolism. Perhaps the Storm Pattern started out as a simple geometric design, which just happened to be a good fit for the creation story.

Other experts told me that the Storm Pattern had deep spiritual roots and meanings, perhaps evolving from an old sandpainting pattern. On my previous year's visit to the Hubbell Trading Post I spoke with a Navajo woman who was now a National Park Service ranger there. She told me that Storm Pattern rugs could be woven only by people who had participated in a Lightning Way ceremony, a long, intricate healing ceremony for people who had been struck by lightning or been close to a lightning strike. Lightning was dangerous magic, and Navajos weren't supposed to even touch a tree that had been struck by lightning. I'd heard all about the dark powers of lightning from my barber, a Navajo lady who owned and farmed land at the bottom of Canyon de Chelly and who cut hair during the week in Flagstaff; for years she'd consulted a famous medicine man, including for the pains brought on by the repetitive motion of cutting hair. As she snipped my hair I thought of how Navajo hands had been snipping sheep hair for centuries and turning it into rugs. She told me about how people exposed to lightning could receive sickness and require healing ceremonies.

The Hubbell ranger said that weavers of the Storm Pattern didn't need to have had a personal encounter with lightning, but at least they needed to have participated in a Lightning Way ceremony for someone else; otherwise, it was strictly forbidden to weave a Storm Pattern rug. Yet the next time I visited the Cameron Trading Post I asked the Navajo man in the art gallery about this, and he shook his head and said he'd never heard this claim before. His mother had woven Storm Patterns for decades, nothing but Storm Patterns, and she had never been through a Lightning Way ceremony. Later I went to Garlands, one of the most prestigious dealers in Navajo rugs, and I asked Sandy, a white woman who'd worked there for twenty years, and she said yes indeed, some Navajos will refuse to weave a Storm Pattern unless they've been through the right ceremony. But few other sources made this claim.

✦ ✦ ✦

Edwin Hubble set up his telescope on the rim of the Grand Canyon and aimed it at Polaris, the star that Hale's tests were using to compare different sites. Polaris was a Cepheid variable, the type of star Hubble had used to prove that Andromeda was another galaxy. Polaris was the Navajos' Central Fire, symbolizing the hearth in the center of the hogan.

We receive only glimpses of Hubble's activities at the canyon, through a letter he wrote to Slipher after he got home. It's likely Hubble stayed at El Tovar Hotel on the canyon rim and explored the nearby buildings. In the Lookout Studio, an ingenious stone building that seemed to grow naturally out of the canyon rim, Hubble would have found a long, shiny telescope for gazing into the canyon. Hubble couldn't have resisted. The eye that had recognized Andromeda to be a galaxy now puzzled over the scale and shapes of things inside the canyon. Hubble probably also went into Hopi House, an imitation three-story pueblo that served as a quality Indian arts gallery, designed by the same architect who designed the Lookout Studio, Mary Colter. The main supplier of Navajo rugs for Hopi House, and for other shops connected with the Santa Fe Railway, was J. L. Hubbell. Hubbell also supplied Hopi House with real Indians to demonstrate weaving or silversmithing and to perform dances outside.

As Edwin Hubble walked through Hopi House he was seeing stacks and walls of Hubbell rugs. He was also probably thinking about the galaxies flying apart. How could he ever stop thinking about it? Flying apart from what? A universe of millions of galaxies was mind-boggling enough. A universe of galaxies flying apart was even more unbelievable. Now he had to face the possibility that an incredible amount of matter had emerged from one place, one moment, one event. Did the laws of physics even allow for such extreme compression? How could the universe have a beginning? How could humans ever understand it? Perhaps the origin of the universe would remain a mystery.

On the wall Hubble noticed a Navajo rug with a center from which energy was flying in all directions.

✦ ✦ ✦

Just as there were many opinions about the symbolism and sacredness of the Storm Pattern design, I found that there were many opinions as to where the Storm Pattern originated. Most people I asked agreed that it came from the western reservation, but the exact spot was all over the map, most often Tuba City, but also Kayenta, Red Lake, Black Mesa, Piñon, Coal Mine Mesa, or just "somewhere between Tuba City and Kayenta."

My most authoritative source was Jim Babbitt, whose grandfather had owned some twenty trading posts in the western reservation. Jim himself had managed the Tuba City Trading Post in the 1980s, and he had restored it to its original elegance as an eight-sided giant stone hogan. Jim said that the Storm Pattern design had always been his personal favorite, partly because the Babbitt trading posts had used the Storm Pattern as a logo on their stationery and other items. Jim had conducted his own inquiry into the origin of the Storm Pattern; he told me it came from the Red Lake Trading Post at Tonalea, sometime around 1900. The trader there wanted to have, like other trading posts, a rug design that was unique to his trading post. But whether this trader designed the pattern himself, or only adopted it from Navajo sources, wasn't clear. Jim thought that a likely source was a sandpainting design that looked a lot like the Storm Pattern. Jim had talked with Navajo elders who said that the Storm Pattern was definitely the Navajo creation story. In one detailed account, the whirling logs were cottonwood trees that the people strapped together as a raft, on which they floated down the Little Colorado River, and when they reached the Colorado River at the bottom of the Grand Canyon, the raft hit a whirlpool, which is what made the logs whirl, but the people survived.

In her book *Navajo Trading Days*, Elizabeth Compton Hegemann, who in the 1930s ran the Shonto Trading Post near Red Lake, said that the Storm Pattern was originally "called the 'Red Lake pattern' because a trader at that post had originated the design sometime after 1900."[2] The next time I passed the Red Lake Trading Post, I had to stop and ask. The 1891 stone building is still there, though in poor shape. The trading post had been famous for its "tuna" sandwiches, actually made from the plentiful local rattlesnakes. But today it was just another convenience store, contagious with junk food. The owner was away, so I asked the teenage Navajo clerk, but she had no idea what I was talking about. A few years later the store put up a new sign featuring a Storm Pattern rug.

A few people told me that the Storm Pattern came from New Mexico, but I noticed that this opinion was coming from whites, often transplants to the Southwest. Navajos who were born on the western reservation and who had learned their weaving there always said that the Storm Pattern came from the western reservation.

I was startled, then, when I walked into one of the most prominent Native art galleries on the square in Santa Fe and asked about the Storm Pattern, and they said confidently that it was created by J. B. Moore at his Crystal Trading Post in New Mexico. I asked in other Santa Fe galleries and museums, and this was all I heard: J. B. Moore invented the Storm Pattern in Crystal in 1911, invented it as a sales gimmick for white customers who wanted religious symbolism. As I inquired in other New Mexico galleries, in Albuquerque and Gallup and elsewhere, I ran into J. B. Moore everywhere. Some said that J. B. Moore had copied the Storm Pattern from some Oriental rug. I realized that there were two basic versions of Storm Pattern origins, an Arizona version and a New Mexico version, with many variations on each version.

As I looked into the literature on Navajo rugs, I found that the J. B. Moore story tended to dominate. Since Santa Fe is the capital city of southwestern culture, it wasn't surprising that a Santa Fe version of events got emphasized in the books. Arizonans who relied on books—not on Navajos—for their Navajo rug knowledge tended to pick up the New Mexico version.

J. B. Moore certainly was an important figure in the history of Navajo weaving. Along with J. L. Hubbell and a few others, Moore helped revitalize Navajo weaving from a decline inflicted by the Long Walk and Bosque Redondo; he encouraged quality materials and workmanship and developed large new markets, especially through his mail-order catalog. Moore's 1911 catalog, the first to use color plates to display Navajo rugs, is now legendary, an extremely rare collector's item that brings many thousands of dollars. Plate #28 is a rug that Moore called simply a "special design," with all the elements of today's Storm Pattern. Certainly, it was this catalog that made the Storm Pattern famous across the reservation and far beyond. But some historians go further and say that this catalog was the origin of the Storm Pattern and that J. B. Moore invented it, or ripped it off from an Oriental rug, as a cynical marketing ploy to sell rugs to mythology-hungry white customers.

The problem with this theory is that Moore's own catalog contradicts it. If Navajo mythology was such a hot marketing trick and Moore was such a hustler, he could have claimed that other rug designs had mythological themes. But of all the rugs in the catalog, the Storm Pattern was the only one to which he ascribed mythological meaning. He also said that it had old, sacred roots: "This pattern is one of the really legendary designs embodying a portion of the Navajo mythology. Not many weavers will do it for superstitious reasons and on that account its production is practically confined to one family or clan. . . . The trouble has been to get enough of them made, and to overcome this is the main purpose of this engraving. With the pattern for a working model, we hope to get other weavers to making it."[3]

It's not clear how this statement got turned into the now widespread theory that Moore invented the Storm Pattern just to make a buck. There's definitely some cynicism going on here, but it may be cynicism on the part of historians. J. B. Moore never wrote another word about the Storm Pattern, for soon after his catalog appeared, Moore left the trading-post business, left Crystal, and pretty much disappeared.

◆ ◆ ◆

My search for the origin of the Storm Pattern led me to Albuquerque's Old Town, the original Spanish plaza that is now a zone of galleries, gift shops, and restaurants. At the Margaret Moses Native American Gallery my arrival was expected, and Tom Moses, Margaret's father, took me to a café for a better conversation. But we weren't talking about Navajo rugs. We were talking about Albert Einstein, specifically about Einstein's 1931 journey home after Einstein met Edwin Hubble at Mount Wilson Observatory and was converted to the idea of an expanding universe. From Los Angeles Einstein took the train across America, and he made two stops in the Southwest: the Grand Canyon and the Petrified Forest. Tom Moses's stepmother, Margaret Wennips Moses, had served as Einstein's translator and tour guide for those stops.

As evidence for an expanding universe accumulated through the 1910s and 1920s, Albert Einstein watched with dismay, for the idea of an expanding universe, which implied that the universe had a beginning, seemed absurd to him. It seemed more logical that the universe had been here forever, stable forever. Poets and scientists alike had long regarded the night sky as the definition of eternity and stability. Even when Einstein was in college there was no obvious evidence for a dynamic universe. Yet Einstein was very aware of a problem with the idea of a stable universe. If the universe had been around forever, gravity would have had time to gather matter together until it ended up in one huge clump. The alternative was that the universe was expanding—absurd! When Einstein was spelling out the cosmological implications of his general theory of relativity, he adopted a new tactic to avoid both cosmic collapse and expansion. He invented a "cosmological constant," a mysterious expansive force, an antigravity that perfectly matched gravity's tendency to contract the universe. Einstein wasn't happy with his cosmological constant, for it was completely arbitrary, unexplained by anything in nature, but at least it preserved a stable universe. The Einstein who had become great by following his equations wherever they led, even into the most outlandish concepts, had now lost his nerve, reining back equations that yearned to fly through space.

When in 1929 Edwin Hubble published his findings showing a correlation between galactic distances and redshifts, consolidating years of accumulating evidence for a dynamic, expanding universe, Einstein knew he had to come to terms with it. At the end of 1930 Einstein made his second trip to America to visit Mount Wilson Observatory and the California Institute of Technology, or Caltech. Einstein stayed several weeks and was given an office across the hall from Edwin Hubble's office at the observatory headquarters at the base of Mount Wilson. Hubble's wife, Grace, helped chauffeur

Einstein around Los Angeles. The observatory bought a new car just for Einstein's visit, since the old truck that usually hauled astronomers up the rough Mount Wilson road was deemed too undignified to be seen by the flock of national media that were following Einstein around. When the day came for Einstein to make his drive—his pilgrimage—up the mountain, he was accompanied by young filmmaker Frank Capra, a Caltech engineering graduate who had aspired to be an astronomer and would always regret he hadn't become one. Capra captured the historic moment for a newsreel. Einstein dutifully posed for Capra, pretending to be gazing into the telescope, though it was daylight and there was nothing to be seen, as Edwin Hubble stood puffing on his pipe beside Einstein. But Einstein was genuinely delighted by the telescope and examined all its workings. Einstein's wife, Elsa, was not so impressed: when told that this was the telescope that had discovered the universe's shape, Elsa famously replied, "Well, my husband does that on the back of an old envelope." That night Einstein looked through the telescope for real.

A few days later Einstein gave a lecture to Mount Wilson and Caltech scientists in the Mount Wilson headquarters library. He announced that he had now accepted Hubble's findings, accepted that his own cosmological constant was unnecessary, accepted that the universe was expanding. "A gasp of astonishment swept through the library," wrote an Associated Press reporter in an article that was published all over the country.[4] The *New York Times* ran the front-page headline: "Einstein Drops Idea of 'Closed' Universe."[5] For many readers this was the first time they'd heard the idea of an expanding universe; they read that the great Einstein had bowed to someone named Hubble.

When the Einsteins left Los Angeles at the end of February a thousand people gathered at the train station to get a glimpse of them. "Their arms were filled with roses," said the newspapers, "and boxes of California fruit were stacked at their feet."[6] The president of the Santa Fe Railway lent his private railroad car to the Einsteins. The railway also lent them Margaret Wennips.

Margaret Wennips had worked for several years as a guide for the Indian Detours, tours run by the Santa Fe Railway's tourist services subsidiary the Fred Harvey Company. The Indian Detours offered car and bus tours of regions around the Santa Fe Railway route, especially of Indian villages like Taos Pueblo and Acoma, and ruins like Bandelier and Mesa Verde. The guides were all college-educated women, uniformed in Navajo velveteen blouses and Navajo turquoise jewelry. The Fred Harvey Company hired experts like author Charles Lummis and anthropologist A. V. Kidder to train the guides in geology, history, and Native American culture. For Margaret Wennips this was the start of a lifelong immersion in Native American culture; her future husband, Horace Moses, was one of the founders of the Gallup Intertribal Ceremonial, still one of the leading powwows. Many of Wennips's tourists were seriously interested in Native cultures, but there were also spoiled rich folks merely looking for diversions, such as the lady who complained to Margaret about the Indians building their ruins too far away from the railroad. Guides had to be prepared for everything, such as the lady passenger who started picking flowers without noticing they were full of bees, which began swarming her brightly colored clothes and stinging her, sending her fleeing and tossing off her clothes, sending Margaret in pursuit to wrap her coat around the now nearly naked woman.

Guides received an extra ten dollars if they used their language skills. Margaret was the only guide who spoke German, which is why she was assigned to Albert Einstein.

If another Indian Detours guide, Margaret Hubbell, had spoken German, she might have been Albert Einstein's guide at the Grand Canyon. Margaret Hubbell was the niece of J. L. Hubbell. (A few years later, the Hubbells would start their own tours of Indian country.) Only a month after Edwin Hubble had stood beside Albert Einstein and pointed into deep space and deep time, Margaret Hubbell would have stood beside Albert Einstein on the rim of the Grand Canyon and pointed into its deep space and time, its expanding and evolving shapes. Indeed, Margaret Hubbell would have been pointing out a serious problem with Edwin's research. Edwin's estimate of the rate of cosmic expansion predicted that the universe was about two billion years old. But some twenty years before, physicists had used new discoveries in radioactivity to date the planet Earth as two billion years old, and recently they had announced that it might be as old as three billion years. How could it be, Margaret Hubbell would have declared to Einstein, that Earth is older than the universe? Clearly, cousin Edwin didn't know what he was doing; silly Edwin didn't even know how to spell the Hubbell name correctly. Einstein would have looked at Margaret Hubbell, nodded sagely, and started thinking... *More time.*

As it turned out, it was Margaret Wennips who stood beside Albert Einstein on the rim of the Grand Canyon and pointed into a rock manifestation of the same depths of time Einstein had seen through the Mount Wilson telescope. Perhaps Einstein even gazed at the canyon through the Lookout Studio telescope.

We don't know what Einstein thought of the Grand Canyon, but it's likely that, as unique as Einstein was, he shared the nearly universal experience of people first seeing the Grand Canyon, the experience of immensity. First-time visitors have seen pictures of the canyon and suppose they know what to expect, but they are usually amazed to see the true scale of the canyon, to *feel* its immensity, to measure it with their suddenly puny human bodies.

Yet we can guess that Albert Einstein also saw the canyon in unique, Einstein, ways. Human brains are busy biolooms for finding patterns in the world, and Einstein's brain was especially hungry and sensitive for patterns. He would have looked at the canyon's strange shapes and colors, its layers and cliffs and slopes and mesas and bends, and tried to glimpse patterns in it and behind it: hidden forces or laws that made sense of its complexity. Einstein stared into the canyon just as humans have always sought out the larger powers that created them.

Having just come from looking through the Mount Wilson telescope, having prompted himself to start seeing an expanding universe, perhaps Einstein glimpsed astronomical time in the Grand Canyon. Here was the one landscape on Earth that best personified the same immensities as the sky.

Most of the details of Einstein's day at the Grand Canyon have been forgotten, but it seems that Margaret Wennips liked Einstein, who wasn't at all stuffy or pompous like many of the other famous people she had guided. She shared the opinion of Frank Capra, who right after filming Einstein at Mount Wilson began filming Jean Harlow in *Platinum Blonde*, in which a reporter comments: "Say, I interviewed a swell guy the other day—Einstein. Swell guy, a little eccentric, but a swell—doesn't wear any garters. Neither do I as a matter of fact; what good are garters?" And Einstein liked Margaret Wennips and enjoyed his Grand Canyon vacation. When the Einsteins got back to Germany Mrs. Einstein wrote Margaret a thank-you letter, in German, of course. Margaret also kept a photo of Einstein on a porch, probably the porch of El Tovar Hotel, with the canyon beyond.

One event in Einstein's Grand Canyon day has become famous and made headlines in the *New York Times* on March 2, 1931:

EINSTEIN IS "GREAT RELATIVE".
HOPIS DECIDE ON HIS THEORY

Yesterday at the Grand Canyon of the Colorado River in Arizona the Hopi Indians made Professor Einstein a chief of the tribe. But the Indian council, which has honored presidents and other notables, was puzzled to assign a name to the scientist.

"What's his business?" the redskins asked.

"He invented the theory of relativity," they were told.

"All right," was the reply, "we'll call him The Great Relative."

This event was loaded with cultural confusion on all sides. It took place at Hopi House, and the Hopis in the article were the Hopis who lived upstairs and demonstrated crafts and performed dances for tourists. Whatever the commercial motives of Hopi House, it was built with respect for Hopi culture. Its architect, Mary Colter, was a deep admirer of Native American culture; her Desert View Watchtower, farther east on the canyon rim, may be the most inspired tribute to Native American culture and spirituality ever built by white Americans. At a time when women found it almost impossible to pursue careers as architects, the Santa Fe Railway and the Fred Harvey Company hired Colter because they felt she was genius, with a respectful vision of southwestern landscapes and peoples, and they gave her the freedom, money, and authority to do what she wanted, however exotic.

Yet most of the tourists who visited Hopi House held cartoonish images of Indians, images reinforced by Hollywood, images taken from Great Plains tribes like the Lakota. Indians were supposed to live in teepees, wear feathered headdresses, hunt buffalo, and smoke peace pipes, none of which was true for southwestern tribes like the Hopi and Navajo. The Fred Harvey Company was ready to pander to tourist stereotypes and expected its Indian employees to play along. The publicity photos for the Indian Detours included Pueblo Indians posing in Plains Indian clothes and headdresses.

The "ceremony" that made Einstein a Hopi chief—the Hopis don't actually have chiefs—included placing a feathered headdress on Einstein and handing him a peace pipe. A now famous photograph shows a feathered Einstein surrounded by the family of Porter Timeche, the Hopis who lived in Hopi House. Einstein is holding the hand of Porter's little girl, Laverne. Today this photograph is usually misidentified as taking place in a Hopi village. The "Indian council" mentioned in the New York Times was merely a few Hopis trying to earn a living by entertaining silly white people. Yet Albert Einstein, smiling happily, appears to be having a great time. Einstein's favorite childhood author was Karl May, a German who wrote a wildly popular series of adventure novels about American Indians. Karl May had never set foot in America, and his ethnology was wildly scrambled. Yet Einstein seemed delighted to be meeting real Indians and becoming an honorary Indian.

A couple of Santa Fe Railway big shots couldn't resist barging in for another photo with Einstein, including Herman Schweitzer, the buyer for the Fred Harvey shops. Schweitzer's largest supplier, J. L. Hubbell, sold Schweitzer twenty-five thousand dollars' worth of Navajo rugs every year.

Another photo, taken with the canyon in the background, shows the Einsteins standing with Margaret Wennips.

It's a safe guess that Margaret Wennips took the Einsteins inside Hopi House. Einstein would have seen a lot of Hubbell rugs, and it's quite likely that his attention quickly zeroed in on a Storm Pattern rug, but not for the best reason. At that time, Storm Pattern rugs included swastikas. In 1931, the year before Adolf Hitler came to power, swastikas were parading threateningly through German streets and through the nightmares of German Jews like Albert Einstein.

Margaret Wennips was astute enough about world events to recognize why Einstein was suddenly distracted. Perhaps she took him over to the Storm Pattern rug to explain it to him.

The swastikas, she would explain, are really whirling logs, logs spinning on the floodwaters of the Navajo creation story. The swastika is also an ancient Navajo symbol, a Hopi symbol too, that conveys a blessing; perhaps she translated the Navajo concept as "a good-luck symbol." The whole creation was a blessing; the lightning bolts carried blessings; even the whirling logs symbolized a blessing. The square in the center of the rug symbolized the place where the world first emerged.

First emerged—thought Einstein. So the Navajos too lived in an emerging, changing universe. He looked at the Hubbell rug more carefully, just as he had stared at the Hubble galactic velocity-distance graph with its sloping line. The first thing Einstein appreciated about the Storm Pattern rug was its perfect symmetry, how each of four quadrants was exactly the same: a lightning bolt heading from the center to a sacred mountain. Symmetry was very important in Einstein's mathematical equations. When equations stuck out ungracefully it was usually a warning sign. Stuck out like the cosmological constant. Einstein admired the lightning bolts, the sheer energy of the Navajo creation. Yet—what a snug universe that is bordered by visible and immovable mountains.

Swastikas represented cataclysmic flood, Coyote's ruining the creation, the power of chaos set loose. Primordial chaos itself was marching down the streets of Berlin. With World War II, the swastikas disappeared from Storm Pattern rugs, or were transformed into water bugs with four bent legs.

That night the Einsteins stayed at the Mary Colter–designed La Posada Hotel in Winslow. At five thousand feet above sea level,

La Posada was nearly as high as Mount Wilson, and its dry desert skies were even clearer. Arching across the sky was the Milky Way, more vivid than Einstein had ever seen it. To the Navajos the Milky Way is Yikáísdáhá, or "that which awaits the dawn," for the way it rises just before dawn in January. The Milky Way was the last pattern that Black God placed in the sky before Coyote stole his crystal pouch and scattered its remaining stars into the sky chaotically.

The next day the Einsteins toured Petrified Forest National Park, where Einstein saw crystals that became not stars but the patterns of trees. Decades later a photo of Einstein, perhaps taken by Margaret Wennips, was displayed in the park's Painted Desert Inn, the former Fred Harvey café. Centered in the inn's main room, hanging on the wall facing the Painted Desert, is a Storm Pattern rug.

◆ ◆ ◆

I arrived at the Hubbell Trading Post early to have a chance to look over the rugs before the auction began. The rugs were laid out on tables, where serious collectors were examining them carefully, discussing every nuance. Of nearly five hundred rugs on the sales list, thirty-three were Storm Patterns. Nearly half of these were woven around Piñon, a remote town halfway between here and Red Lake, but no one I asked could tell me why Piñon had become today's center of Storm Pattern weaving. In color and design, the Storm Pattern rugs ranged from traditional to jazzy. In age the weavers ranged from their teens to their eighties. The target prices ranged from forty dollars to four thousand. Most rugs were new, but auctions often dredged up one or two Storm Patterns that had been locked up in a trunk in 1939 or on December 7, 1941, and never seen again, which meant they were in excellent condition, but they were still hard to sell.

Before he got busy I talked with one of the auctioneers, Hank Blair. Hank's parents had run the Kayenta Trading Post, and today Hank ran the Lukachukai Trading Post. Hank said that no one was really sure where the Storm Pattern originated. It was first published in J. B. Moore's 1911 catalog, but it could have been a Navajo design of some sort before that. Was it a sacred design? Hank was wary of this claim, for both traders and collectors had imposed so many false meanings onto Native art that the truth could be hard to sort out. But Hank seemed pretty sure how the Storm Pattern had come to be identified with the western reservation. From J. B. Moore's catalog, the Storm Pattern design was adopted by the Hayden flour mill in Tempe, Arizona, as the logo on their flour sacks. The Babbitt trading posts got their flour from the Hayden mill. The Babbitts were distributing many tens of thousands of pictures of the Storm Pattern all over the western reservation. Every Navajo who traded at a Babbitt post was looking at the Storm Pattern as they cooked fry bread. Thus the Storm Pattern became a yummy design to weave. Now those flour sacks had cooked up the myth that the Storm Pattern actually originated in the western reservation.

I also ran into a professional rug appraiser from Tempe. She wasn't convinced that J. B. Moore had invented the Storm Pattern. The whole subject of trader influences on Navajo designs was highly controversial. For various reasons, whites often give too little credit to the Navajos, who had plenty of creativity of their own. She suspected that the Storm Pattern evolved through a process of give-and-take between Moore and local weavers. She also doubted that the Storm Pattern had any religious origins; this was merely a later interpretation. She also agreed that the Storm Pattern had gone from the J. B. Moore catalog to the Hayden-mill flour sacks to the Babbitt trading posts to the kitchens of the western reservation, and thus it became a popular design there.

A few days after the auction I went back to Jim Babbitt and asked him about the Hayden-mill flour-sack theory. He shook his head with pity. He'd been hearing this story for years. There wasn't any evidence for it. He'd never seen one of those Hayden-mill Storm Pattern flour sacks, and he didn't know of anyone who had ever actually seen one, including the people repeating the flour-sack theory. The Babbitt family had a museum's worth of artifacts from their trading-post history. In fact, I was visiting Jim in his office above the 1888 Babbitts store in Flagstaff, his walls full of Babbitt history, his desk loaded with old photos he was turning into a book. You would think, said Jim, that if the Babbitts had been distributing tens of thousands of Storm Pattern flour sacks, someone in the Babbitt family might know about it, and one of those sacks might have survived. There were still plenty of 1890s Arbuckle's coffee crates nailed to reservation walls, including the walls of the Red Lake Trading Post.

Jim thought that the flour-sack theory might be a garbled version of Babbitt trading-post history. In fact, the Babbitts had done a lot to popularize the Storm Pattern design by putting it on company supplies such as stationery, jewelry boxes, and shopping sacks—not flour sacks: paper shopping sacks. Perhaps some elderly Navajo weaver told someone that she had learned her Storm Pattern from a Babbitt sack, and this mutated into the flour-sack theory.

The Babbitts adopted the Storm Pattern for their logo because it was already representative of the western reservation areas they served. Jim suggested I look into the book *Navajo Trader* by Gladwell Richardson. The Richardsons were another of the great trading-post families, who still ran the largest Native gallery in Gallup. When I had stopped in the Richardsons' store they had told me that the Storm Pattern originated in the western reservation. In all the other Gallup galleries, they told me J. B. Moore. Gladwell Richardson had run various posts in the western reservation, including Cameron around 1930, and later Sunrise. In his book Richardson discussed the origin of the Storm Pattern design: it was already being woven around Sunrise in 1890, two decades before J. B. Moore's catalog. He also said that the Storm Pattern symbols derived from sacred sandpaintings. Jim Babbit's own research led to the Red Lake Trading Post, and beyond that, it got mysterious.

Perhaps J. B. Moore had merely taken an obscure western reservation design and made it famous in his catalog. Because Moore's catalog was so historically significant, it has cast its aura onto the Storm Pattern design, getting credit for its origin, even when Moore himself said otherwise in the catalog.

As I walked down the stairs of the old Babbitt store, I was puzzled indeed. As I turned the sidewalk corner, I saw in the distance the white dome of Lowell Observatory, the dome where Vesto Slipher had measured the redshifts of the galaxies. It was puzzling indeed that humans could calculate the exact time and intensity of the creation of the universe, but we were at a loss to figure out the origins of a rug design, barely a century old, that depicted—some people claimed—the creation of the universe.

♦ ♦ ♦

Edwin Hubble walked up to the canyon rim at Desert View. He looked down at the best view of the Colorado River he had seen, the river curving through a more open section of the canyon. It looked right: it looked like the view in George Ritchey's photo-drawing. But it didn't take any scientific instruments to notice something wrong. On the canyon rim the air was often turbulent. Desert heat in the canyon depths sent heat waves boiling out of the canyon and mixing energetically with the much cooler rim air. Turbulence was bad for astronomy; it blurred the images of stars.

Hubble looked up and imagined the world's greatest observatory right here. He imagined a giant telescope tracking the stars all night, measuring the redshifts of galaxies farther and farther out, finding the largest patterns of the cosmos.

In the distance Hubble saw the gorge of the Little Colorado River, which hid the Sipapuni, the Hopis' place of emergence. Directly west of the junction of the Little Colorado River with the Colorado River was Hubbell Butte, named for J. L. Hubbell.

♦ ♦ ♦

The Navajos say they were taught to weave by Spider Woman. Spider Man gave them the loom, and Spider Woman gave them the secrets of weaving. The people carried the loom with them when they escaped the flood. The loom was made of earth and sky. The warp sticks were sun rays; the batten was a sun halo; the spindles and tension cords were made of lightning bolts. There are prayers for building a loom, prayers and songs for weaving. Weavers talk to their rug as if it is a child. When weavers come upon a spiderweb in their hogan, they gently remove it and rub it on their hands to acquire the skills of the spider. The steady thumping of the weaver's comb, used to pat the weave tight, is like a ceremonial drumbeat, like a heartbeat. Navajo babies are soothed by the rhythms of weaving.

I was sitting in the rug room of the Cameron Trading Post, watching an older weaver weaving a Storm Pattern rug. Public demonstrators like her were a century-old southwestern tradition, promoted by the Hubbell family, but a problematic tradition, since some white tourists took it as merely exotic entertainment. Yet for Navajos there was honor in representing your people to the world; demonstrators were often the only chance whites had to talk with Navajos about their culture. Most questions were technical: "How long does it take you to weave a rug like that?" But some tourists asked about the meaning of a rug design. I had noticed that public demonstrators seemed less likely than other weavers to volunteer information about the sacred. For this weaver, the symbol in the center of the Storm Pattern was simply her own hogan.

I watched the rhythms of the weaving, her hands going back and forth, in and out, up and down. Back and forth, in and out, up and down. She worked from no pattern, only from her own mind, her sense of what was right. Her heartbeat became the thumping of the weaver's comb and a cardiogram of wool. Dangling threads of many colors slowly coalesced into patterns. The ancient sandstone was sedimented into strata of deliberate beauty. The floodwaters of last year's thunderstorms welled up into the lightning bolts of sanctification.

I was watching an emergence of order, a creation of patterns, that was far more ancient than Navajos or humans or life or sandstone; it had begun with the universe itself. In its first moment the universe exploded into order. The raw energy of the Big Bang flashed into patterns, into particles and forces that quickly built more elaborate particles and forces and gradually built stars and galaxies. The tsunami of gas racing away from the Big Bang shaped itself into billions of spiral galaxies spinning and spinning, spinning themselves into webs of greater order. The galaxies spun themselves into stars and pulsars and black holes, into planets and comets and moons. Planets spun and spun and spun themselves into oceans and atmospheres, volcanoes and mountains, rivers and canyons, sandstone and thunderstorms and lightning. Some planets spun themselves into highly patterned carbon molecules, and then into cells, which turned out to be master weavers. Cells wove whole oceans of molecules into cells, then into multicelled creatures. Cells wove billions of patterns of life. Cells wove the land into green forests. Cells wove fish and birds and dinosaurs and mammals. The universe's genius at weaving patterns became a spider weaving a spiderweb. The universe's long quest for patterns became brains searching for patterns in events, patterns on the earth, patterns in the sky. The master weaving that began with the creation of the universe became the weaving of a rug symbolizing the creation of the universe. The flash of the Big Bang became the lightning bolts of sanctification.

◆ ◆ ◆

As Edwin Hubble lay sleeping beneath his Storm Pattern rug, a spider was spinning a web in the ceiling corner.

Around 1640, astronomer William Gascoigne was looking through his telescope when a spider dropped across his field of view, leaving a spider thread across the stars. Gascoigne was impressed by what a thin line it made. He arranged two spider threads into a crosshair, creating a telescopic sight that greatly enhanced the aiming of his telescope and the mapping of the sky. Three centuries later astronomers were still using spider threads for telescope crosshairs. At Royal Greenwich Observatory astronomers plucked their spiderwebs from hedgerows. At Mount Lick Observatory in California, director Robert Aitken fed bugs to a nest of black widows, whose webs, he insisted, were superior. George Hale used spiderwebs at Yerkes Observatory, but astronomers and historians at Mount Wilson aren't sure whether Hale used them there. It's possible, at least, that Edwin Hubble was gazing through a spider's web to discover the source of all weaving.

◆ ◆ ◆

Waiting for the auction, I wandered through J. L. Hubbell's house, full of rugs and art and books. I noticed two astronomy books from the 1890s. Then there was *The Light of Western Stars* by Zane Grey, who had stayed in this house. In this biofilter of astronomy Grey wrote: "She had shunned the light of the stars as she had violently dismissed every hinting suggestive memory of Stewart's kisses. But one night she went deliberately to her window. There they shone. Her stars! . . . Those shining stars made her yield. She whispered to them that they had claimed her—the West claimed her—Stewart claimed her forever."[7]

In the trading-post rug room I asked Steve, the Hubbell buyer, about the origin of the Storm Pattern, and he said there was a mystery about it. Most books said J. B. Moore. I told Steve what Jim Babbitt had said, and Steve said that the Babbitts knew the history of the western reservation better than anyone, so Steve was inclined to accept Jim's account. But then a Navajo woman who worked with Steve said she'd always heard it was J. B. Moore.

During the auction Hank Blair pointed out the weaver of one of the Storm Pattern rugs, a woman who looked old enough to have been the daughter of an original weaver of Storm Patterns, and I edged my way through the aisle to speak with her, convinced that at last I would learn the secret from the source, but it turned out that she spoke only Navajo. If she knew the secret, it was going to remain a secret.

Along with Hank Blair, the other auctioneer was Bruce Burnham, a fourth-generation trader. Hank and Bruce, both married to Navajos, were two of the last old-time traders, still doing some business in barter. Like traders from the Hubbell era, Burnham had given direction to a new rug design, the Burntwater, though this design started with a creative mutation, with one weaver combining elements from two other designs. Hank and Bruce knew their rugs well, and in the auction they were careful not to hype a rug, but they were also quick to scold the audience for not recognizing the quality or value of a rug. Unfortunately, when the rug I had decided to buy came up for bid, Bruce announced that it was a great deal, a very nice rug for too low a price.

The previous year I'd been here only as an observer, free to enjoy everything, but now I had a biologized role, competing for resources against unpredictable others, and needing to decide a rug's value for me. During the preview I'd made a list of seven possibilities, but since I preferred #345, I had to let most of the others get away. I liked #345 because it had Ganado colors—red, white, black, and gray, the colors of J. L. Hubbell's Ganado Red rugs—and because it was the traditional design, the design the Hubbell or Cameron Trading Post might have been selling in 1928. The lightning had to be white, not red, as weavers often made it—real lightning was white.

Encouraged by Bruce Burnham, the bidding on #345 took off. Most rugs got only one bid, but for #345 the price quickly jumped by 60 percent. What was the value of a creation-story rug that Edwin Hubble might have seen when he was in the middle of becoming the first human to see the creation of the universe? SOLD!

The rug identification tag gave the weaver's name and home-town, but as I asked around, no one knew her. She too would remain a mystery.

For twenty years I'd kept a Ganado Red rug on the foot of my bed to keep my feet warm, to guard them against the unbiological night. Now the Storm Pattern rug would join it.

A few weeks later I ran into Bruce Burnham at another Navajo rug auction and asked him about the origin of the design he'd sold me. Bruce adhered to the J. B. Moore theory, though he thought that Moore "worked out the details" of the design with local weavers, maybe just the one weaver he'd mentioned in his 1911 catalog. Bruce said that the design then got picked up by the Hayden mill for their flour sacks, which the Babbitts distributed all over the western reser-vation, which is the only reason the Storm Pattern became so identi-fied with the western reservation. Bruce admitted that he had never actually seen one of those Storm Pattern flour sacks, but he sug-gested that I go talk with Jim Babbitt, who had a museum's worth of trading-post artifacts; Bruce was *sure* that Jim Babbitt would have some of those flour sacks. I did contact the historical museum in Tempe, where the Hayden mill is a famous landmark. The museum had a collection of Hayden-mill flour sacks. They told me that no one there had ever seen or heard of a Storm Pattern flour sack. But they told me to go talk with Jim Babbitt, who had a museum's worth of trading-post artifacts and who might have a Storm Pattern flour sack.

The next time I went to Sedona I stopped at Garlands again and asked them, again, about the origin of the Storm Pattern. They said that no one knew; it was a big mystery. I replied that it was refreshing to hear someone admitting that no one knew.

When I looked at my Storm Pattern rug I saw the creation of the universe, densely woven with mystery.

✦ ✦ ✦

As Spider Woman spun her white galaxy in the ceiling corner, Edwin Hubble lay protected from the cold, immense, mysterious night, protected by a thin layer of human stories.

Yet Hubble was restless; Hubble was dreaming energetically; Hubble couldn't stop imagining the galaxies flying apart. Hubble woke up in the middle of the night. Starlight glowed imperceptibly from the spiderweb. Hubble woke up in a shock of wonder. Was it a dream that the universe was expanding? Could it really be himself who was transforming the universe? He had always been so cautious, so shy of exotic ideas—like Einstein's theories. He avoided using the word *galaxy* even after the galaxies had made him famous. In his public writings he stuck to the facts, avoiding any sense of wonder.

Yet people seldom become astronomers without a sense of wonder. There must have been at least one night when Edwin Hubble woke up in a shock of wonder at the mystery of creation, a mystery that no thin layer of human stories or theories or numbers could prevent from sinking deeply into human bodies.

✦ ✦ ✦

The weather forecast was perfect. A 100 percent chance of thunderstorms. Some possibly severe. Strong winds. Dangerous lightning. A chance of hail. Flash-flood warnings for large areas. Perfect!

I drove up to the Grand Canyon, and along the rim. Already the clouds were building up above the canyon, a line of clouds that curved this way and that, imitating the canyon's curves. The July heat welling out of the canyon energized condensation above the canyon before there was much condensation around it. The clouds spread out and linked up and rose taller. The canyon built a mountain range of clouds above it, the ghost of the mountain ranges from which the canyon rocks had come. The clouds started out bright white and then grew gray and blue and black. Far away, the rumbling began.

I arrived at the great astronomical observatory at Desert View. George Ritchey never built his Grand Canyon observatory. His plans were too technologically ambitious, and he couldn't find financial backing. Ritchey's dream was also strangely oblivious of astronomical realities. One of the most important requirements for an observatory is the "seeing," the calmness or turbulence of the air. Calm air is essential for clear star images. But the heat waves roiling out of the Grand Canyon make the air along the canyon rim very turbulent, good for keeping ravens and condors soaring for hours, and good for triggering thunderstorms, but very bad for astronomy. Ritchey did have valid reasons for selecting the Grand Canyon: its high elevation, dry air, usual lack of clouds, and remoteness from city lights were all good for astronomy. Yet Ritchey knew the Grand Canyon well enough that he should have recognized a big problem with turbulence. Ritchey first vacationed at the canyon in 1907, and the next year he may have become the first person ever to take color photographs of the canyon. Ritchey's ignoring of the turbulence problem suggests that he had become obsessed with the idea of an observatory on the rim of the canyon, on the rim of deep time and deep beauty. Ritchey's vision seems to have captured the imagination of the *New York Times*, which in one of its articles about the Grand Canyon observatory dubbed it "the desert watch tower."

George Hale too may have become obsessed by the Grand Canyon observatory, if in a negative way. Two years after Hale sent Hubble to the canyon, he sent Hubble's assistant, Milton Humason, to make further tests, to make sure Ritchey was wrong. It was even odder that Hale sent Hubble to Cameron, three thousand feet lower than Desert View and much hotter and dustier, very wrong for astronomy. Hale built his observatory on Palomar Mountain after all.

Yet someone did build an observatory at Desert View. At least, Mary Colter thought of her Desert View Watchtower as a Native American astronomical observatory.

We know quite a bit about Mary Colter's thinking about the Watchtower, for she wrote a one-hundred-page book about its inspirations and motifs. Colter modeled her watchtower on the Puebloan tower ruins in the Four Corners region, especially at Hovenweep.

Colter spent six months studying tower ruins, even hiring a plane to search for them in remote areas. Colter studied them more extensively than had any archaeologist. In her book Colter discussed theories of the purpose of the towers. She dismissed theories that they were granaries or habitations. She admitted that they were often defensive, but she pointed out that many towers were connected by underground passageways to kivas, which didn't make any sense for defensive purposes. But it did make sense for ceremonial purposes. The Puebloans were farmers whose survival and ceremonial cycles depended on the seasons, and they watched the sky closely. Colter endorsed the theory of anthropologist Jesse Walter Fewkes that the towers were used by priests to track the sun and moon and stars and seasons. A watchtower connected Puebloans with the sky, and allowed a priest or katsina to arrive from the sky into a kiva ceremony. Colter built her watchtower with a connected kiva.

I walked through the kiva room and up the narrow stairs into the seventy-foot stone Watchtower. The tower's first floor held murals by Hopi artist Fred Kabotie, depicting the Hopi universe, especially their connection with the Grand Canyon. The ceiling was full of astronomical motifs, whose Hopi meanings Colter explained in her book. I climbed through two more mural-rich floors, then reached the top floor, with its eleven large windows, about three feet high. Colter had planned to install telescopes here or on the roof, just like in her Lookout Studio. Colter finished her architectural plans for the Watchtower less than three years after Edwin Hubble had stood on the canyon rim here. Given all the publicity about the Grand Canyon observatory, Colter must have known about it, and it's the kind of idea that would have inspired her.

I gazed into the canyon, now densely patterned with cloud shadows and sunbeams, constantly changing. I gazed north at the gorge of the Little Colorado River, the Hopis' place of emergence, an idea given historical flesh when the Hopis really did emerge from the Grand Canyon and migrate to the mesas where they live today. Far to the west several cloud banks were already raining, dropping blue warp threads that curved in the wind and sometimes evaporated before they reached the ground. Some rain streaks fell into the canyon and darkened the cliffs. A lightning bolt hit somewhere behind the rim, and after a while its washed-out thunder arrived. Then a lightning bolt hit one of the buttes inside the canyon.

I watched the clouds building up a few miles away, rising, spreading, darkening, rumbling, and then they released their rain, first a few strands, then a curtain dropping into the canyon, obscuring the shapes behind it. As the clouds moved, the rain streaks hiked through the canyon, and then a sunburst followed them, and the canyon buttes gleamed. Far to the west a rainbow was growing.

The sky above me darkened. The wind whooshed around the tower, gaining stranger tones from the roughness of the stones and the cracks between them. Raindrops spotted the windows, streaked the windows. The blue curtain wrapped itself around the tower, eliminating my view of the canyon. Then the rain drifted off, and I got a cloud's-eye view of rain falling into the canyon.

Along dozens of miles of the canyon, half a dozen clouds were raining into it, and raining much larger shadows, and through them the sun rained jigsaw patterns of light. Thunder continued rumbling from far and near. A lightning bolt struck a cliff, which flared with an odd glow.

On a normal summer afternoon the thunderstorms dissipate after an hour or two, but today they continued building up, the clouds growing blacker, the rain and lightning more intense. I watched a huge storm cell building up just west of me, very dark, loud with thunder, moving my way. An eerie twilight. Then the storm exploded. The windows became waterfalls; the wind roared; the tower vibrated; thunder boomed very loud, very near. I stepped well back from the windows, not trusting the tower's lightning rods. The storm raged for fifteen or twenty minutes, and when it drifted off I could see waterfalls erupting from cliffs, flash floods frothing down drainages, creeks combining into larger flows. I watched the floods working their way layer by layer, turn by turn, down to the river.

I was seeing a power that had been at work on Earth for aeons. The power of thunderstorms had melted mountain ranges down rivers to the sea and built the strata of Grand Canyon rocks.

Thunderstorms had nurtured aeons of life, supporting its evolution, welding its limbs, building it into the mile of fossils in Grand Canyon strata. Then thunderstorms had carved that strata away and created the canyon. The lightning had signed its jagged name deep into the ground. Yet thunderstorms were a small part of much vaster energies and aeons. A lightning bolt was but a planetary mirror's glimmer of the power of the sun. A thunderstorm was but a microeddy of a galactic hurricane. A lightning bolt was but the memory flash of the Big Bang.

I was seeing the power of order and the power of chaos, the power of Emergence and the power of Coyote. I was seeing the power that curled the sandstone desert into green grass and white wool, yet also flash-flooded away soil and sheep. I was seeing the power that grew forests, yet also set them afire. I was seeing the power that built a mile of stone, yet also eroded stone into canyons. I was seeing the power that had welcomed Hopi ancestors to grow corn in the bottom of the Grand Canyon, yet then withheld the rain and forced the Hopis to abandon their homes. I was seeing the power that provided Navajo ancestors with a lot of rabbits to hunt, yet also provided a lot of coyotes to snatch rabbits away. I was seeing the power that gave life, yet also gave disease. I was seeing the mysterious power that filled the world with both blessings and evil omens and that challenged humans to tell them apart and to encourage the omens to become blessings. I was seeing the power of pattern and the power of storm.

Occasionally, I went to the window facing away from the canyon. I was looking for a mountain fifty miles away, but clouds blocked my view. Finally, one of the gaps in the storm aligned with me, and I saw Dook'o'ooLííd, one of the Navajos' four sacred mountains, this one better known as the San Francisco Peaks. Above the mountain was a huge dark mountain of clouds. I waited. I watched the streaks of rain curling down. Then it flashed: a lightning bolt. A lightning bolt connected the mountain and the cloud. This mountain was one of the four sacred mountains in the Storm Pattern design. I waited. I watched. Then it flashed: a lightning bolt arced from the mountain, just like in my Storm Pattern rug.

Then nearby clouds drifted across my view.

I stayed in the tower for as long as the storms continued coming, for maybe five hours. The storms came in waves that advanced through the canyon for a dozen miles or more. The clouds turned on and off, built up and melted away. The tower was engulfed in rain, then in sun. Mist rose out of the canyon, white snakes of mist curling up the drainages and over the edges of cliffs, ballooning into strange shapes, into ghosts, rising to meet the much darker rain clouds. Rainbows sprouted and changed shape and intensity and melted away. Dozens of lightning bolts proclaimed that powerful and invisible forces connected the sky and the earth.

When the storms were over I headed down to the Cameron Trading Post for dinner. I went into the original trading-post building and peeked behind the on-the-wall rug that hid the original doorway, the doorway through which Edwin Hubble had walked billions of years ago, when the universe was much younger, the doorway now sedimented shut by ancient sand dunes. On the dining room walls there were a dozen rugs, five of which were Storm Patterns, including the largest. Another rug blended the Storm Pattern design with the Tree of Life design, filling the lightning bolts with colorful songbirds. The lightning bolts offered a Navajo blessing onto my food.

At sunset I headed for the San Francisco Peaks, still wrapped in clouds. I lived at the base on the mountain, in the forest, with no other human structures between me and the mountain. Occasionally, Navajo medicine men came up my driveway and harvested some of its bordering wild roses for ceremonial uses, but they would never tell me exactly what uses.

I looked anew at my Storm Pattern rug. I looked at the symbol in one corner, the San Francisco Peaks. I looked just beyond it, and I picked out one little crest of red wool. This is where I live: this is me. This is the purpose of creation stories. They are maps that locate humans amid the forces of creation. They are clouds that make visible the secretly flowing energies that generate life. They are lightning rods that turn dangerous energies into blessings. I looked anew at the Storm Pattern, and I saw the flash of the Big Bang turning into outrushing galaxies and weaving a further pattern that praised the journey and the patterns and even the storms of the universe.

Yet in the middle of the night, when humans are even more oblivious than usual, when dreams only hint at the strangeness of reality, the black boundaries of my rug merged with the blackness of the night; the thin layer of human stories was engulfed by space; the compass of the map of creation was overwhelmed by electricity from the stars; and the origins of creation remained a mystery.•✦

NOTES

1. Vesto M. Slipher Papers, Lowell Observatory, Flagstaff, Arizona.

2. Elizabeth Compton Hegemann, *Navajo Trading Days* (Albuquerque: University of New Mexico Press, 1963), 302.

3. Facsimile page of Moore catalog in H. L. James, *Rugs and Posts: The Story of Navajo Weaving and Indian Trading*, 3rd ed. (Altgen, PA: 2005, Schiffer Publishing Company), 86.

4. Quoted in Gale E. Christianson, *Edwin Hubble: Mariner of the Nebulae* (New York: Farrar, Straus, and Giroux, 1995), 210.

5. *New York Times*, February 5, 1931.

6. *Arizona Republic*, February 28, 1931.

7. Zane Grey, *The Light of Western Stars* (New York: Harper and Brothers, 1914), 345.

·6·

SANDPAINTINGS

THE SAND was full of footprints.

There were lizard tracks, with a zigzagging line where the tail had dragged and swished. There were mouse tracks and jackrabbit tracks wandering from flower to flower, bush to bush. There were beetle tracks and spider tracks, wandering a bit more randomly than mammal tracks. There were raven tracks in a cluster where a raven had landed briefly. There were the tracks of rocks, rocks journeying across a quarter of a billion years.

For a quarter of a billion years this sand had been sandstone, hard and well buried. Before that, this sand had been sand dunes hundreds of feet deep and hundreds of miles wide, sand washing down from distant mountains, sand blowing on the winds from a nearby ocean. Only georecently had this sandstone been unearthed. It felt the sunlight again, the rain again, the wind again. It dissolved back into sand.

When this sand had last felt the imprint of animal feet, they had been the feet of small lizards. This sand had never known the footprints of dinosaurs, for the dinosaurs hadn't evolved yet. It had never known the footprints of mammals or birds, ants or butterflies. Now the sand was reading the news of a quarter of a billion years. Scorpions weren't news; they were indistinguishable from ancient scorpions. The news was that Earth had flourished with new forms of life. The news included a creature who could look at sand and see in it images and meanings much larger than footprints.

I wandered off the trail to a slope of deeper sand, leaned down, and reached out my finger. I traced a line in the sand. I drew a spire, tall and straight and thin. I drew a larger monolith, taller than the spire, connected to it by cliffs and slopes. I filled this outline with vertical lines to emphasize the skyward reach of the monolith and spire.

I looked up at the real landscape, at the real monolith and spire. I was looking at Monument Valley, full of spires and monoliths, buttes and mesas, rock and sand. It was full of empty space, without which the monuments would not be themselves, defiant of high and empty space.

I was looking at the most famous monument of Monument Valley, an image seen in numerous movies, calendars, magazines, book covers, and posters. In his 1939 movie *Stagecoach*, director John Ford sent his stagecoach around and around this monument, pretending the stagecoach was on a long journey across the West, leaving viewers imagining that the West held endless monuments like this. This monument is called West Mitten Butte, which is west of the similar-looking East Mitten Butte. The name "mitten" refers to the thumb-like spire and the hand-like monolith. These names were given by a Colorado-born, mitten-childhood white pioneer, not by the desert-born Navajos who had lived here for centuries. Yet the Navajos did recognize the monuments as hands, the dormant hands of the gods, left as signs that the gods would return here someday. The Navajos have their own names for these monuments, names full of time and generations, living and dying, sun and wind and rain and sand, piñon trees and horses, gods and ceremonies.

West Mitten Butte is the only part of Monument Valley that holds a hiking trail open to the public, a three-mile loop. Aside from a rough and sandy driving loop, the rest of Monument Valley is private, for it is still home for many Navajos, who live in hogans among the monuments, herding sheep and weaving rugs and performing ceremonies as they have for generations. I was starting out on the hike, dropping from a ridge, down a sandy slope, and onto the valley floor.

I was being followed. I was being followed by footprints, deep and distinct in sand that had gone without rain for weeks. I was adding a new shape to all the other shapes that only cells, with their geometrical skills, could make against the formlessness of sand. Yet the wind was already quickening, this early in the morning, already starting to blur my identity, erase my journey. Already the wind was starting to erode my picture of the monument back into mere sand.

+ + +

It is to fight against erosion that the Navajos make sandpaintings, an act at the center of their most important religious ceremonies. It is to fight the erosion of the body, the disharmony of the mind, the imbalance of the cosmos. It is to summon the gods that the Navajos paint sand images of the gods, images of perfect harmony that would please the gods enough to lure them to inhabit their images. From sandpaintings, the powers of the gods would flow into humans and restore them to harmony.

The Navajos developed sandpainting into a richer ceremonial form than it was for almost any other people on Earth. For the Navajos sandpaintings bore greater spiritual power, so the Navajos gave them greater artistry and symbolism. Perhaps only the Tibetan Buddhists, with their complex mandalas, developed sandpainting with greater sophistication. Navajo sandpaintings are similar to mandalas in being mirrors of the cosmos, lenses through which the powers of the cosmos could be focused into human lives.

An elderly Navajo woman in Monument Valley told me that sandpainting was a stronger tradition in the Monument Valley area than it was in many other areas of Dinétah—Navajo lands. Perhaps Monument Valley's long isolation and traditional lifeways had helped preserve spiritual traditions that were fading away elsewhere, in towns where stories came not from the night sky but from television, where spirituality came from the white man's church, and where medicine came in the form of pills.

Sandpainting ceremonies are performed in hogans, traditional Navajo homes whose eight sides and sunrise-facing door are already full of spiritual symbolism. Some hogans are built just for ceremonies, but most often sandpainting ceremonies are performed in the hogan of the family with the person who needs healing. In front of the door the medicine man hangs prayer feathers to request the coming of the gods.

The ceremony begins with the clearing out of the earthen floor of the hogan. The medicine man brings in a large amount of ordinary sand and spreads it across the floor, smoothing it out with a weaving batten into a layer a couple of inches thick. Then he brings in bowls full of colored sands. The sands have been carefully gathered and prepared. A mano and metate, just like those used for grinding corn, are used to grind sandstone into sand. The sands have five sacred colors. The red sand comes from red sandstone. The white sand comes from white sandstone or gypsum. The yellow sand comes from yellow sandstone and yellow ocher. The black sand comes from charcoal, burned from the roots of special trees, mixed with sand to make it less powdery. The gray sand, serving as blue, is a mixture of white and black.

The medicine man dips his fingers into a bowl and scoops up sand. He reaches out and lets the sand slip between his fingers and thumb. He draws a thin, straight, precise line. The sandpainting must be done precisely or it will not work, and it may even do harm. The medicine man is reproducing a holy painting that the gods, persuaded by the quest of a hero, showed to the Navajo people. The gods drew the original images on clouds, but humans have to settle for drawing them upon sand, which they give cloud-like designs. The medicine man has no pattern to copy. He carries the whole complex design in his head, as did the generations of medicine men from whom he inherited it.

◆ ◆ ◆

West Mitten Butte loomed above me, the hand of a medicine man.

As I walked I watched the butte changing shape. It seems that most photographs of the butte are taken from the same angle, the same location where a photographer can park a vehicle and set up a camera without much effort. As I walked, the butte broke out of the photographs and became real. It grew larger and taller as I approached. Its general shape turned into a thousand shapes, cliffs full of curves and angles, recesses and shadows, colors and splotches. The spire became thicker, then thinner. The monolith turned out to hold a little slice of blue sky, a window where the cliff was beginning to crack open and create a new spire, or perhaps only a new pile of rubble below.

Beyond West Mitten Butte I looked at other buttes and spires, this strange geological city.

What was the fascination of Monument Valley? Many visitors came here looking for the Wild West they had seen in movies, a realm of adventure, freedom, and beckoning wealth. Yet John Ford himself had seen something greater here. Ford was trying to elevate the western movie from cheap melodrama into national mythology, and he saw Monument Valley as a mythic landscape, larger than life, powerful and glorious and strange. Even when Ford's scripts were about the national conquest of the land, the land itself was telling a different story, a story of ancient, powerful inhuman forces, a story of strange, epic events. The land itself was whispering the stories that the Navajos heard as stories of gods and creation and magical transformation.

By any telling, Monument Valley is a strange landscape. Even nineteenth-century Navajos who spent their entire lives in Monument Valley were told by traveling Navajos that Monument Valley was a strange place. Even by the standards of a Colorado Plateau full of geological strangeness, Monument Valley is strange. Rocks are not supposed to look like this, standing so tall and narrow and smooth. Geology is supposed to be a more disorderly process. Erosion is allowed to create canyons and rubble, but not to stack rocks into spires. Monument Valley seems unnatural, surreal. The spires partake of an order that seems more biological, the order that builds trees. The spires seem more like human architecture, like skyscrapers or cathedral towers; the valley's very name implies human-made memorials. Humans love to see in landscapes the shapes of human architecture and human bodies and faces. Across the West humans have named rock formations "castles." In Monument Valley one trio of spires is the "Three Sisters." Finding human shapes in nature makes nature less inhuman, more reassuring. Yet rocks with human faces are even more surrealistic.

The spire of West Mitten Butte did indeed have a head-like cap. I thought of it as the head of a *yei*, a Navajo god. Monument Valley does have a set of spires the Navajos saw as "Yei Bi Chei," dancers from a *yei* ceremony.

I stepped off the trail and reached down to the sand. I drew a spire, thoroughly geological at its base, but evolving into the biological, with a human head. I gave it the face and feathers of a *yei*.

The rocks had grown a face surrealistic enough to see the surrealism of the universe.

✦ ✦ ✦

The sand fell onto the ground, forming a thin, straight, precise line. The line began to curve in a steady, precise curve. The sand stopped, formed a corner, and headed back, paralleling the first line, forming a shape. The sand couldn't understand what it was doing. It had never done anything like this before.

The sand did know about lines. It had formed the many curving lines of sand dunes, formed them, shifted them, shifted them, shifted them endlessly. The shifting sand had been steered by the wind, but this was not the wind steering the sand now. The sand knew about being steered by rains and floods and rivers, but this was not water steering it now. The sand was forming a long, elaborate shape. The sand knew about being long shapes, for it had stood tall as sandstone mesas and spires, stood for tens of thousands of years. But the shape it was forming now was far more elaborate. The sand had always been only itself, only many forms and actions of itself, but now it was being turned into something new, a picture of something else, a symbol, charged with energy from brains. As sandstone spires the sand had felt great pressure and upheld great weight, but now it was upholding a different kind of weight. It was upholding the order of life, the order of the cosmos, the order of the sacred.

The sand formed the image of Mother Earth. On her belly, at the place of emergence, is a lake, and radiating from it are the roots of plants. Rising from the lake toward her head is a cornstalk.

✦ ✦ ✦

Rounding a bend in a drainage, I startled a rabbit at her breakfast bush. She tensed and bolted and ran. I followed the rabbit tracks a little ways into the brush. I reached down and touched a track, and from it I drew a rabbit, and at the rabbit's mouth I drew a bush, plump and delicious and safe. There were no coyotes or hunters in my sandpainting, no hunger, fear, or chaos.

✦ ✦ ✦

Alongside the image of Mother Earth, the medicine man begins drawing Father Sky. He lays out the image of Father Sky carefully, for in length and shape it has to have a precise symmetry with the image of Mother Earth. He fills the body of Father Sky with black charcoal, for Father Sky is the night sky, and he will be filled with stars.

This image of Mother Earth and Father Sky is the most important, sacred, and powerful of all sandpaintings. It is a map of the Navajo cosmos. Creating it is a reenactment of the creation of the cosmos. It is an altar summoning the gods, an affirmation of cosmic order against the forces of chaos. It is the final sandpainting done in elaborate ceremonies that might require nine days, with a new sandpainting done every day. Medicine men were wary of the power of this sandpainting and did it only when the most powerful healing was required.

When the medicine man is finished creating the black body of Father Sky, he begins filling it with constellations. He places the constellations carefully, with the right number of stars, the right configuration, and the right relationships between constellations. He is placing the constellations as carefully as had Black God in the original creation. Black God had placed the stars with an order that would uphold and guide the lives of his people. The medicine man is not including any of the stars that had been thrown into the sky by Coyote. Coyote had ruined the planned order of the sky by stealing Black God's star-filled pouch and tossing its remaining stars into the sky with no order at all. Coyote had introduced chaos into the cosmos. It is to fight against chaos that the medicine man creates this sandpainting, which restores the original order and benevolence of the cosmos and summons it into a disordered human body.

Father Sky's constellations have Western names and stories—Orion, the Pleiades, Scorpius, Cassiopeia, the Big Dipper, the Milky Way. Yet the Navajos have their own names and stories. To the Greeks and their predecessors Cassiopeia was an arrogant queen whom the gods punished by chaining her to a chair. To the Navajos Cassiopeia is Revolving Female, a strong and wise mother or grandmother who circles Central Fire (the North Star) in the center of the Hogan, circles it with her husband, Revolving Male (the Big Dipper), circles it with a harmony that proclaims the importance and reliability of the Navajo family. To the Greeks Scorpius was a giant scorpion, sent by Gaia to kill Orion the hunter and silence his boasting that he could kill all the animals on Earth. The Navajos divide Scorpius into two constellations. One is an elderly man who holds a basket of seeds, a symbol of agricultural abundance. The other one is Gah heet'e'ii, or Rabbit Tracks, named for how its two sets of stars look just like the tracks a rabbit leaves in sand. Gah heet'e'ii is a symbol of hunting abundance, a tribute to rabbit for his important gift to the Navajo diet and a warning against overhunting. When Gah heet'e'ii is in one position in the sky, hunters must cease hunting, for deer and pronghorn are nursing their young. When Gah heet'e'ii reaches another position, the animal babies are grown, and hunting can resume.

When the medicine man has finished the sandpainting, he takes a handful of sacred corn pollen and flings it into the air over the painting. The pollen covers the painting. The sandpainting is ready to be inhabited by the gods.

❖ ❖ ❖

In the distance I noticed a hogan. To Navajos the spires of Monument Valley are the posts of a giant hogan, which has a central fire and a sunrise-facing door.

Some Navajos regard their four sacred mountains as the posts that uphold the sky, which is a giant, transparent hogan.

Every hogan is a representation of the Navajo cosmos. It has poles in the four sacred directions. It is domed like the sky and round like the sun, and it faces the sunrise. It is a house made of dawn. Its central hearth represents the North Star, the hub of the cosmos. Its floor is Mother Earth. Its structure is a physical embodiment of hózhó, of the balance of the cosmos. The building of a hogan is accompanied by chants that ask for the blessings of the gods and invoke their building of First Hogan. The gods built First Hogan at the Place of Emergence, built it to be a model for Navajo life. It was in the sky of First Hogan that Black God drew the constellations in harmonious order. It is First Hogan that appears at the center of the Storm Pattern rug design, which portrays the Navajo creation story.

I stepped off the trail, which here was hard dirt and gravel, and found a sandier patch. I drew the dome of a hogan, and I filled it with stars.

◆ ◆ ◆

The sandpainting is ready to heal. The ill person enters the hogan and walks onto the sandpainting and sits down upon it. This blurs the sandpainting, but it doesn't matter: the sandpainting was created for a person to sit upon, at the focal point of the Navajo-cosmos telescope.

Around the ill person are placed four wide boards, painted with cosmological motifs and scenes from the mythic story being enacted in this ceremony. The boards help focus the power of the sandpainting onto the ill person. One board shows the black of night on one side and the white of dawn on the other. The second board shows the moon on one side and Mother Earth on the other. The third board shows the sun on one side and Father Sky on the other side, with the sun's rays across Father Sky's face. The fourth board shows one of the Thunder People carrying a sacred hero through a skyhole into the dawn sky.

The medicine man begins to chant. He shakes a rattle. With words, with prayers, with songs he creates another sandpainting in the air, a complex, sacred pattern that summons the gods. He rolls out long verses, varying and building, full of poetry and meaning. He sings the words from memory, from centuries of memory. The chants must be done precisely or they will not work, and they may do harm. The power of the sandpaintings and the chants comes from their sacred symbolism, not from the medicine man himself. The Navajo medicine man is not a shaman; he does not become possessed by a spirit or see original visions. The Navajo medicine man is a priest who presides over a symbolic language that the gods gave to their people long ago and expect to hear when their help is needed.

There are hundreds of sandpaintings and hundreds of chants and ceremonies that go with them. One of these chants, from the Nightway ceremony, summons the gods with these words:

In the house made of the dawn,
In the house made of the evening twilight,
In the house made of the dark cloud,
In the house made of the he-rain,
In the house made of the dark mist,
In the house made of the she-rain,
In the house made of pollen,
In the house made of grasshoppers,
Where the dark mist curtains the doorway,
The path to which is on the rainbow . . .
With your moccasins of dark cloud, come to us.
With your leggings of dark cloud, come to us.
With your shirt of dark cloud, come to us.
With your head-dress of dark cloud, come to us.
With your mind enveloped in dark cloud, come to us.
With the dark thunder above you, come to us soaring.
With the shapen cloud at your feet, come to us soaring.
With the far darkness made of the dark cloud over your head,
    come to us soaring.
With the far darkness made of the he-rain over your head,
    come to us soaring.
With the far darkness made of the dark mist over your head,
    come to us soaring.
With the far darkness made of the she-rain over your head,
    come to us soaring.
With the zigzag lightning flung out on high over your head,
    come to us soaring.
With the rainbow hanging high over your head, come to us
    soaring. . .[1]

The gods come. The gods come soaring. The gods come out of
the sky and the earth and come into the hogan. The gods recognize
themselves in the sandpainting of Mother Earth and Father Sky.
The gods recognize the original order and harmony and goodness of
creation. The gods recognize the reverence that humans are showing
for creation and for the gods. The gods flow into the sandpainting.
The powers of the universe, of the stars and the sun and the moon,
flow into the sandpainting. The powers of the rain and lightning and
rainbow and rivers flow into the sandpainting. The powers of the soil

and seeds and plants flow into the sandpainting. The powers of the
animals and reptiles and birds and insects flow into the sandpainting. The order and harmony and goodness of creation pulse within
the sandpainting.

And from the sandpainting, the gods flow into the ill person.
The powers of the universe flow into human flesh.

In the Nightway ceremony the identification of the ill person
with the gods is encouraged with this chant:

This I walk with, this I walk with.
Now Talking God, I walk with.
These are his feet I walk with.
These are his limbs I walk with.
This is his body I walk with.
This is his mind I walk with.
This is his voice I walk with.
These are his twelve white plumes I walk with.
Beauty before me, I walk with.
Beauty behind me, I walk with.
Beauty above me, I walk with.
Beauty all around me, I walk with.[2]

The gods fill the ill person with the original order and harmony
and goodness of creation. The gods overpower the powers of chaos.
Chaos melts out of the human body. Illness melts into the sandpainting. With this reminder and model of cosmic order, the human
body realigns itself, restores itself. Now with harmony, now with
beauty, now with *hózhó*, humans may walk.

◆ ◆ ◆

As I walked, the restlessness and chatter of the human ego had a
chance to settle down. With no humans present to mirror my identity, my only mirrors, my only society, were the monuments. I began
to hear their silence, to see their colors and shapes. I began to feel
their ancientness. I was reminded that the ancient powers of the
earth that had built these monuments had also embodied themselves
in human bodies. The monument beside me walked very slowly
through time. I walked more quickly.

I reached down and drew a human torso and head. Inside the

torso, where the heart would be, I drew the monument, its spire reaching up only because it was falling down, its spire so tall only because space was so empty.

✦ ✦ ✦

When the healing is finished, the sandpainting must be obliterated. The sandpainting was created not for the sake of art but for ceremony, and the ceremony must conclude with the dispersal of the sandpainting. The sandpainting now holds the evil that had caused the illness, and this evil must be sent on its way. When in the twentieth century Navajos began making sandpaintings as art for permanence and for sale, they always made the sandpaintings differently than ceremonial sandpaintings, leaving out sacred elements, introducing deliberate errors, so as not to violate sacred rules.

The sandpainting, started after sunrise, must be obliterated before sunset. In nighttime ceremonies, such as the Big Star Chant, the sandpainting must be started after dark and obliterated before dawn.

The medicine man reaches out a wooden staff with a prayer feather, touches it to the sandpainting, and stirs the sand. In the proper order, and from foot to head, the gods blur. The gods disappear. The gods are now streaks of color. The medicine man sweeps all the sand into a basket or blanket and carries it out the door of the hogan. He carries it to the north, to a far, safe distance from the hogan, and there he pours the sand onto the ground. He recites a final prayer over the sand to release the power from it, both the sacred power and the evil power.

The sand begins blowing in the wind.

✦ ✦ ✦

The next morning I went for another hike around West Mitten Butte. All of my sandpaintings were gone, as far as I could figure out. I had stepped off the trail to make my pictures, so I wouldn't impose them on other hikers, and now I wasn't sure of where I had stepped off. I was fairly sure about the first spot, but when I looked there it seemed my sandpainting of West Mitten Butte had been eroded away, in a day. My second sandpainting, the spire with a yei face, was also gone. Or was it only my memory, drawn upon the sands of the human brain, that had eroded away? Yesterday had been a very windy day, with veils of sand blowing across the valley. Even my foot-prints on the trail had been reduced to a vague disturbance.

Yesterday afternoon I'd gone on the seventeen-mile drive through Monument Valley. The wind was blowing hard and the sand was streaming. On the bumpy descent into the valley I came upon a car stuck in a sand drift. A young guy was out pushing hard on the rear, a young woman was gunning the engine, the rear wheels were spinning, the sand was flying up, but they were going nowhere, except deeper into the sand. I stopped to help. They were tourists from Spain, and like quite a few young Europeans they had been tempted by American status symbols: they had rented a Lin-coln Town Car, badly unsuited for this road. Now they had plenty of status, the status of fools who were barred from a land where the Navajos had been walking in beauty for centuries.

On my drive the wind was driving sand and tumbleweeds across the road. The manes of eight horses in a corral were blow-ing like flags, and so was the long black hair of the Navajo tending the horses. Where the prevailing winds ran into the long, curving Thunderbird Mesa, the sands were trapped and over centuries had built up long and tall sand dunes, perhaps one hundred feet tall. The lower dunes had vegetation growing out of them, but on the upper dunes the ever-shifting sands had smothered or uprooted anything trying to grow, so the dunes were bare. Waves of sand blew along the dunes and billowed up into ghostly shapes.

Near Cly Butte the road was especially sandy, and a sudden dust devil swept right past me, rocked my truck, and wrapped my win-dows with sand and dust. Cly Butte was named for a Navajo family that had lived at its base for generations. At one of the most popu-lar valley viewpoints there is a stone memorial—a monument—to Ericson Cly, whose thirty-two-year life included being a US Marine, a Christian missionary, and a computer science major in college, but who was struck by lightning at his family home here and killed.

The sand around Cly Butte billowed up into ghostly shapes.

Now on my morning hike the wind was stirring again, and beginning to stir the sand and dust.

This sand had once been tall sandstone spires. It had been West

Mitten Butte in an earlier and larger version, or other buttes. It had been buttes and spires that long ago had crumbled and disappeared. It had stood tall and strong and resisted the rain and wind that was trying to dissolve it, defying the rain and wind for tens of thousands of years. But it was outendured. Nothing could outendure time. The spires and buttes drained down like the sand in an hourglass. They drained into piles of sand that wouldn't even hold onto a footprint or a drawing. They drained into piles of sand that turned against the surviving spires and buttes and began sandblasting them, pulling them down into sand. In a few thousand years West Mitten Butte's spire would fall, and another spire would separate from the butte, and then it too would fall. The butte would continue to shrink, and someday it would disappear.

It would disappear just like my sandpainting of the butte. The real butte had been painted by a hand far more powerful than mine, a geological hand full of time and strength and creativity, applying all the geochemical secrets of endurance. The butte too would disappear.

I had hoped that by hiking early in the morning I would beat the heat and the wind, but already the wind was warm and on the trail to hot. I could feel the warm wind sucking the moisture from my skin. I could feel the same power that sandblasted hard, ancient spires back into sand, now trying to erode me. I could feel myself weakening, disintegrating. I too was a sandpainting. I felt time draining through the hourglass of my body. I too would disappear just like my sandpainting of the butte.

◆ ◆ ◆

The sand discarded from the sandpainting began blowing in the wind.

In the sandpainting the sand had portrayed and pulsed with the powers of the sky and earth, the powers of the rain and wind, the powers of the gods. Now this sand felt the warmth of the real sun and was animated by the real rain and wind. Now the charcoal and the white sand that had portrayed the night sky were engulfed by the wheeling lights and blackness of the real night sky. Now the sand had rejoined a far more ancient ceremony.

The sand remained a blur of unusual colors for a while, and gradually it dispersed and mixed with ordinary sand.

The charcoal was carbon, and it went on a different journey. In the desert, carbon is too precious to ignore. It was sucked into the roots of trees and cacti and grasses and flowers. It was raised into the air and arranged into precise lines and shapes. It became green, brown, red, yellow, purple, and white. It opened to greet the rising sun. It absorbed the night sky.

The charcoal jumped from plants into animals. It joined bees and buzzed from flower to flower. It joined lizards and basked in the sun. It joined deer and with large gentle eyes saw a horizon full of red buttes and mesas and spires. It joined birds and migrated hundreds of miles.

It was Father Sky that was now living in these plants and animals, filling them with immensities of time and space and power, infusing cells with harmony, with *hózhó*. Father Sky was pleased at how these lives meshed with the cycles of the days and seasons. Father Sky was delighted to wear animal bodies and to experience the world through their senses and minds. Father Sky watched the night sky with deep recognition.

It was the gods that had flowed into plants and animals and infused them with the inspiration that ran the universe.

♦ ♦ ♦

That evening I had wanted to go for another hike around the butte, but thunderclouds gathered in the distance and began rumbling and raining and moving this way. Lightning struck a sandstone cliff and set it glowing for a moment, perhaps cooking the sandstone harder, perhaps blasting some of it free to become sand blowing in the next thunderstorm. I imagined this newly freed sand being used in a future sandpainting, yet even this lightning-charged sand would not possess the energy of sand that had been struck by the symbolic, mythological energies of the cloudy human mind.

The storm came this way and rained for a while and set winds swirling, and then a rainbow broke out above the monuments. Many sandpaintings hold rainbows, or the rainbow deity, framing three sides of the painting, the west, north, and south sides, leaving the east side open for the Holy People to enter. For a desert people, rainbows are a special blessing.

When the clouds seemed discharged enough to make it safe for me to be far out in the open, I set off on my hike. The sand dunes were now imprinted with tens of thousands of little craters, and the dune crests were blurred. The storm had created its own sandpainting, a self-portrait of the sky's raw power.

I was halfway along the hike and rounding the butte when I looked back at the eastern horizon and saw a bank of dark clouds, near the ground. Their color was odd, and it was odd that they were there at all, for the rain clouds had been dissipating, and in this region and in this season thunderstorms seldom started near sunset. I watched the clouds growing, swirling, darkening, moving. They formed a long curtain that blocked my view of everything behind them. The clouds engulfed one monument, then another. They were heading toward me. It was a sandstorm, dense and turbulent, throwing sand and dust high into the sky. The curtain loomed taller as it approached. I quickened my pace. There were sections of this trail that were not entirely obvious even under clear skies, and other sections that were largely the sandy footprints of previous hikers.

The dark curtain rolled toward me, a tsunami of sand, engulfing another butte, another mesa, another butte, all of Monument Valley except for the two buttes nearest West Mitten Butte, and then they too disappeared. I was measuring the pace of the oncoming cloud against my pace back toward the trailhead and my truck—I wasn't going to beat the cloud. It loomed high above me. West Mitten Butte grew cloudy, then ghostly, and then it disappeared. I stopped and kneeled down and touched the sand.

I drew a mighty storm. I drew streaks radiating outward from a center, a wind blowing outward in all directions. I drew galaxies, spiral galaxies with hundreds of billions of stars, galaxies spinning, galaxies flying outward in all directions, including the four sacred directions. I drew an expanding universe vibrant with light and motion and planets and life.

The air quickened; the wind swirled; the sand and dust were activated; the sky disappeared; the sandstorm engulfed me. Sand stung my face. I closed my eyes and tried to turn my back to the wind, but the wind continued circling. My hat was trying to escape, its brim flapping like a panicked bird, and I grabbed it down. Hot wind and sand thronged my ears and nose and sucked the moisture from my skin.

I had been engulfed in solid rock, encased inside a sandstone spire that had stood tall for ten thousand years. I had been engulfed by time, enough time to bring down sandstone spires that had stood tall for ten thousand years. I had been engulfed by erosion, erosion that brought down sandstone spires and dissolved their boulders into rocks and pebbles and sand and dust. The forces of erosion were now bombarding me, trying to erode me, trying to break me down into my particles. I was no rock spire that could resist storms for ten thousand years—I could not resist a sandstorm for two days. I felt small and soft and vulnerable. I felt the enormous size and power and endurance of the forces of erosion. Erosion outendured everything. I felt the power that erased mountain ranges, that melted plateaus into spires and canyons and then plains, that swept plains into the ocean, that erased rivers and lakes and entire oceans. I felt the power that wore out entire planets, cooling their internal fires, evaporating their oceans, bleeding their atmospheres into space, pounding them into craters and rubble and dust, engulfing them in supernovas and black holes. I felt the power that wore out stars, exhausting billions of years of fuel, leaving space swarming with dead stars. I felt the power that outendured galaxies, that watched patiently as galaxies drew dim and went dark. On my fast-eroding face I felt the unstoppable momentum that over hundreds of billions of years would carry the entire universe from light into darkness, from action into inertness, from order into disorder, from life into death.

When the storm eased, I walked back and looked at the universe. The universe had disappeared.

✦ ✦ ✦

From its Place of Emergence, the universe emerged. The universe exploded with light, energy, matter, space, and motion.

The universe expanded into the four sacred directions, in millions of directions, all of them outward. The universe expanded in order, unfolding form upon form. The universe became atoms and nebulae and galaxies, stars and pulsars and black holes, planets and comets and moons. The planets became skies and rocks and oceans, mountains and volcanoes and canyons, rivers and clouds and lightning. The universe built sandstone spires standing tall, carefully balanced.

But the universe was not balanced. The universe was not whole. The universe was ill.

The universe was blind, unable to see its vast flowings of light, its paintings of shapes and colors, its rainbows and mountains and sunsets.

The universe was deaf, unable to hear the music of the surf and rivers and wind and rain.

The universe had no sense of touch, no fingers and no feelings with which to know the motion of water, the smoothness of river cobbles, the soft flexing of grass.

The universe had no senses of smell or taste with which to turn molecules into rich experiences.

The universe was mute, unable to speak its secrets or its own name.

The universe was torn by extremes. It was too hot and too cold, too bright and too dark, too energetic and too frozen, too full and too empty.

The universe was somewhat mad, a mad rushing and swarming of energy and matter.

The universe needed balance, the balance of a tall sandstone spire. The universe needed hózhó.

So the universe reached out and drew upon space a circle, a mandala. It drew a balance of land and water, ice and deserts, mountains and plains, rock and soil. Out of carbon created inside stars, the universe drew two circles and gave them eyes with which to see the stars and the blackness of space. It gave them ears, noses, mouths, and tongues. It gave them skin abuzz with sensations. It gave them emotions in which the storms and lightning and rainbows became the energies of awe. It gave them minds that could recognize the order of the universe. It gave them hands that could draw symbols of the order of the universe. It gave them voices that could chant for the order of the universe.

Into this sandpainting the powers of the universe came, came soaring, came soaring. The powers of the stars and sun and moon flowed into the sandpainting. The powers of the rain and lightning and rainbow and rivers flowed into the sandpainting. The powers of the soil and seeds and plants flowed into the sandpainting. The powers of the animals and reptiles and birds and insects flowed into the sandpainting.

Through this sandpainting, the universe was healed and balanced. It was no longer blind, no longer deaf, no longer mute, no longer without a sense of touch or smell or taste. It was no longer without consciousness. It was no longer dead. The universe would not race onward forever as a swarm of oblivious matter. Now the universe could live its journey. Now the sandstone spires could be inspired. Now the rainbows could glow even brighter. Now the silence of space could chant its own name. Now the carbon blackness of the night sky could brighten into the light and colors of celebration.

Eventually, the sandpainting would be erased. It would dissolve back into sand, into rivers, into wind, into rock. Eventually, Earth would dissolve into solar fire, into stardust, into nebulae. Eventually, the stars would burn out, the galaxies go dark. The galaxies would fly onward into the blackness, dissolving back into chaos.

Amid all the matter drifting and dissolving, there was a tiny portion of matter that had once been alive and aware. It had saved the universe from being forever dead and blind and oblivious. It had been puzzled by the bodies and the role it had worn, and afflicted by the excessive residue of cosmic chaos that surfaced within its flesh. But thanks to these atoms, thanks to their troubled flesh, cosmic chaos had been able to gaze out through human eyes and proclaim the universe to be Father Sky and Mother Earth and to walk with them for a while, to walk among the sandstone inspires, to walk in beauty.•✦

NOTES

1. Washington Matthews, *The Night Chant: A Navaho Ceremony* (New York: American Museum of Natural History, 1902), 143.

2. Ibid., 76.

·7·

TRANQUILITY BASE HERE

NEIL ARMSTRONG has returned to the moon.

Forty-three years and one day after Neil Armstrong took step by careful step down the ladder of the lunar lander, reached the bottom rung, dropped onto the landing pad, lifted his foot, placed it onto the lunar soil, and announced that this was only one small step for him, I am watching his feet carefully, actually both of his feet, since I am not sure which foot it was that took our first step onto the moon.

I am watching his feet as he walks down the carpet. His feet appear to be ordinary feet, not heroic bronze-statue feet, not science-fiction antigravity aerodynamic feet, not noticeably athletic feet. They appear to work just like everyone's feet: one step at a time, performing a mixture of momentum and balance and steering. His shoes are ordinary shoes. He leaves no iconic footprints.

Half a century ago Neil Armstrong and the other Apollo astronauts went walking near here to learn how to walk on the moon. Here they explored how to explore the moon—they did their geology training. In the early 1960s many basic questions about the moon were wide open. How had the moon formed? What was it made of? Were the lunar craters created by volcanic eruptions or meteorite impacts? What process had created those large, smooth, dark basins such as the Sea of Tranquility? To deal with all the unknowns and possibilities they might encounter on the moon, the astronauts needed hands-on and feet-on training in a variety of geological landscapes. To find all those landscapes in one place, they came here to northern Arizona.

The first draw was Meteor Crater, the best-preserved major meteorite impact crater on Earth and the perfect model for the craters the astronauts would find on the moon. Meteor Crater is 570 feet deep, which could easily swallow the 360-foot Saturn V rocket that boosted astronauts to the moon. Gouged out fifty thousand years ago, its dry environment hadn't eroded it seriously, so its features were still sharp. Geologist Eugene Shoemaker led the astronauts on hikes along the crater rim and to the bottom, showing them its large-scale features and its mineralogical details. Only a few years previously, Shoemaker had proven that Meteor Crater really was a meteorite impact crater and not the result of a volcanic explosion. Shoemaker was also convinced that the craters on the moon were impact craters, but many other geologists held that they were volcanic craters. This question wouldn't be decided until astronauts brought home rocks from lunar craters.

The astronauts also needed to understand volcanic landscapes. Whether the lunar craters were volcanic or not, other lunar features gave plenty of signs of being volcanic. The maria, the dark basins that included the Sea of Tranquility—the first Apollo landing site— were best explained as ancient, huge lakes of lava that had hardened into smooth surfaces.

Just west of Meteor Crater was a fifty-mile volcanic range that included six hundred volcanoes (all extinct), from a 12,600-foot stratovolcano to numerous small cinder cones, with many types of lava and lava flows. Here the astronauts studied some of the landforms and rocks they might find on the moon.

The best training ground was an artificial moonscape created in a field of volcanic cinders (gravel-size nuggets of lava) thrown out by Sunset Crater, the most recent volcano, which erupted nine hundred years ago. Geologists selected a photograph of one patch of the lunar surface that held dozens of craters of various sizes and depths. They drilled dozens of holes into the cinder field, packed them with various amounts of explosives, and exploded the cinders upward and outward, leaving a crater field that matched the photograph.

The geologists built a mock-up of the lunar lander, from which the astronauts practiced climbing down. Neil Armstrong's one small step onto the moon was practiced here. Wearing moon suits and life-support backpacks and carrying the geology tools they would take to the moon, the astronauts practiced picking up rocks, drilling holes into the ground, and walking in and out of craters. With a version of the lunar rover that would be used on later Apollo missions, the astronauts practiced driving on the moon, steering around or through craters. On the day Neil Armstrong and Buzz Aldrin walked on the moon, CBS News had used this moonscape to broadcast a simulated moonwalk.

◆ ◆ ◆

I look at Neil Armstrong's hands. These were the hands that steered *Eagle* toward the surface, over the craters and boulders, taking command when the computer was steering *Eagle* toward a crater ringed with rubble. These were the hands that gripped the ladder to the moon, picked up moon rocks, and snapped the photographs that became world famous. I look at these hands, and I see rather ordinary hands.

Perhaps those iconic photos of the superhero costumed in brightness and helmet and gloves have left me surprised to see a secret identify that is not even Clark Kent but simply an ordinary human body. I watch Armstrong's hands working, the knuckles bending, the fingers folding, the wrist twisting, a hand rising into the air. The hand that gripped moon tools now grips a fork, excavating his dinner, lifting his food to his mouth. The mouth that had said "That's one small step..." opens and takes one small bite and chews and smiles.

The astronauts also trained at the Grand Canyon, the world's best display of geological strata. No one was expecting to find the canyon's sedimentary rocks—ocean deposited and fossil rich—on the moon, but the canyon still offered a dramatic classroom for learning basic geological principles. The astronauts made a two-day hike to the canyon bottom and back out. They were accompanied by geologists who showed them the basic types of rocks, the laws of stratigraphy (older rocks are beneath younger rocks), and how faulting and erosion could remove and distort the original strata. The geologists taught the astronauts how to read geological maps, how to match aerial photographs with the landscape in front of them, and how to recognize and describe distant features. The geologists had selected the Grand Canyon hike as the first event in the astronaut's geology training in hopes that it would inspire them with the grandeur and power of geological forces and convince them that geology could be an adventure worthy of macho pilots. At first many of the astronauts had been openly hostile to the prospect of studying geology, for it was too nerdy and they were seriously preoccupied with learning how to fly new, complicated, dangerous spacecraft. The Grand Canyon hike did indeed succeed in knocking the right-stuffiness out of the astronauts and getting them hooked on geology.

Neil Armstrong was one of the few Apollo astronauts who had hiked into the Grand Canyon before. In 1952 he and his brother, Dean, had taken a long road trip through the American West, visiting ten national parks, camping most of the way. At the Grand Canyon they hiked to the bottom and camped overnight. Armstrong was impressed by the canyon's geology. A decade later NASA's geologist-trainers noticed that Armstrong was more motivated than most of the astronauts; on the moon Armstrong proved to be a keen observer, which validated the idea that astronauts could be trained to be skilled geologists.

Shortly after stepping onto the moon Armstrong had described the scene: "It has a stark beauty all its own. It's like much of the high desert of the United States. It's different, but it's very pretty out here."[1] Armstrong was probably comparing the moon with the landscapes and moonscapes he had seen in northern Arizona.

The astronauts also made use of Lowell Observatory in Flagstaff, where they looked through a major telescope at the moon. Founded in the 1890s to study Mars, and proud of its discovery of Pluto in 1930, Lowell Observatory had continued studying the planets and moons through the decades when almost all other astronomers were studying the stars, the galaxies, and cosmology. This made Lowell Observatory a backwater in the world of astronomy—until Sputnik in 1957, when suddenly America needed to know everything about the planets and moons.

Cartographers at Lowell Observatory drew the lunar-surface relief maps that the astronauts used in lunar orbit to recognize landmarks below, including their landing sites, and the maps they used to find their way on the lunar surface. On Apollo 17 the astronauts accidentally broke a fender off their lunar rover, and the wheel was spraying dust all over them—dangerous, for their moon suits needed to be white, not dust-black, to fend off the 243°F heat. Using duct tape, the astronauts turned one of the laminated Lowell maps into a replacement fender.

Today the Lowell museum displays a guest book signed on January 16, 1963, by many Apollo astronauts, including Neil Armstrong.

It was for the sake of Lowell Observatory that Armstrong has now returned to Flagstaff. He is dedicating a new telescope that would put Lowell Observatory back on the cutting edge of astronomy. He is talking about the importance of exploring the universe, whether by spacecraft or by telescope.

I watch the one-small-step mouth making words, some of them the same words I'd heard him speak from across a quarter million miles of space. His voice is recognizably the same, soft and modest, though at age eighty-one he is more than twice as old as he was then. He has the same smile that made going to the moon appear to be a happy, boyish adventure. I see the persistence of the human face and voice and personality through a lifetime.

❖ ❖ ❖

Yet I know that this is not the same Neil Armstrong who walked on the moon. Few of the atoms of this Neil Armstrong walked on the moon. Most of the atoms that made up the Neil Armstrong of 1969 cycled out of this body long ago. Every year, 98 percent of the atoms in the human body are replaced. Two-thirds of the substance of the human body is water, and almost all of the water in a body is replaced every two weeks. Heavier atoms like carbon, which make up the structure of cells, persist a lot longer than water, but not nearly as long as the cells themselves. Many generations of atoms succeed one another at keeping a cell intact and functioning. The atoms that make up heart cells are replaced every six months, but the heart cells themselves are replaced at a rate of about 1 percent per year. About half of Neil Armstrong's heart cells are the same cells that powered his moonwalk, but most of the atoms that did the work had disappeared by the end of 1969. The atoms that make up the human skin are replaced every four weeks, so some of the skin that walked on the moon had disappeared before Armstrong even got back to Earth.

Of course, these atoms didn't disappear; they only left Armstrong's body for further adventures. They flowed back into the great cycles from which they had come. They flowed back into rivers and lakes and the sea. They flowed back into the wind and the rain and the rainbows. They flowed back into mountains and canyons and volcanic fields. They flowed up into trees and flowers. They flowed into the cells of fish, the hearts of butterflies, the skin of zebras, the wings of eagles.

They are still out there, somewhere. The atoms that walked on the moon. Now they are walking on African savannas, on polar ice packs, on desert cliffs. Now they are eagles gliding onto a tree branch and thinking, "The eagle has landed." They are bear cubs climbing down a tree and taking one small step onto the forest floor. They are kangaroos taking giant leaps. They are roadrunners printing footprints into the desert dust. They are peacocks raising their flags of pride. They are badgers digging into the ground. Now the atoms that had proclaimed human progress are making birdsongs that proclaim the journey of the silent, formless earth into the patterns of life.

It was the patterns that persisted. It was the pattern of Neil Armstrong that persisted and inducted new atoms into itself. At dinner I watched the old pattern absorbing new atoms. Already some of the water Armstrong had absorbed was plumping his cells and supporting his metabolism and carrying his oxygen; already it had assumed its new identity as Neil Armstrong. A body full of atoms that had never been to the moon was speaking about being the first human body on the moon, speaking with sound waves that were also patterns that moved onward while the atoms that conducted them jostled for a moment but stayed behind. He was being taken quite seriously by his listeners. Many of them imagined that they had watched Armstrong's moonwalk on television, when in fact all the atoms that watched the moonwalk cycled out of these bodies long ago.

It is the patterns that persist. It is the patterns that are recognized as the true identity of human beings. Solid matter is merely a ghost; it is the pattern that is alive; it is the pattern that is the "I." It is the shape of a face, the color of eyes, the sound of a voice, and most of all the recognition in memory. A living body is a vast memory of shapes, the ancient shapes of DNA and cells and bones, and the unique shapes of one body. Some of those memories hold the places and beings and events a body has experienced.

The atoms inducted into Neil Armstrong are given careful training in storing his memories. They are locked into complicated molecules and neurons, and tuned to precise energies. They grasp the torch of images of the moon: the grayness of the dust; the shapes of craters and boulders; the feel of that first footstep; the stark beauty of it all. They become convinced that they were really there.

In introducing Neil Armstrong, the master of ceremonies asks for a show of hands of everyone who remembers the first moonwalk. A good portion of the audience raise their hands. Neil Armstrong raises his hand.

Forty-two years ago, on the first anniversary of the Apollo 11 lunar landing, "I" had seen Neil Armstrong and his crewmates, Buzz Aldrin and Michael Collins. The "I" here was a much younger version of my pattern, which imprinted memories strong enough to be passed down to "me" today. The Apollo command module *Columbia* was touring all fifty states, and it happened to be in my state on the first anniversary of the landing. The astronauts hadn't seen *Columbia* since they had climbed out of it; they decided to reunite with it to mark the anniversary. They flew into my hometown. The astronauts still retained some of the atoms that had been to the moon, that had imprinted footsteps and memories. When the astronauts spoke of their journey, it was the real atom-nauts speaking. Yet even then, most of the atoms that walked on the moon had already jumped ship.

They are still out there, oblivious. Atoms that felt the moon with the intensity of human consciousness are now bobbing on the ocean, faintly sparkling with moonlight. Atoms that had been part of Neil Armstrong's eye now belong to the eye of an owl and are looking at the moon without any recognition. Atoms that fused strong memories of lunar beauty have forgotten everything.

It was the patterns that persisted. Skin might wrinkle, bodies might lose strength, and memories might fade, but the patterns worked hard to persist. Bodies might die, but the patterns passed themselves onward into new bodies. The patterns focused much of their energy into passing themselves onward. Species of patterns persisted for thousands of generations, millions of generations, millions of years. The patterns changed slowly from one shape into another, unfolding new layers, new limbs, new abilities. The patterns changed shape until they no longer recognized themselves. Yet they remained the same fundamental pattern, the same cells within all their millions of combined shapes, the same wellspring drawing order out of chaos, the same life. Life had drawn an entire planet out of chaos and into patterns. Life had filled the seas and the land and the sky with patterns. And finally, life tossed a few of its patterns through the atmosphere and into space and to the moon.

The moon remained chaos. Its only pattern was wreckage. Every mile was saturated with wounds that had never healed, with craters and rubble and dust. Its lava seas hadn't flowed or rippled for billions of years.

The day after Armstrong's talk I went out to the volcanic cinder moonscape where the astronauts had trained. About two dozen craters remained, but they were badly eroded, for the cinder field had been turned into a playground for all-terrain vehicles. From the edge of the cinder field, I walked half a mile to where the craters started. I could see them from a distance, not just from their holes but from their darker color; the explosions had excavated darker material from underground. I walked from crater to crater. I walked into craters. One of them was still deep enough that I was looking up at the rim.

I was crunching and kicking the cinders that taught Neil Armstrong how to walk on the moon and how to grasp moon rocks both physically and intellectually. If only I could read the code, I would see how these cinders had been permanently rearranged by Armstrong's footsteps. The same force that had acted here left impressions on the moon that will last a million years. Perhaps it was this flat plain of cinders and the odd-colored volcanoes around it that imprinted within Buzz Aldrin the feeling of "magnificent desolation" that he applied to the moon. The energy that had welled up here from deep within Earth traveled much farther than that of other volcanoes.

I was walking on the moon. I lifted my foot and set it down on the primordial lava. That's one small step...I looked at the imprint I left. On Earth, it was so common. On the moon, it was an outrageous wonder.

The moon was walking on Earth. Humans had transported this small patch of the moon onto Earth. This was the moon that watches over us in the night. Perhaps this was a cell from the eye of the Man on the Moon or the Rabbit on the Moon. Now the moon was looking at Earth close up. It saw the clouds brewing toward rain. It saw the ponderosa pines on the fringe of the moonscape, as tall as rockets, aiming toward a long future for the ponderosa pattern. It saw a human body standing amid its craters, form amid formlessness, connection amid incoherence, activity amid inertness, memory amid forgetting. It felt me taking one small step and showing the moon what had been happening on Earth for four billion years while the moon had been lying dead.

At Meteor Crater the moon was staring upward like a giant empty-skull eye socket. Here space itself had transported a small patch of cosmic chaos onto Earth. The moon's eye gazed at the humans standing on its rim and looking into it. The human eyes were full of form and energy. They were full of patterns seeking outside patterns. They were full of wonder seeking understanding. They were full of Earth seeking the cosmos that gave their lives the largest patterns. The human eyes looked at the bottom of the crater and saw an Apollo astronaut standing there, a wooden cutout of an astronaut in a moon suit, a reminder that the astronauts had trained here. Trained to look into a moon crater and see one circle of the cycles of the cosmos.

On the moon the astronauts did succeed in finding decisive evidence about the moon's origins. Before the moon landings there were three theories about the moon's origins: the moon was flung out of Earth when Earth was still new and molten; or the moon formed elsewhere in the solar system and was passing close to Earth and was captured by Earth's gravity; or the moon congealed alongside Earth from the same gas cloud. Each of these theories had problems. After scientists analyzed the moon rocks, the problems got worse. Yet the evidence fitted well into a new theory. When the solar system was new and unstable, a Mars-size object crossed Earth's path and collided with it. Earth was nearly its present size and had a solid, rocky crust. The collision tore the impactor apart, and tore a massive, hot wound into Earth. The debris from the explosion flew into space. Much of the debris rained back onto Earth, but some of it went into orbit about Earth, a dense, hot swarm. From this swarm, a mixture of material from the impactor and Earth, the moon formed.

Some of the material of the moon had been part of Earth for tens of millions of years before it was ejected. This moon material should have remained part of Earth. It should have joined in all of Earth's geological and biological adventures. It should have formed tectonic plates, volcanoes, mountains, and oceans. It should have become cells, fish, trees, and birds. It should have become an eagle calling out as it landed in a tree beside a field of volcanic cinders.

Instead, it became gray boulders lying motionless and silent for billions of years. It became a sea of lava and then the Sea of Tranquility. It became craters staring blindly at the living planet it should have been. It became lunar dust waiting for a foot to print the news it had missed.

And then there was material that was part of the impactor and could easily have become part of the moon, but instead it joined Earth. Would-be moon rocks became Earth rocks recording in the Grand Canyon their long and elaborate transformations. Would-be moondust became green leaves that absorbed the light with far more skill and purpose. Would-be moon craters became eyes that gazed up at the moon and felt the moon's beauty and mystery.

I felt the would-be moon within myself, walking upon the cinder field. I felt the impactor within myself, making little impacts. I felt the would-be formlessness loaded with form, form within form within form, pulsing with oxygen and heartbeats and electricity and consciousness. I felt the would-be moon feeling wonder about the moon. I saw the dead formlessness that Earth might easily have remained.

✦ ✦ ✦

My thoughts returned to Neil Armstrong.

Toward the end of his half-hour talk he had presented a new video showing his view of the lunar surface as *Eagle* approached it. The four-minute video, shown on a giant screen, had been derived from images taken by the Lunar Reconnaissance Orbiter, which in 2008 began circling the moon and taking the best-yet images of it. Because *Eagle's* path had been east–west and approaching the surface, and the LRO's path was north–south and in a steady orbit, computer-nauts had to do some ingenious work to translate LRO's images into a re-creation of *Eagle's* view. Clearly, Armstrong was impressed. Shown alongside the new video was the original, blurry 16mm movie taken through *Eagle's* window, actually Buzz Aldrin's window, not even offering Armstrong's view. The new video offered very sharp images and a wider view, the view Armstrong had seen.

As Armstrong played the video he gave us a narration of what he'd been seeing and thinking. He told us how *Eagle's* computer was taking *Eagle* toward a crater "the size of Dodger Stadium," and how he had taken control to aim for a smoother spot. He explained that the "1202 Alarm" that sounded on the original movie was a computer overload. At one point he paused the video to explain something. He started it again, and we saw the landing as only Neil Armstrong had ever seen it. We cleared the stadium crater and its rubble and watched the ground grow closer and more detailed. Still a lot of smaller craters and rubble. Thirty seconds of fuel. *Eagle* was heading toward another crater, but Armstrong made it descend and hover and waver to the right and then the left. We were getting very close.

Hands that could have been the motionless dust of the moon were now gesturing in the air, as if Armstrong was gripping *Eagle's* controls and reenacting a deeply remembered action. Eyes that could have been blindly staring at lunar craters were now staring at craters that might make the difference between life and death, passionately felt life and death. A voice that could have been the silence of the moon was now filling the air with intricate patterns.

The living Earth reached out and touched the formlessness from which it had arisen.

The audience, riveted and tense, sighed with relief. "Tranquility Base here," Armstrong spoke from the original movie. "The *Eagle* has landed."

+ + +

This would be Armstrong's final public appearance. Two weeks later, he required heart surgery. Complications developed, and Neil Armstrong died.

He melted back into the formless from which all life flies upward, briefly.

He returned to the moon.₊₊

NOTES

1. Quoted in Don E. Wilhelms, *To a Rocky Moon: A Geologist's History of Lunar Exploration* (Tucson: University of Arizona Press, 1993), 202.

·8·

THE BLOOD OF THE MARTIANS

I WAITED FOR MY TURN to look through one of the world's most famous telescopes, to look at Mars.

Built by Alvan Clark and Sons of Boston in the 1890s, the Clark telescope was one of the last great refracting telescopes ever built, as the age of refracting (glass lens) telescopes yielded to the age of reflecting (mirror) telescopes at the start of the twentieth century. Lowell Observatory's twenty-four-inch-diameter lens was still well short of the world's largest, a forty-inch lens at Yerkes Observatory in Wisconsin, but Lowell's location at more than seven thousand feet in the dry Southwest gave it better observing conditions than any other observatory at the time.

Lowell Observatory had the strangest origins of any major observatory. Most observatories were built by institutions to last for decades and do a full range of astronomy; Lowell Observatory was built as one man's personal observatory to do one specific project in one specific year. Percival Lowell wanted to observe Mars in 1894, when Mars's orbit brought it closer to Earth than it had been or would be for years. Lowell had become obsessed with the idea that Mars held a planet-wide system of canals, built by a great civilization.

Well into the 1800s, Mars remained at the boundaries of human perception. The best telescopes showed Mars as a blur of blotches. As telescopes improved, astronomers became confident they were seeing actual surface features on Mars, not just clouds or atmospheric tricks, but those surface features remained vague blobs and streaks and shades. Different astronomers reported seeing different shapes, and they interpreted them in different ways, some seeing Earth-like continents and oceans, some seeing zones of vegetation.

When Mars orbited closer to Earth in 1877, astronomer Giovanni Schiaparelli reported seeing a series of islands separated by curving, relatively narrow channels. As Schiaparelli observed Mars over the next ten years, his drawings increasingly showed the channels as straighter, longer, and thinner. Astronomers debated the nature of these lines. Perhaps they were rivers, or geological fissures caused when the planet had cooled and cracked, or furrows dug out by crashing meteorites. Other astronomers didn't see the lines at all and suggested they were optical illusions or psychological illusions. A few astronomers wondered if the lines could be artificial, not channels but canals, built by intelligent beings. This idea enthralled Percival Lowell, and he built his observatory to prove it.

On his last map of Mars, Schiaparelli had placed seventy-nine canals. As Percival Lowell and his assistants observed Mars in 1894 they discovered more than a hundred additional canals. In the years to come, Lowell added hundreds more, giving each a name. Lowell drew elaborate maps showing all the canals, then turned his map into a wooden globe. Many canals started in the polar regions and radiated toward the equator, running thousands of miles, crisscrossing one another. Lowell recognized that for a canal to be visible from Earth it would have to be about twenty miles wide, so he proposed that he wasn't seeing a canal itself but the zone of vegetation around it, like the green agricultural zone along the Nile, surrounded by desert. One time when Lowell observed a canal he hadn't seen before, he declared that he hadn't seen it because it hadn't been there: the Martians were still building new canals. The canals could not be natural features—they were far too straight: "No railway metals could be laid down with more precision."[1] When other astronomers complained that they could not see any canals, Lowell replied that his observatory had better viewing conditions than other observatories, which was true.

The line was moving slowly tonight; I was still outside the dome. Perhaps other people were taking special pleasure in seeing Mars through this telescope.

Percival Lowell also elaborated a theory about Mars, Martians, and why the Martians were building canals. Lowell connected his canal observations with the most powerful idea of his era, the idea of evolution. Lowell started with the evolution of the solar system and linked it with new, Darwinian, ideas about the evolution of life.

In 1796 French astronomer Pierre-Simon Laplace proposed "the nebular hypothesis," in which a rotating nebula would collapse into a disc and then into a sun, then planets revolving around the sun. In Percival Lowell's version, planets developed through different stages, at different rates. A younger planet had plenty of water, but as a planet aged it dried up, its oceans turning to deserts. Because Mars was smaller than Earth, it was aging faster and had already lost its oceans. Now the only water source left on Mars was its polar ice caps.

To this astronomical picture Percival Lowell added an optimistic interpretation of biological evolution, saying that on planets of the right size, life was inevitable, and life inevitably evolved into intelligent life. Because Mars was evolving faster than Earth, it had a civilization older and more advanced than Earth's. Facing the drying of their planet, the Martians had built their vast canal system to take water from the polar caps and carry it to the temperate zones, where it supported agriculture and cities. Water could flow over long distances on Mars because as planets aged, their mountains eroded away, so Mars was fairly flat: "With the greatest magnification we can produce, the Martian limb still appears perfectly smooth."[2] In spite of their inevitable doom the Martians were heroically building masterful technology.

When Lowell's critics complained about his elaborate Martian scenarios, he replied that he was defending the scientific, evolutionary worldview against religiously motivated people who wanted humans to be the center of creation, the only life in the universe. Lowell closed his 1895 book *Mars* with: "If astronomy teaches anything it teaches that man is but a detail in the evolution of the universe.... He learns that, though he will probably never find his double anywhere, he is destined to discover any number of cousins scattered through space."[3] Lowell had now filled the Martian canals with the energy of two powerful ideas: ancient human wonderment over whether the universe holds other beings, and the new authority of the scientific, evolutionary worldview.

Percival Lowell was a master at publicizing his ideas about Mars, writing three books and numerous magazine and newspaper articles. He organized his facts in a way that seemed thoroughly scientific, presented his ideas with eloquence, ignored all the evidence against him, and made his critics seem ignorant and unreasonable: "If Martian philosophers are of the pattern of some earthly ones, they must incontrovertibly prove to their own satisfaction the impossibility of our existence."[4] Lowell created such enthrallment that the public hardly noticed that the idea of intelligent life on Mars was fairly dead in the scientific world years before Lowell died in 1916. Two-thirds of the way into the twentieth century, science-fiction writers were still filling Mars with canals, cities, and a superior species, and Martians were a familiar part of popular culture.

At last it was my turn to look through Percival Lowell's telescope. I saw a red-orange dot, a distant marble. It had a white cap, and vague streaks. As my eyes had a chance to focus, more details dialed into clarity. Suddenly, I was seeing them, clearly, undeniably, hundreds of straight lines crisscrossing the planet—the canals! A spiderweb of canals. I saw canals flowing with polar water, whiteness turned blue turned green, the green swaths of farms. I saw cities, the ancient, great Martian cities, their spires rising taller than the Flatiron Building, their streets swarming with horseless carriages, their skies full of zeppelins, their homes full of kinetoscopes and wireless telegraphs. Martian cities were far ahead of Earth cities: art-nouveau and arts-and-crafts architecture had been old-fashioned for a long time; the Martians were already building art-deco cities. I saw the Martians themselves, and clearly they were superior, wise, and peaceful.

◆ ◆ ◆

The sands of Mars blew onward; the ancient red sands flowed onward as they had flowed for billions of years. The ancient red sands flowed across plains, through canyons, down volcanoes, into craters, piling up into large dunes and blowing onward again. The sands were oblivious of their own flowing. They were also oblivious of the dreams with which they sparkled, oblivious that the sands of another planet had arisen into life and now were even more restless, haunted with wonder, tortured with dreams, projecting their dreams onto the ancient red sands of Mars.

The sands didn't arrange themselves into long straight canals but were engineered by the winds. The lines of Mars were curving and jagged, drawn by tectonics, by volcanoes, by meteorites, by ancient floods. Mars was a highly organized society of natural forces, surviving without even trying or caring.

✦ ✦ ✦

In truth, I really had seen many Lowellian canals, years ago. I had gazed into them, noticed their engineering design, and thought about the social values they embodied. These canals weren't on Mars, but on Earth, in a city named Lowell. The Lowell family fortune, including the money that built Lowell Observatory, had come from the city and the textile mills of Lowell, Massachusetts, a city and an industry built around an intricate system of canals. Percival Lowell's vision of Martian society came directly from the way Percival's ancestors had run Lowell, Massachusetts.

In some accounts, Percival Lowell's vision of a canal-filled Mars resulted from simple error. Giovanni Schiaparelli had claimed to see only "channels" on Mars, natural channels, which in Italian were *canali*, but *canali* got mistranslated into English as *canals*, implying artificial design, and simple-minded Percival simply misunderstood. Or the error was perceptual. The human brain is designed to recognize lines, even to impose lines upon vague shapes, and the vague shapes on Mars were right at the threshold of human recognition. Two astronomers who were critical of Percival Lowell's canal claims conducted experiments, one with schoolboys and the other with professional astronomers, to test how people would draw a distant ball with vague shapes upon it, and both groups drew straight lines, though the ball itself had none.

Yet Percival Lowell's enthusiasm for Martian canals was no accident of translation or perception. He was in the grip of powerful ideas: the idea of life beyond Earth, the idea of an evolutionary universe that sprouted life as readily as trees sprouted leaves, and the idea that heroic technology—which on Earth was then building the Suez and Panama Canals—could advance to the point where it could reshape an entire planet. These ideas were powerful enough to generate the Martian canals. Percival's line-forming brain may have helped him to see canals, but it didn't prompt him to envision Martian society in the specific ways he did. This arose from more personal sources.

When Lowell's ancestors, along with other investors, built Lowell, Massachusetts, in 1823, it was America's first factory town and the beginning of the Industrial Revolution in America. Until then, England had carefully guarded its monopoly on textile manufacturing; the clothes worn by Americans were often American cotton that had been shipped to English textile mills and then shipped back to America. At a falls where the Merrimack River fell thirty-two feet, the founders of Lowell diverted the river into a network of seven canals, a total of 5.6 miles, which provided the power to run the mills. The canals often flowed red or other colors from the dyes being used to color the cotton. Lowell became famous as a technological wonder, the Silicon Valley of its time. It also became famous as a sociological wonder, a proof that industrialism could be civilized.

In England industrial towns had attracted the most degraded part of the population and further degraded them, offering low wages, long hours, unhealthy and dangerous working conditions, slum housing, and quick repression of labor unrest. Lowell was a rationally designed town with pleasant streets and parks, and its employees were young farm girls who lived in clean new dormitories, ate good meals, attended church regularly, and produced a nationally famous magazine of their own writings. Charles Dickens, with his keen eye for social injustice, came to inspect Lowell and was very encouraged by it. Lowell seemed a proof of the utopian dreams that ran deep in the American psyche.

Yet the owners of Lowell were not quite as benevolent as they seemed. In the 1820s the only available workforce for factories was the unmarried daughters of New England farm families, and their parents were often reluctant to let them go off to a morally questionable life in a factory town. To reassure everyone, Lowell's owners required "the Lowell girls" to live in supervised dorms with curfews and to attend church every Sunday. Everything about Lowell was managed with smug, self-serving patrician pride.

As a young college graduate Percival Lowell went into the family business for six years, and his job included making a regular trip to Lowell to deliver the payroll. Percival would have had plenty of time to study the canal system that had made the Lowells rich and world famous. But in the 1880s Lowell was no longer a utopian city. As the decades had passed, conditions had worsened, the Lowell girls had left, Irish and Italian immigrants had arrived, wages were too low, and labor unrest was rampant. The Lowell family hated the emerging world of labor unions and clung to a world ruled by an oligarchy, where workers knew their proper place.

Nearly a century after Percival Lowell had worked in Lowell, I lived there for several months. I walked downtown every day, past textile mills long abandoned and decaying, and I looked into deep redbrick canals long dry and full of garbage. The roaring energy of utopia had become a deep silence.

When Percival Lowell first heard about Mars having a vast system of canals, it may have triggered some personal, positive associations with a vast system of canals. When Percival imagined Mars he saw a patrician utopia, ruled by an oligarchy, where the workers knew their place and did their jobs without complaining. The superior Martians couldn't possibly have labor unions. Building and maintaining a planet-wide system of canals required enormous leadership, discipline, and cooperation. This couldn't be the cooperation of socialism, for both socialism and democracy meant that the rabble ruled, the inferior smothered the superior, the stupid suppressed the smart. It meant chaos. Mars required total subordination to the challenge of surviving on a dying planet. In his public lectures Percival Lowell often used the Martians as models for human society. He told a group of Arizona miners that the Martians would never go on strike, that "the average man. . .calls progressive what Mars stamps exactly the reverse. . . . [W]e may be very certain that in the Martian world-economy, the fittest only have survived."[5]

Percival Lowell was also confident that he was superior to the astronomers who failed to see the Martian canals.

✦ ✦ ✦

Once again I looked through Percival's telescope. Or perhaps it was really a movie projector, projecting human fantasies onto the sandy screen in the Mars Theater. It was a kaleidoscope offering ever-changing, entrancing images. It was a carnival mirror reflecting back our own image in ways we didn't even recognize. It was a Star Trek transporter delivering people to alien planets where the historical events and social problems seemed oddly familiar. Each person brought their own Mars with them to a telescope; each person saw their own Mars, confirmed their own Mars, and carried away their own Mars.

Once again I saw a Mars of canals and dead seas, but this time it held not a patrician utopia but races of different colors, constantly warring against one another with swords and spears. I saw green Martians, red Martians, four-armed Martians, egg-laying Martians, giant Martians, savages and superiors, palaces and princesses, tribes and warriors and cannibals. Into their midst there suddenly appeared Captain John Carter of Virginia, magically transported from a cave in Arizona, where Carter had been fighting Apaches. John Carter arrived on Mars with perfect timing, for the Apache war was the final drama of the Wild West, and America would have little further need for Arthurian knights like Carter. Mars's feudalistic society was a good match for John Carter's southern aristocratic codes. Carter plunged right in to the slaughter, slaying warriors left and right, and he won the love of a lovely Martian princess. This Mars, this Barsoom, was a utopia for adolescent male fantasies. Percival Lowell got into trouble for having too much imagination, but Edgar Rice Burroughs got rich from his imagination.

✦ ✦ ✦

The sands of Mars blew onward; the ancient red sands flowed onward as they had flowed for billions of years. The ancient red sands flowed across plains, through canyons, down volcanoes, into craters, piling up into large dunes and blowing onward again. The sands were oblivious that the sands of another planet had arisen into life and were projecting their dreams onto the defenseless ancient red sands of Mars.

The sands of Mars were red for the same reason that the blood of Earth was red, because of its iron. Iron is blood's carrier of oxygen. Every second, the human body creates 2 million red blood cells to maintain a total of 25 trillion blood cells, each containing more than 250 million molecules of hemoglobin loaded with iron and blood. Iron races through the human body to uphold the skyscraper of life, the Eiffel Tower of consciousness.

The iron of Mars had never flowed as blood, only as sand. It had never pulsed faster as it climbed up Olympus Mons or climbed down the great canyon of Valles Marineris, as it beheld a super-red sunset, as it held the pulsing hand of its sweetheart. It had never pulsed faster as its body tripped on a rock and fell and cut its hand on a sharp rock and began to bleed, as blood dripped onto rock, as blood was reminded of how precious blood was, how irreplaceable life was. The iron of Mars couldn't gaze up at the blue dot in the night sky and envy it for the talents of its iron, for its gift of life. The iron of Mars also never imagined the possibility of lifting an iron sword and cutting open a body and spilling the talents of iron back into oblivious iron sand.

On Earth, iron had arisen from formlessness, arisen from obliviousness, arisen into a being who could gaze up into the night sky and see a universe full of iron asteroids, iron planets, iron moons, and iron stars, and who could see how rare was the iron of blood.

Yet, somehow, the iron of Earth didn't appreciate its gift. To the iron of Earth the greatest glory, honor, and thrill came from lifting iron swords and iron rifles and iron bombs and spilling blood back into chaos. To John Carter the greatest thing about Mars wasn't that it was another living planet in a lonely cosmos but that it held the same warrior code as humans, that he could make himself feel valuable by treating life as valueless. How had it happened that iron had become imprisoned— imprismed—in such a mind? Iron was forced to view the universe through the prison bars of human eyes. The iron of Earth could not recognize itself in other human or animal bodies. The iron of Earth had become an asteroid aimed at Earth. The iron of Earth could not hear the sands of Mars crying iron tears for the life it had missed out on.

◆ ◆ ◆

Again I looked through Percival's telescope. I saw explosions on the Martian surface, numerous red flashes with boiling smoke, and from each smoke cloud arose a plume, many dark, boiling plumes rising up, rising straight, rising fast, rising high, rising out of the Martian atmosphere. The rockets sped away from Mars, into space, toward Earth. H. G. Wells: "No one would have believed in the last years of the nineteenth century that this world was being watched keenly and closely by intelligences greater than man's . . . that as men busied themselves with their various concerns they were scrutinized and studied, perhaps almost as narrowly as a man with a microscope might scrutinize the transient creatures that swarm and multiply in a drop of water."[6] The Martian invasion rockets, packed with giant war machines and ray guns, sped straight for Britain.

+ + +

The sands of Mars blew onward; the ancient red sands flowed onward as they had flowed for billions of years. The ancient red sands flowed across plains, through canyons, down volcanoes, into craters, piling up into large dunes and blowing onward again.

Occasionally, a dust devil scooped up sand and swirled it into the sky, a red plume, but if it was aimed at Earth it was only by accident. The sands' only imperialism was that of covering other sand, only by accident. The sands of Mars knew no lessons to teach the British about being the victims of imperialism. The sands of Mars continued blowing obliviously on Halloween night of 1938 as millions of Americans panicked at the radio news that the Martians were invading, panicked and fled and gathered in the streets, even committed suicide. Humans were really fearing their own darkest impulses, their own greed and power hunger and aggressiveness and disregard for life, dressed up as Halloween Martians.

+ + +

Again I looked through Percival's telescope. Once again I saw a Mars of canals and dead seas, and this time of dead cities. Martian civilization had been dying for a long time before humans arrived. The Martian cities had been wonders. In the vision of Ray Bradbury, they had crystal houses with crystal pillars and crystal art. They had wine trees, flower gardens, and fountains. They had great sculptures, libraries, museums, and music. With their musical voices the Martians sang ancient, ethereal songs. With their golden eyes the Martians finger-read hieroglyphic books, which sang out Martian stories. The Martians were graceful, wise, philosophical, telepathic beings. But then the Americans arrived, with their 1950s confidence in the superiority of their tail fin and fast-food society, and they also brought smallpox, silly smallpox, which killed off most of the remaining Martians.

I saw a human settler promising to show his children some Martians, now so rare and reclusive. He took his children on a picnic, and they continued asking to see the Martians. He led his children to a canal and told them to look down into it, into its mirror waters. They looked down and saw themselves, only themselves. You, said the father, you are the Martians now.

But this had always been true. Humans had been the Martians all along, seeing only themselves in the canal mirrors.

✦ ✦ ✦

The sands of Mars blew onward; the ancient red sands flowed onward as they had flowed for billions of years. Their Martian chronicles consisted of counting the years by piling up dry sand dunes and blowing them away again.

✦ ✦ ✦

Once again I looked through Percival's telescope. This time I saw a Mars that had been thoroughly explored by orbiting spacecraft and roving robots. This was a Mars without canals, without cities, without life, without dreams or nightmares. This was a Mars of volcanoes and canyons and sandstorms. Out of the sand I saw a shape emerge briefly, a huge face, the Sphinx of an ancient civilization, the last gasp of the human dream of companionship in the solar system. Then the face faded away, returning to sand.

Next I saw a new human dream projected onto Mars, the dream of terraforming, of transforming a dead planet into a living planet, giving it oxygen and water, plants and animals, human cities and mines and industries. Perhaps this was merely the newest version of American Manifest Destiny, of a new frontier to conquer and exploit. Perhaps it was the hubris of humans stealing the powers of the gods. Or perhaps it was the old cosmic loneliness, finally able to create its own answer.

I saw the sand stirring and arising, not into a dust devil but into solidity, into shape, into a body. Formlessness swirled into the forms of legs, a torso, arms, a head, a face. The ancient red sands of Mars now pulsed with breath and a heartbeat, with blood, with consciousness. The Martian opened her eyes and looked out upon the formless red sand she had been for billions of years. She looked down at her own body. She reached out her hand and stared at her fingers and wiggled them. She reached her hand to her face and felt it, tracing the shapes of her mouth, her ears, her eyes. She felt the wind blowing in and out of her nose. She opened her mouth, and she blew out wind, then sounds, then words.

"Oh...oh...oh...aye...aye...eye...eye...I...I...

"Mars...Mars...me...me...

"So this is myself. Red sand and red cliffs and black lava, this is myself. This was myself all this time, all these ages, unsuspected, unseen, for unknowing was also part of myself, the essence of myself.

"And now, this body, these eyes, this life, this is myself. How strange a body. Too soft, far too soft, dangerously soft, yet it seems to be stable, holding its shape. How wet it is, plump with water, so wet it should be flowing, raining, eroding away, yet it seems to be stable. It seems to be flowing on the inside. It makes its own motions from within, like volcanoes, not like sand moved by the wind. And out of its inner motions come outer motions, the motions of fingers, feet, eyes, lips. How strange these limbs, too flimsy, yet so attached, so servile, so talented, so active. How strange this flesh, so warm, its own sunlight, so vibrant, so full of feelings. How strange these senses, the outside world turning into the inside world, sunlight into vision, air into sound, dirt into smell. How strange this touch, the touch of the wind on flesh, the touch of the fingers on rock, how rich, how sensual, how alive. How strange this consciousness, the reports racing through it, the images

swirling, a weather all their own, the dreams that dream themselves, the feelings that sneak like snakes and pounce like jag-
uars, the thoughts you can construct layer by layer, the knot of
me-ness at the center of the swirl, how strange, how wonderful,
how outrageous, how impossible.

"Yet this was what Earth was doing all this time, while I, Mars,
was only sand blowing onward for aeons. I was content being
only sand, but only because I didn't have the capability for
discontent, and now that I do, I am content being alive. Thank
you, Earth, for giving Mars this gift, for setting Mars free from
rock and sand, for letting Mars live. We will use our new voices
to praise this gift of life.

"Yet now that Mars has the capability for discontent, we need
to express discontent over your abusing our reputation. You
have called us the god of war. You have made statues and temples and processions and offerings to Mars, the god of war.
You have claimed that Mars caused, sanctioned, or celebrated
the slaughter of armies and cities and nations. We did not. We
knew nothing of death, for we were nothing but death, and
now we have had enough death and would not advocate death.
You were the advocates of chaos, the deniers of life, the painters with blood, the betrayers of Earth's greatness. You were the
Martians all along."

◆ ◆ ◆

Again I looked through Percival's telescope. The red dot of Mars
wavered, like a mirage. The red began to flow downward, like paint
being poured from a can. Redness began spreading out onto space.

When Percival Lowell's reports of canals on Mars were met with
derision by other astronomers, he tried to marshal scientific evidence to support his theories about planetary evolution, why Mars
was ahead of Earth in developing life and civilization and in drying
out into a desert world that required canals. Percival Lowell believed,
as did most astronomers, that spiral nebulae were nearby clouds of
gas and dust that were turning into new stars and new solar systems.
Lowell set his astronomer Vesto Slipher to work studying the spiral
nebulae with his new spectrograph, which could reveal the motions

of objects by showing how their light was Doppler shifted toward the red end or blue end of the light spectrum. A redshift meant that an object was moving away from us, a blueshift meant it was moving toward us, and the extent of the shift revealed a precise speed. Percival Lowell was hoping to see the nebulae spinning and condensing to form planets, and forming planets in ways that made some of them evolve faster than others.

Slipher was astounded to find that the spiral nebulae were almost all redshifted, and at fantastic speeds. This was inconsistent with the spiral nebulae being nearby embryonic solar systems, for their speeds would have slung them far away from us long ago.

Some astronomers had wondered if the spiral nebulae might actually be other galaxies far outside our Milky Way galaxy, but they had no way to measure the distances to the spiral nebulae. If the spiral nebulae were galaxies, then the universe was outrageously large, and if the galaxies were racing outward, then the universe was undergoing a very strange, very dynamic, very fast process of expansion.

Slipher recognized the implications of his redshift discovery, but he remained cautious and quiet about it. The Martian canals had already branded Lowell Observatory with a reputation for eccentricity. Was Slipher going to push the far more eccentric idea of an expanding universe? This idea would wait a few years until Edwin Hubble proved that spiral nebulae really were other galaxies, and found a method for measuring their distances. When Hubble correlated his distance measurements with Vesto Slipher's redshift measurements, Hubble found a strong correlation: the galaxies were flying outward from a common origin.

I gazed through the telescope that had revealed both the Martian canals and the expanding universe, and I saw the redness of Mars melting into the redshifts of the galaxies. I saw the Martians, the noble dying Martians, bleeding into vast swirls of red light, a cosmos of vibrant afterbirth red lights. As in the creation myths in which a god's body becomes the universe, the Martians' flesh decayed into the expanding universe. Martian dust devils became spinning galaxies. Martian sandstorms became a storm of billions of galaxies.

The Martian canals became long filaments of galaxies. The Martian deserts became vast zones of emptiness. The Martian cities became endless skylines of stars. The Martian invaders were now invading an infinity of space.

Percival Lowell had dreamed up the Martians out of the old loneliness of humans in the cosmos, the desire for companions who could acknowledge our own sense of wonder. Lowell's dream had led to a cosmos with far more room for life than he'd ever dared to dream, a cosmos loaded with stars and planets and evolutionary power and, no doubt, intelligent life. Yet Lowell's cosmic loneliness had also made the cosmos lonelier. The cosmos had become much larger, and humans much smaller. The distance between us and our companions, which once was only the distance between Earth and Mars, bridgeable by telescopes and signal beacons and radio waves, was now the distance between galaxies. Our cosmic companions were now so far away that we had zero chance of ever discovering most of them. The Martians were still out there, billions of planets of Martians with cities and canals, awed by being alive, lonely for companionship, but they would forever remain hidden and unknown to us, a universe of Martians upon which to cast our dreams.✦

NOTES

1. Percival Lowell, *Mars and Its Canals* (New York: Macmillan, 1911), 206.
2. Ibid., 97.
3. Percival Lowell, *Mars* (Boston: Houghton Mifflin, 1897), 212.
4. Percival Lowell, *Mars as the Abode of Life* (New York: Macmillan, 1908), 90.
5. Percival Lowell, "Two Stars," lecture delivered at Kingman, Arizona, October 20, 1911, Lowell Observatory Archives.
6. H. G. Wells, *The War of the Worlds* (New York: Penguin, 2005), 5.

·9·

UNIDENTIFIED MOUNTAINOUS OBJECTS

I THOUGHT I WAS HIKING on solid rock, but then the rock began to dissolve and flow.

My boots told me that the rock was hard, and so did my muscles and sweat and breath. My eyes told me that I was hiking up a mountain. The mountain told me that it had tall cliffs and steep slopes because its rock was strong, stronger than gravity and thunderstorms and time. The mountain warned me that if I slipped and fell, it would prove to me how hard it was.

Yet my eyes were also noticing the redness of the rock, and all the lines and thin layers in it. My boots were confirming that this was sandstone, for the sandstone was dissolving back into sand, and in places the slopes were coated with enough sand to make them slippery. In little pockets in the ground, sand was gathering into small dunes, dunes with the same slopes and shapes as the lines and layers in the sandstone.

Time too began to dissolve, to get slippery. I began to see the cross-bedding in the rocks as ancient sand dunes, sand once roaming with the wind. I saw the winds of 280 million years ago, winds made visible by all the sand they carried. I saw sand blowing across a vast desert, piling up into long dunes, then blowing down again, the dunes dissolving, the dunes migrating downwind to build new dunes—a herd of millions of sand turtles crawling for miles, for millennia. I felt the desert heat and heard the whooshing of the wind. I saw the sand dunes glowing softly from the star dunes of the night sky. I left my footprints in the sand, and then I turned and watched my footprints dissolve away. Even when the sand dunes buried one another and piled up higher and higher, they showed no talent for being a mountain. Then I stepped out of the past and back into the present, stepped upon the solid, hard sandstone of a mountain.

I reached the top, and abruptly reality shifted from vertical to horizontal. The top of Bear Mountain was flat. Bear Mountain wasn't a mountain at all, but a plateau, and not just its own plateau but the edge of a plateau that stretched for hundreds of miles. I had just climbed up the edge of the Colorado Plateau, two thousand feet up. To the north some twenty miles away I saw the San Francisco Peaks, beneath which I lived. These peaks were a genuine mountain. From the base of Bear Mountain I had thought I was seeing a mountain: I'd been looking up at the sky and seeing an arc of rock. But now that I was standing on the same plateau on which I lived, my perceptions changed, and I felt that I was looking down into the earth, earth bear-clawed away by erosion. I was X-raying the rock layers that lay beneath me all the time, the rocks that upheld my land and my life, unseen and unappreciated. I was looking down as if from the rim of the Grand Canyon, except that here there was no opposite rim, only one rim eroded into ridges and side canyons, peaks and spires.

I was looking down on the red-rock formations that surround the town of Sedona, formations that humans have neglected to give any name of their own and so simply refer to as "Sedona." It's as if people called Yosemite, Yellowstone, or the Grand Canyon by the name of the closest tourist town. The red rocks had been there for aeons, the town of Sedona only since 1902. Sedona had remained a village for half a century, and had legally incorporated itself into a town only in 1988. Yet this blip of human activity had imposed its identity onto the ancient rocks. Originally, the name "Sedona" wasn't even a village, but just the name of the wife of the area's first postmaster. It was as if Yosemite was referred to as "Patty." At least the name "Sedona" had some poetry; if we used Sedona's last name, we'd be calling the red rocks "Schnebly."

A name was only the beginning of the projections of human identities and desires onto the ancient rocks.

✦ ✦ ✦

After my hike I stopped at Sedona's little bookshop and petted the store cat, and then I walked to another bookshop a few doors away, which offered mostly New Age books. On a doorway flier I noticed that this evening there was a meeting of Sedona's MUFON chapter. MUFON, or Mutual UFO Network, was the world's leading organization devoted to investigating reports of UFOs. Sedona was famous for its UFO activities. For anyone with a curiosity about the subject, a MUFON meeting in Sedona should be interesting. I had always been curious about the subject.

I was born a year before Sputnik, before humans had gotten a close look at the rest of our solar system. Some scientists were still hoping that our neighborhood planets might hold life, at least lichens, and science fiction writers were still placing civilizations on Mars and Venus. It had been less than twenty years since Orson Welles had landed Martians in New Jersey, where they were greeted quite seriously. In one human lifetime human technology had jumped from the Wright brothers to Sputnik, and in the 1960s it was leaping toward the moon and promising to soon take us to Mars and Venus. With no limits to technological progress, it seemed reasonable that if there were Martians and Venusians their technology would be far superior to ours and they would be flying to Earth to investigate us. As I was growing up, the media was full of reports of alien spacecraft in our skies, and the US Air Force took this seriously enough to conduct a scientific investigation of UFOs. It was true that even before Sputnik some astronomers were warning that the planets appeared to be inhospitable: Venus was quite hot, Mars was cold and dry, and Jupiter's clouds were so thick that sunlight might not reach its surface—if Jupiter had any surface. But in the years before human spacecraft reached the planets, anything seemed possible.

Flying saucers became part of the culture of the 1960s, alongside the space race, the Beatles, secret agents, and John F. Kennedy. Aliens made appearances on television every week. I was fascinated by *Star Trek*, in which humans traveled out to meet aliens, and by *The Invaders*, in which the aliens were traveling to Earth and disguising themselves as humans. I did find it puzzling why the real flying saucers didn't seem very good at disguising themselves; if the aliens were trying to observe us secretly, why did they place bright-colored flashing lights on their saucers?

As our spacecraft began landing on Mars and melting on Venus, the aliens made a rapid retreat, entirely out of the solar system. They also seemed to be losing ground when it came to the credibility of their advocates. Eventually, I tuned out the entire subject. Over the years I was aware that the aliens were becoming odder and odder: now they were abducting people, cutting off the tongues of cows, cutting patterns in fields of crops, channeling messages through psychics, and, though the aliens had mastered the technology of interstellar travel, they were incredibly incompetent pilots who were constantly crashing their saucers.

Still, I retained a vague nostalgia for the subject, though perhaps this was basically nostalgia for innocent-and-gone childhood, nostalgia that could have been triggered as easily by a 1964 Beatles song. Now, in Sedona, I found that I liked the idea of seeing what the aliens were up to these days.

To keep myself busy for the several hours before the meeting, I bought a copy of *Life on Other Planets*, written by Emanuel Swedenborg in 1758, two hundred years before Sputnik. I headed for the Red Planet Diner, which had a science fiction decor, with murals and decorations of Martian landscapes, flying saucers, aliens, *Star Trek*, and *Star Wars*. I ordered a Roswell Burger.

The Red Planet Diner fitted in well with Sedona's architectural anarchy. While some American towns have an architectural theme that is true to their historical identity—the Spanish of Santa Fe, the French of New Orleans—Sedona never had much of an identity, and the efforts of developers to invent one has resulted in a chaos of contradictory themes battling one another from every corner. The most prominent building downtown is the Matterhorn Lodge, as if no one would notice the difference between the Swiss Alps and the Arizona desert. Much of the rest of the downtown was done in Old West style, and some shops and restaurants have cowboy themes. Just down the road is Tlaquepaque, an upscale shopping center built in the 1980s to look like an elegant Spanish village; tourists often assume that it is an old Spanish mission. Many of Sedona's resorts have Spanish names and styles, though Sedona has almost zero Spanish history. Many other buildings are done in Native American pueblo style. Some franchises like McDonald's have tried to dress themselves in pueblo or Spanish style, but many remain anywhere-and-everywhere, building-as-logo franchise style. Sedona has art-deco buildings, modern buildings, space-age buildings, arts-and-crafts buildings, Victorian buildings, and just plain bland buildings. Only the mountains were secure in their ancient identities, as humans tried to make their confused identities as solid as wood and brick and concrete.

Mr. Spock watched over me as I read *Life on Other Planets*. It actually had a lot to say about the roots and motives of today's UFO culture.

Emanuel Swedenborg was a Swedish polymath, a scientist, inventor, politician, Christian theologian, and mystic. God opened up Swedenborg's "interior faculties" and allowed him to speak freely with angels and the spirits of the dead, who taught Swedenborg the secrets of the spiritual world, secrets traditional Christianity hadn't grasped. Later, Swedenborg began meeting spirits from other planets, who revealed to him the vast spiritual plan of the cosmos. Far ahead of astronomy, Swedenborg declared that the universe held hundreds of thousands of solar systems. God had created these planets and planted them with humans in order to breed spirits to fill heaven with glory; all the beings and spirits in the universe were Christians, but they were more spiritually evolved than the dimwitted Christians of Earth, and they had important lessons to teach us.

The spirits of each planet had unique attributes.

The spirits of Mercury took the form of round crystals, the shape of spiritual knowledge, and were so spiritually advanced that they disliked encountering spirits who were still preoccupied with material realities, even with the beauty of mountains, a fraud compared with the beauties of heaven. The spirits of Mercury were appalled by the Christians of Earth, who pretended to be religious but who behaved otherwise.

The inhabitants of Mars were so spiritual that their speech was almost silent, like the speech of angels, heard with inner faculties.

When Martians spoke, their feelings registered precisely on their faces, making it impossible for Martians to practice deceit or hypocrisy. Martians could speak openly with angels, and God was so pleased with Martians that he walked visibly among them. Martians didn't have kings but lived in democratic equality. Occasionally, a Martian began to value power or wealth or ego, but got exiled into rocky deserts until they recognized their errors.

The inhabitants of the moon had thunderous voices because the moon's atmosphere was too thin to carry sounds like Earth's atmosphere.

Venus was divided into two halves, with one half inhabited by gentle, benevolent beings, and the other half by giants as fierce as wild animals.

The inhabitants of Saturn were so spiritual that they didn't worry about the body, about appearances, clothing, food, or even burial when the body died.

The inhabitants of Jupiter were jovial, with round, happy faces. They went naked without embarrassment or lust, for they were pure and innocent. They were so spiritual that they couldn't conceive of greed, crime, murder, or war. The spirits of Jupiter refused to associate with the spirits of Earth, who still reeked of human corruptions.

Angels transported Swedenborg to several planets of other stars. To the inhabitants of one planet he explained that humans communicated the Word of God by printing it as symbols on paper, and the inhabitants were dumbfounded by this primitive method, unknown elsewhere. For spiritually advanced beings, divine wisdom was received directly, telepathically, from the angels.

Mr. Spock, watching me eat my Roswell Burger, agreed fully that humans were an inferior species, hopelessly illogical.

The MUFON meeting was at the Episcopal church, which I found a bit reassuring, suggesting that UFO folks were sober and conservative, not Pentecostals speaking in alien tongues and cheerleading the end of the world. And in fact, MUFON had a reputation as a conservative organization, relatively speaking. They trained members to investigate UFO reports, interview witnesses, search for physical evidence, and weed out aircraft sightings and outright hoaxes. While it had become trendy in UFO circles to think of UFOs not as space-craft but as interdimensional energy beings, MUFON remained committed to "nuts-and-bolts" highest-tech spacecraft, piloted by alien astronauts.

The Episcopal church did give one sign that it was located in Sedona. On its parking lot was painted a large, mazelike circular design. A crop circle? More likely it was a labyrinth, an old spiritual symbol that has become popular again. The fifty or so people at the MUFON meeting included ladies dressed in full Sedona style, with long purple dresses, crystals, turquoise, and Egyptian symbols.

Our guest speaker tonight was Louise, who had just published a book about her long acquaintance with one alien. Louise admitted that her book was partly fictionalized, but this was only to protect the identity of the alien. Aliens, of course, were all around us. There were aliens working at Burger King and at the car wash. Just the other day Louise was walking in Boynton Canyon, the site of one of the vortexes, when she recognized that a woman was really a reptilian alien. In Sedona New Age stores it was an everyday experience to hear someone mentioning that they were from Andromeda. At the average meeting about UFOs, Louise said, the crowd included two or three aliens. I glanced around the crowd; I didn't notice anyone glancing at me. The aliens, she explained, had been on Earth for a long time; in previous centuries people had mistaken them for angels. The aliens/angels were indeed highly evolved, benevolent beings, here to guide our spiritual evolution, to prepare us for Ascension to a higher vibrational level, scheduled for 2012. They came from planets where spirits had no further need of bodies, and they traveled the universe as interdimensional energy. Aliens lived inside of Earth, which was hollow, and their flying saucers—she didn't explain why interdimensional energy beings required flying saucers—were often seen around Sedona and Mount Shasta because these were portals into the hollow Earth, as well as maximum energy nodes from which the aliens charged their saucers. The US government knew all about the aliens and was masterminding a massive conspiracy to hide the truth. President Eisenhower had signed a treaty with the aliens, but the US government had broken the treaty many times.

The audience added their comments. Several people reported their recent encounters with aliens, including waking up in bed, totally paralyzed, as a gray alien examined them or fondled them. One woman had seen luminous energy beings in her backyard and recognized that they'd just emerged from the hollow Earth. Another woman said she was sure that one famous UFO had come from Venus.

Venus? Half a century ago, the Venusians had been melted by their 900°F degree heat.

＋ ＋ ＋

The rocks pulsed with energy. The rocks that tricked my feet into experiencing them as solid and hard were actually bee swarms of energy. In every atom, points of energy swirled around and around, swirled as they had swirled without a second of hesitation for nearly fourteen billion years, swirled with the energy unleashed by the Big Bang. The energy of the Big Bang had also fused atoms together and now become the hardness of rock. The rocks also contained the energy of stars and supernovas, which had fused atoms into heavier atoms, into the heaviness of stone and metal, the heaviness of mountains. The red color of the rocks was iron that had been fused in the final stage of the life of stars. After stars fused a series of atoms— carbon, oxygen, nitrogen, sodium—they created iron atoms that refused to fuse into still heavier atoms and thus fuel a star's burning. When too much iron had accumulated, a star shut down, collapsed, exploded as a supernova, and shredded itself into space. The iron in these rocks was the blood of stars, the heart attacks of stars. With every sunset, every day's dying of the sun, the red rocks glowed redder, its iron remembering the glory of the stars it had been, the stars it had killed. The red-rock mountains glowed like candles of commemoration.

Yet in triggering supernovas, the iron had also triggered the instant fusing of the elements heavier than itself, the completion of atomic evolution. It had sent itself and other elements wandering onward to become planets with red-rock mountains glorious with sunset, with the blood of birth. The red rocks were the astronomical footprint of my own journey.

The rocks also contained the energy of a cloud of gas and dust knotting itself into our solar system. They contained the heat of the newborn Earth, erupting as volcanoes. They contained the impacts of comets and asteroids. They contained the energy of continents moving and colliding and pushing up mountain ranges and triggering earthquakes. They contained the winds that drove the sands for miles and piled them into massive deserts. They contained the rains and sudden waterfalls of millions of years, and the crumpling of the earth into forms on its way to formlessness.

The rocks also pulsed with human imagination, with the images and names humans had imposed upon them. One ridge is called Snoopy Rock for its profile of Snoopy lying atop his doghouse. Another ridge is Submarine Rock; local lore says it was named by Walt Disney, who was taking a Sedona vacation during the filming of his *20,000 Leagues Under the Sea*. Many ridges or buttes, like the one named Steamboat Rock in 1880, bear the energy of the American national story, of the conquest of a vast continent. Some landmarks were named from the sixty western movies filmed around Sedona, such as Zane Grey Wash. The Jimmy Stewart western *Broken Arrow* gave its name to the Broken Arrow Trail. Other human meanings imposed onto the rocks are Castle Rock, Chimney Rock, Coffeepot Rock, the Teacup, Courthouse Butte, Capitol Butte, and Bell Rock. Even geologists had shown a limited imagination: they had named one rock layer after a nearby real-estate development.

At least I liked the name of the rock formation I was climbing now: Cathedral Rock, its many spires pointing upward.

A young couple on the trail asked me eagerly: "Is all of Cathedral Rock the vortex, or is the vortex concentrated in one spot?"

I didn't like to pinpoint anyone's bubble, but I wasn't interested in being hailed as another vortex pilgrim. "There aren't any vortexes," I answered.

They looked at me with surprise, as if I were an imbecile, or a satanist shouting in a cathedral. "Why do you say that?" the guy asked indignantly.

"You know how in the grocery-store checkout line the *National Enquirer* headlines talk about psychics predicting the Super Bowl or the return of Elvis? It was a *National Enquirer* psychic who invented the vortexes around 1980."

Actually, in the 1970s some people were already talking about Sedona being a "power place," but it was psychic Page Bryant who channeled, from her spirit guide Albion, the revelation of which specific rock formations were vortexes. Bryant also suggested how the vortexes worked, the differences between them, and their connections with other points in Earth's chakra system, and with cosmic ley lines. The Bell Rock vortex, for example, was a receiver of astrological energies from the planet Pluto, energies that facilitate healing. The vortex at Red Rock Crossing, right below Cathedral Rock, greatly enhances psychic powers, allowing you to see and talk with spirits. In an amazingly short time the Sedona vortexes became a firmly established part of the New Age cosmos, drawing thousands of pilgrims from all over the world. Yet within ten years Page Bryant was disgusted by how shabby the vortex craze had become, with all sorts of bogus claims about them and with rent-a-shamans charging pilgrims large sums of money for vortex spiritual experiences.

The guy scolded me: It was a well-known fact that the vortexes were ancient and sacred shrines for Native Americans, who made pilgrimages here from hundreds of miles away. The vortexes were quantum-energy nodes connected with similar energy nodes at Stonehenge, the Egyptian pyramids, and Machu Picchu, which is why those shrines had been built in those locations. *Sedona* spelled backward was *Anodes!*

My mood marred, I finished the hike without noticing that the red-rock cathedral was celebrating the journey of iron from supernovas to blood that quickened with red-rock sunsets.

◆ ◆ ◆

This time I had planned my Sedona hike to coincide with MUFON's monthly meeting.

Tonight's speaker, Gary, had written a book proving that the Hopis had arranged their villages and sacred sites in a pattern that matched the constellation Orion, just as the ancient Egyptians had arranged their pyramids in the pattern of Orion. The three stars of the belt of Orion coincided with the three Hopi mesas. Gary admitted that the real sky map of Orion didn't fit the real Earth map of Hopi villages, but if you turned the Orion map upside down and backward, then it did fit, and it fitted a lot of other Hopi landmarks, too. Orion's arm lay atop the Grand Canyon, even if it curved in the opposite arc, and one star lay atop the Sipapuni, the Hopis' place of emergence. Other stars matched the layout of famous ruins. All these matches couldn't possibly be a coincidence. If you extended one of the lines of Orion into New Mexico, it pointed straight at Roswell, and if you extended another line into Nevada, it pointed straight at Area 51. This was proof that the Hopi prophets had received—from aliens—a revelation that Roswell and Area 51 would hold great significance in the twentieth century. The Hopi god Masau'u had gray skin, just like the gray aliens. The similarity of Hopi and Egyptian words proved that the ancient Hopis were also communicating with the ancient Egyptians. The San Francisco Peaks, sacred to the Hopis, had three peaks, and there were three pyramids at Giza. Gary showed us a photo of the Phoenix lights, a famous UFO sighting, and reminded us that Phoenix, Arizona, was named for the Egyptian god Phoenix. Phoenix, Arizona, was located on the thirty-third latitude, and the Masons, masters of Egyptian lore, called the highest degree of Masonry the thirty-third degree. Harry Truman had been a thirty-third-degree Mason, and he was also the thirty-third president of the United States.

In connecting the Hopi dots, Gary was practicing geomancy, or sacred geometry, which had become an occult fad in England in the 1920s. By connecting ancient ruins with "ley lines," you could find larger meaningful patterns. There was an entire book on the geomancy of Sedona, connecting the vortexes and mountains, finding pentagrams or the outlines of serpents or birds. Extending geomancy into the sky was a more ambitious attempt to find patterns in the world.

All animals seek patterns in their experiences. Deciding whether a shape in the forest is a fruit or the head of a predator is a matter of life and death. In humans this pattern seeking had expanded until it included the entire universe. As with patterns of food and predators, weather and disease, the human mind sifted the patterns in the sky for their meanings for human life and death. Sometimes astronomical patterns did indeed fit into human events: a star or constellation might appear at the right time for spring planting, summer hunting, autumn harvesting, or winter solstice. But other times, in grasping at something far outside their earthly experience, humans made erroneous connections. In this room tonight I was seeing the ancient human radar that searched for patterns in the sky, for connections with the cosmos. Here the drive to find cosmic meaning was so powerful that it overrode every fact or logic or gap that stood in its way, and it had little conscience about inventing things that served it.

After the meeting I went to the grand opening of Sedona's telescope store, which offered state-of-the-art Celestron telescopes. The telescope store doubled as a New Age art gallery, with paintings of Egyptian pyramids, Native American ruins, and astronomical objects mixed with sacred symbols and spirit beings. The store belonged to Bearcloud, an Osage Native American who had discovered secrets of the Egyptian pyramids that had eluded scholars for five thousand years. The passageways inside the pyramids, their bends, stairs, dead ends, and chambers, spelled out a hidden star language, which Bearcloud recognized because it was similar to his own Osage shamanic tradition. Bearcloud also recognized Osage symbols in crop circles in England, to which he had traveled many times, one time witnessing an alien spacecraft landing. A few years ago Bearcloud received a vision that he should build a great spiritually themed garden in Sedona, centered around a glass pyramid 481 feet tall, the height of the Great Pyramid at Giza. Bearcloud was opening this gallery/ telescope store to raise funds to build his pyramid.

The grand opening was a big social event, with wine and cheese, fancy clothes, and a white guy playing a Native American flute. The biggest excitement was in the back parking lot, where several telescopes were set up. Many people had never seen a telescope before, and they made many amazed comments about the telescopes and the views through them. I hung out for an hour, going from scope to scope. The conversations I overheard seldom came from the astronomical universe. There was much talk of astrological signs. One woman asked what, exactly, are stars, and she was amazed to learn that stars are suns just like our own, only far away. She was reassured to hear that astronomers recognized the constellation Aquarius, which was what was going to usher in the Age of Aquarius. One person wanted to see the Face on Mars. One telescope was trained on the Pleiades, the home of the Pleiadians, one of the most prominent alien races, who live on a crystal planet and frequently channel their messages through Sedona psychics. Pleiadian energy is transmitted by the Cathedral Rock vortex. The Pleiadians will play a key role in planetary Ascension.

When a flashing light flew overhead, one person declared it was an alien spacecraft. It was heading for Airport Mesa, the mesa that held the Sedona airport. Airport Mesa is a hotbed of UFO activities.

◆ ◆ ◆

Is it possible to see a mountain while you are climbing it?

I am climbing Bear Mountain again. Normally, I would use the word *hiking* and not *climbing*, but Bear Mountain's steepness—two thousand feet in about two miles—shifts my emotional gears into climbing.

From the trailhead parking lot I can see the whole of Bear Mountain, and though the trail isn't visible, I can surmise the contours it needs to follow. After a flat zone, I am face-to-face with a cliff, and I lose sight of Bear Mountain. In the course of the hike, Bear Mountain disappears many times. It disappears even when I am staring right at it and feeling its firmness and measuring it with my muscles and lungs. Bear Mountain shrinks into one square foot of rock around my foot. The trail requires constant close attention, for it has a lot of ledges, loose rocks, slippery sand, oddly torquing slickrock slopes, manzanita branches, yucca bayonets, and cairns. As long as I am moving, I can't afford to look at the mountain. As if the mountain gets annoyed at me for not seeing it, it steals my breath away and forces me to pause, and then I can look at the mountain. Yet even then I often can see only the slope I am on, not the mountaintop, not the bulk below me. I see other mountains better than the mountain I am on. Casual tourists at Sedona shopping centers can see Bear Mountain better than I can.

As my climb goes on, Bear Mountain shrinks not just my vision, but my identity. Hadn't I started this hike as a human searching for beauty? Now I am just an animal searching for danger, searching for a safe place to place my foot and not slide or trip or fall. Now I am an animal laboring hard, sweating hard, breathing hard, muscling hard, feeling the limitations of biological matter against geological matter. I can't avoid feeling an adversarial relationship with the mountain. I resent it for making me work so hard, and I dislike its potential for making me turn back before the top, a defeat for my pride. Can you see a mountain while you are seeing only yourself?

Can you see the planet Earth, as large as it is, while you are standing upon it? Can you see the planet Earth while you are struggling upon it? Can you appreciate being alive while you are an animal and are forced to struggle to be alive? Can you appreciate being alive while you are a human and you can see the illogic of the universe? Can you see the universe while you are a human and can dream of better universes?

✦ ✦ ✦

Tonight's speaker, Jim, was one of the best-known alien abductees. Jim was living a normal life as a successful North Carolina real-estate developer until he was thirty-four years old, and then the alien abductions began and continued for eight years. Unlike most abductees, who didn't remember their abductions until they were hypnotized, Jim remembered nearly everything. The aliens visited Jim frequently, communicated telepathically, and used their field technology to transport Jim through solid walls to their spacecraft, where they conducted long, often painful medical procedures on him, extracting all kinds of tissues and fluids. Jim was so traumatized by these encounters that his emotions and life fell apart and he became a recluse, hiding in his house, his hair and beard long and dirty. The aliens wouldn't stop coming. There were gray aliens, reptilian aliens, Nordic aliens. They had been on Earth for thousands of years. They were neither benevolent nor hostile; they were simply using humans as cattle, to grow useful organs and genes. But now humans were bringing environmental doom upon themselves, and the aliens were intervening to save their investment. The aliens went to Earth's leaders and offered them advanced alien technologies that would solve all of humankind's energy, pollution, food, and poverty problems, but Earth's leaders had refused, since solving these problems would undermine their political power and corporate profits. Now world leaders were orchestrating a massive cover-up to hide the presence of the aliens and to ridicule the people who knew the aliens were real. Now the aliens had turned to Jim to save humankind, to warn the world about the danger of global warming. The aliens were also using Jim's superior genes to breed an alien-human hybrid. Jim was also visited by future humans who were traveling back in time to harvest genetic materials to heal themselves.

During a break I went outside, under stars that appeared to be real, and soon I was joined by Jim and three women coming out to smoke. One woman thanked Jim for his testimony. Her life had been a wreck; she'd even had a drunken car wreck, careening down a slope. She'd been having crazy hallucinations, and she'd thought she was mentally ill, but then she read Jim's book and realized she was being abducted by aliens.

UFO culture had changed a lot since my childhood.

The first time aliens had contacted humans with an important message, back in 1952, the aliens had been wholly benevolent, their message one of spiritual enlightenment. The aliens had come straight out of Emanuel Swedenborg, who had left a large imprint on Western mysticism. A century later Madame Blavatsky combined Western mysticism, Eastern religions, and occult traditions like Atlantis, Egyptian pyramids, and the channeling of higher spirits into theosophy, a spiritual system complex enough to have enduring appeal. In the 1950s theosophy underwent a sudden, major mutation. George Adamski was a devoted theosophist who, in 1934 in California, founded his own vehicle for it, the Royal Order of Tibet, and wrote several books about it. No one paid much attention. In 1947 the idea of flying saucers burst out in the media and captured the public imagination, including George Adamski's imagination. A few years later Adamski reported that he had been contacted by an alien from Venus, a Nordic-looking youth named Orthon, who had an urgent message for humankind. Orthon's message was pure theosophy, some of it taken word for word from Adamski's books. This time,

Adamski became a worldwide celebrity. Theosophy had latched onto the cultural energy of a powerful science-flavored, high-tech idea. Now alien theosophy was offered as the answer to the anxiety of a lonely species fearing its own imperfections in the new atomic age. Theosophy coming from the mouths of aliens worked much better than theosophy coming from the mouths of Native Americans, who for two hundred years had been abducted by whites to serve as their mediums, the Hopis the most abused and exasperated of all.

One of Adamski's true believers was a Swiss woman, the cousin of psychologist Carl Jung; she wrote a book lauding Adamski and did her best to convince Jung. In reply, Jung wrote his book *Flying Saucers: A Modern Myth of Things Seen in the Sky*, in which he said that flying saucers were psychological projections, but possibly healthy ones, their round shapes symbolizing a quest for wholeness. Jung was fascinated by how ancient religious impulses were trying to grapple with the bold, new raw materials of the space age.

✦ ✦ ✦

By the time I reached the top of Bear Mountain, I felt the mountain inside me. Bear Mountain had translated geology into biology, translated the tightness of rocks into the tightness of muscles, the striations of dunes into the cross-bedding of muscles, the bonds of motionlessness into the chemicals of motion, the redness of sandstone into the rallying of blood. I was weighing the mountain on a scale of bones and flesh, and it was heavy. The energy of ancient winds emerged from the rocks and triggered the energy of my breathing—my breathing out the same molecules that had piled up these dunes and that now blew with a greater aspiration. The ancient raindrops that had left tiny fossil imprints in this rock now fell as sweat that propelled me upward. The gravity that had worked this sand into angle-of-repose slopes now spiraled through my ears and brain to build a balance that defied gravity.

When I reached the top I looked back down at the huge cone of sandstone beneath me. It was like the cone of sand in the bottom of an hourglass. This hourglass contained the flowing sands of 280 million years. All of those aeons had flowed through me on my climb, and they did not find any landscapes they did not recognize.

All of those aeons and all of the forces that had built this mountain had been within me all along. The wind, the rain, the earth, the sunlight, all of it had flowed onward and built shapes far more sophisticated than sand dunes. The mountains, the rivers, the canyons had flowed onward. The lizards, the birds, the mice, the plants had flowed onward. The atoms had flowed onward. The energy pulsing within these rocks, the energy of stars, supernovas, and the Big Bang, had flowed onward.

All along, human bodies contained mountains, unidentified.

✦ ✦ ✦

Tonight's speaker was Ann, who for years was the assistant to Dr. J. Allen Hynek, the dean of UFO researchers. Hynek was a professional astronomer who in 1948 was tapped by the US Air Force to analyze UFO reports and find natural explanations for them. In 1966 Hynek dismissed one UFO sighting as "swamp gas," and the national media ridiculed him. Chagrined, Hynek set up his own university-based institute to research UFO reports in a scientific way, without any agenda of either belief or debunking. But now Ann was reassuring us that Hynek's scientific persona was just a facade. Hynek was really one of us—a true believer. He was secretly a member of the Rosicrucian Order. He had seen an alien spacecraft for himself.

Ann told us of how, after Hynek's death, she had been contacted by "the Sisters of Light," a group of female aliens who gave her an urgent message for humankind. Planet X was going to return very soon! Planet X was four times larger than Earth, and was inhabited by superior aliens who had created humans as slaves. Planet X had been in the outer solar system for a long time, but now it was approaching the inner solar system, and it would trigger catastrophic earthquakes and tsunamis on Earth. Planet X was already clearly visible in the night sky. Ann showed us a photograph from the website of a psychic channeler, showing Planet X right next to the sun and just as large and nearly as bright as the sun. Someone from the audience asked why, if Planet X was already as large as the sun, it wasn't being reported by amateur astronomers?

Amateur astronomers? I thought. What about you? Didn't

anyone in this room ever look at the real night sky? Didn't anyone know even the elementary facts of astronomy?

Ann answered that the US government had forced all astronomers to remain silent about Planet X. The government knew all about Planet X and had built massive, secret underground facilities to save the elite of humankind. One audience member recalled how in the 1970s Sedona was swarming with government trucks, undoubtedly building the underground facilities for the coming of Planet X. Ann said that when Planet X was destroying Earth, the Sisters of Light, who were pure benevolence, would transport their true believers to the fourth and fifth dimensions, where humans would exist in pure bliss. One audience member asked if the Sisters of Light would also transport our cats and dogs to the fourth and fifth dimensions, and for once Ann seemed unsure. She said that of course the Sisters of Light loved animals, but she wasn't sure about their pet policies.

I thought of how UFO culture had started out so innocently. Aliens were once next-door Spocks from Venus and Mars, paying us a neighborly visit; it was only a matter of time before they landed and introduced themselves. Yet as the decades passed and the solar system turned out to be barren, the aliens retreated to distant stars. The aliens failed to leave even one bolt from a spacecraft, one footprint, one document, one compelling photograph, so the aliens retreated into interdimensional energies or into a massive government conspiracy. With every decade without good evidence for aliens, belief in a cover-up became more crucial, for if the cover-up did not exist, neither did the aliens. As the cover-up became more elaborate and aggressive, so did anger at the government for denying a truth that was deeply important to believers. UFO culture descended into a spiral of paranoia, which seemed to affect the aliens themselves. The aliens went from being human to being reptilian, went from friendly spiritual lectures to abductions, medical tortures, cattle mutilations, and dark plots against humanity. MUFON had been the bulwark of the original idea that UFOs are nuts-and-bolts spacecraft, and it had waged a long battle against the idea that UFOs are interdimensional energies, but now, in Sedona at least, MUFON had been thoroughly abducted. When George Adamski introduced the idea of aliens offering spiritual messages to humans, he'd remained peripheral, an embarrassment in a UFO culture that was largely nuts and bolts, but today the spiritual impulse was the core of UFO culture.

Like Carl Jung, I was fascinated to watch human religious needs trying to digest space-age ideas. Yet I was amazed by how disconnected this process was from the astronomical universe, and how ready people were to believe anything. In all the MUFON meetings I attended, the only peep of doubt I heard was the guy who asked why no one was seeing a sun-size planet in our sky. Some UFO ideas did offer a good fit for human religious templates: aliens make pretty good angels and devils. Yet in other respects, UFO ideas are too limited and specialized to add up into a comprehensive religion, which needs a cosmogenesis, a theology of good and evil, and personal affirmations from God. It was not surprising that UFO culture was struggling terribly in its efforts to turn UFOs into a religion.

◆ ◆ ◆

I stepped outside into the clear night sky. The mountainous horizon was dark and mysterious. The sky held mountains of stars.

The sky was full of human shapes and stories, star dots that humans had connected into patterns that offered meaning. The sky was a movie screen onto which humans had projected the passions and events of biological beings. The sky held the shapes of hunters with clubs, and warriors with swords. The sky held heroes and villains, gods and demons, angels and monsters, kings and prisoners, queens and maidens, animals and rivers and mountains. The sky held humans driving chariots, carrying water, planting crops, herding goats, making offerings, winning contests, finding love and losing love, giving birth and dying. The sky was full of promises and warnings, rewards and punishments, lessons and hopes.

And somewhere beyond the blinding fog of human desires, there was a real universe, the one that had projected its brilliant energies into the shapes of Earth and of humans.

I had become convinced of one thing. The MUFON group was indeed full of aliens. Earth is full of aliens. Humans are deeply alienated, alienated from the planet and the cosmos that gave birth to us.

Humans could spend whole lives walking upon the hard earth and never make contact with it. They could see the starry night twenty thousand times and barely notice it. They could climb many mountains and never feel any affinity for them. They could see in their fellow humans nothing but threats of violence and targets for conquest. When humans see the mystery of their existence, they are frightened by it and try to hide from it.

I looked into the sky, and I saw a mysterious light. At long last, I was seeing a flying saucer. It was a disc, with a dome on top. It was huge; it filled the sky; it was the mother ship. It was full of lights, thousands of lights, like the windows of an airplane or an ocean liner, proclaiming the unknown lives going on within. Beyond my perception, it had billions of lights. It was the Milky Way galaxy. Our Milky Way saucer was a vessel of mysterious origin and unknown purpose.

Looking beyond our galaxy, I saw billions of other disc-shaped galaxies, a fleet of galaxies, flying alongside one another in formation, streaking from the Big Bang and into the deepening night. I saw the enormous power of creation, the Big Bang that would not stop burning, the light that became life. I saw a great journey out of mystery, a journey that left spaces behind but never left behind mystery. I saw a universe of unidentified beings groping for identity, asking the mountains and the lights in the sky to tell us the secrets of ourselves and our journey, asking because we were unwilling to admit that the entire universe will forever remain unidentifiable.◦✦

·10·

FIRE AND ICE

SOME SAY THE WORLD was created in benevolence, some say in chaos.

All I really knew at this moment was that climbing the highest mountain in Arizona was a mixture of both, of hard beauty and hard stress. I sat down to allow my left-behind breath to catch up with me.

I sat down next to a patch of wildflowers. I watched them lollipopping to the breeze. I didn't recognize some of them, didn't know their name or range or life cycle, so it was easier to see them less biologically and more as poetic flowers. From Blake's seeing "a Heaven in a wildflower" to today, a million poems have made flowers serve as symbols of affirmation. It was fair enough for flowers to serve as emblems of beauty; even the hummingbirds and the bees would agree. But frequently, flowers serve as symbols of a larger order of beauty, the beauty of creation, the benevolent structure and purpose of the cosmos. For the romantics flowers became the thoughts of God, proofs of a master plan, promises of divine love, intimations of heaven. In romantic poetry a weary traveler is making his way through the Alps, feeling the gloom of its abysses, when suddenly his heart is lifted by a flower, a rainbow, an eagle, and now he sees the divinity manifest in nature and in himself. The romantic response to nature became so entrained in the Western imagination that today even nonbelievers continue it in watered-down forms.

As I gazed at the flowers I also saw their biological beauty, their graceful architecture, life's creativity. I saw life's boldness in growing here, on poor soil that only two months ago was buried in snow. I saw the crude volcanic soil being transformed into form, color, and talent.

I turned and looked up the steep slopes of the mountain. I imagined it as it had once been, as an active volcano. I saw massive dark smoke clouds boiling out, roiling miles into the air and mushrooming out. I felt the ground shaking. I heard a thunder roaring on and on. I saw volcanic debris raining down, and rivers of lava flowing down the slopes. The air was dark and deadly with heat and poisonous gases and flying rocks. There was no life for many miles around. The volcano was a monstrous black flower.

The volcano had been taller then, perhaps three thousand feet taller. It was a classic stratovolcano, majestically isolated, its slopes curving up to a tall point, like Mount Fuji or Mount Kilimanjaro. Eventually, the volcano died and went cold and its top collapsed, leaving a ring of peaks.

I gazed up at one of those peaks, Agassiz Peak. It was named in the 1860s for Louis Agassiz, at the time one of the world's most famous naturalists, at a time when naturalist-explorers were major cultural heroes. Louis Agassiz was most famous for proving the power of glaciers and the reality of ice ages. Later he became one of the staunchest scientific opponents of Charles Darwin's theory of evolution. It was an argument over whether the world was created in benevolence, or in chaos.

The ancient human argument over the nature of the cosmos would swirl around this volcano, starting with its names.

For the Hopis, whose ancestors lived at the base of the volcano a thousand years ago, the volcano was Nuvatukya'ovi, or "the Place of Snow on the Very Top," and it was the home of their katsina spirits. In the 1620s the Spanish conquistadores and missionaries arrived and gave the mountain a Christian name, San Francisco Mountain, for Saint Francis. In 1868 Americans replaced Christianity with science, calling the mountain Mount Agassiz. At the base of Mount Agassiz they founded a village and called it Agassiz. Both names faded. The village became Flagstaff, and Mount Agassiz was reduced to one peak in a complex of peaks called the San Francisco Peaks—now, the scientist was subservient to the saint.

The three names represented three conceptual universes.

For the Hopis the world was—and still is—full of spirits who empower the forces of nature and give or withhold those forces for human benefit. Nature holds vast, powerful cycles that humans need to respect and fit into. The katsinas are generally benevolent, but they can be offended by human misbehavior and decline to help humans.

The katsinas live in the Hopi villages for half the year to preside over the planting and growing season. Then they head home to the mountain to preside over the rainy season. In the summertime the Hopis keep an eye on Nuvatukya'ovi about sixty miles away, for it is here, out of a clear sky, that the first rain clouds of the day begin to form. White streaks begin pulsing over the mountaintop and solidify and grow taller and wider and darker, then begin sending out lightning bolts and streaks of rain, streaks represented on Hopi pottery and katsina dolls and even in Hopi hairstyles. From the mountain the clouds spread into the desert, toward the Hopi villages. Other clouds form overhead, like seeds growing into crops. Raindrops fall and patter the cornstalks, setting them dancing. Lightning crashes and rain pours, soaking into the soil and into the corn, on its way into human bodies.

When the Spanish conquistadores arrived in the Hopi villages, they weren't seeking the secrets of farming or living humbly in a desert environment. They were seeking conquest and empire and gold. With the conquistadores came Franciscan missionaries, who named the greatest landmark on the horizon for Saint Francis. In his humility and love of nature, Saint Francis was closer to the Hopi worldview than any other Christian leader. As the centuries passed, Saint Francis would be honored across denominational boundaries, even by atheists. Yet Franciscans remained loyal to a worldview, monotheism, that for ages had been doing battle against paganism.

In nature religions the powers of nature and the forces of good and evil are divided among dozens or hundreds of gods, who contend against one another to control the world and human loyalties. In monotheism there is only one god, who is outside of nature and superior to nature, which he created for the benefit of humans. God is both all-powerful and all-benevolent. If there is evil in the world, then it was the fault of humans, of Adam and Eve, who ruined God's plan. Or it was the fault of the devil and the humans who gave the devil an entrance into the world.

The Spanish missionaries set out to save the Hopis from devil worship, from an eternity of burning in hell. They discarded Hopi "idols" and suppressed Hopi ceremonies. In one village they filled a kiva with sand and built their altar on top of it. They forced the Hopis to build churches and take baptism.

The missionaries met strong resistance, more than they got from many other tribes. They were meeting the power of human memory, memory that had kept the Hopis alive for centuries. The Hopis needed strong memories, embedded in their religion, to guide them in their inherently unlikely survival strategy of farming in the desert. They also remembered how their society had failed in a drought five centuries before. A widespread Puebloan society, which had built great centers like Chaco, collapsed into hunger, thirst, and chaos. Cities were abandoned. The survivors retreated to a few areas with reliable water and soil, such as the Hopi mesas. The drought and social collapse were carved into Puebloan memories like canyons into stone plateaus. The Hopis became even more devoted to the spirits and ceremonies that brought rain and life, that fended off the chaos always waiting to attack humans.

Now the Christian missionaries were demanding that the Hopis cease the ceremonies that made the difference between life and death, and betray the katsinas who had kept them alive for centuries. And what were the Christians offering instead? Only one god to do the work of many. A god who didn't seem to know anything about ceremonies for bringing rain. A god who didn't seem to comprehend the nature of reality. A god who claimed that chaos wasn't real, that the universe was made with entire benevolence. A blasphemous god who held himself apart from and superior to nature. A god who was insane—dangerously insane.

He looks at the earth
and it trembles.
He touches the mountains
and they smoke.
—Psalm 104

He touches the Hopis and they smoke. Hopis caught commit-
ting idolatry were whipped, starved, dressed as penitents in haircloth
shirts and forced to carry a cross, and even doused in hot turpentine.
Finally, in 1680 the Hopis rebelled, expelled the Spanish, demolished
the churches, and went back to their reliable ways.

Two centuries later a third conceptual cosmos arrived at the
Peaks, science, in which the universe is made up of physical forces
that operate according to highly predictable laws. Rain falls and volcanoes erupt according to laws, which may not fit into human needs.
But science also glorifies human reason, which can harness the forces
of nature and turn them into machines and medicines. Evil is just a
temporary obstacle to human progress.

The man who turned San Francisco Mountain into Mount
Agassiz was a strong believer in human progress. General William
Palmer was surveying a southwestern route for a railroad from the
Midwest to the Pacific Coast. His railroad would cut, tunnel, bridge,
and embank its way through mountains, volcanoes, mesas, canyons, and deserts. No obstacle could withstand human progress and
Manifest Destiny. As a western surveyor and a former executive of a
coal-mining company, Palmer knew geology, knew it as a science that
was the latest triumph of human reason and the key to vast wealth.
The greatest American geologist was Louis Agassiz. Mount Agassiz
would proclaim the gospel of human progress over Palmer's trains,
over the lumberjacks clearing the forests, over the miners enriching
the nation, over the ranches turning wild grasslands into prosperity,
over the booming towns like Agassiz.

I continued my climb up the volcano. Human progress can be
hard to believe in when you are climbing a mountain. The peak
doesn't seem to be getting closer. Every step upward is work and
three hundred steps is tiredness, but the mountain still looms. The
upward efforts of humans are a microscopic energy compared with
the upward powers of the earth. The earth had climbed upward
here for aeons, climbed into the empty sky by building the trail of
itself, climbed with the mass of billions of human bodies, climbed
without tiredness or rest, without desire or doubt or pride, climbed
because the earth climbs, the earth builds, the earth hikes the Escher

stairways of its own logic. The earth wasn't interested in building any kind of symbol for human needs. Not a home for katsinas who bring rain. Not an arrow pointing to the god of all creation and judgment. Not a lighthouse of national destiny. Not a tribute to human reason. Not a trophy for athletes and adventure lovers. The mountain acted only for itself, murmuring only to itself of power and time and endurance. The earth builds bodies that are far harder and more enduring than human bodies. Step by step I was measuring the strength of the earth, following in the footsteps of a giant, feeling small. I was a GPS receiver for locating the place of humans in nature.

Louis Agassiz began hearing the mountains murmuring of power and time when he was growing up in Switzerland. Perhaps it required a Swiss to conceive of ice ages. Switzerland was loaded with glaciers and the marks of glaciers past. Swiss sheepherders had been noticing these marks for centuries. They saw that glaciers were packed with boulders, boulders scraping the cliffs. Where glaciers were retreating, they saw scratch marks on the cliffs, boulders left perched high up on slopes, and boulders left piled into ridges on valley floors. They also noticed that many valleys without glaciers still held scratch marks, oddly perched boulders, and long snaking ridges of boulders and gravel. For a long time even scientists regarded such debris as remnants of Noah's flood. But a few geologists began suspecting that Earth was much older than Christian theology allowed. Given enormous time, the forces humans saw at work around them today—rain, rivers, erosion, sedimentation, earthquakes, glaciers, volcanic eruptions—could work dramatic changes, building mountain ranges and erasing them again.

Louis Agassiz roamed the Alps studying glaciers and identifying the marks of glaciers past. He found glacial footprints a hundred miles from current glaciers and decided that Alpine glaciers had once been much more extensive. Then he roamed northern Europe and found abundant signs of glaciers far from any mountains, and he decided that all of northern Europe had been covered with massive ice sheets. Even Charles Lyell, the prophet of an ancient Earth and gradual change, resisted the concept of ice ages. Theologians too resisted, for the idea of God ice-bulldozing half a continent and destroying its creatures was disturbingly incongruous with the Christian story. Yet Agassiz triumphed, partly because he insisted that ice ages were the secret to reconciling geology and theology and proving God's benevolent master plan.

For six generations Louis Agassiz's forebears had been Protestant ministers, and Louis was expected to continue their calling. Instead, Louis heard the call of natural history. He was left acutely aware of the discrepancies between the story in Genesis and the story in the rocks. Agassiz turned the fossil record into a Christian testament. Fossils showed that life had been around long before humans and that there had been repeated large-scale extinctions. Agassiz asserted that major destructions of life meant that there must have been subsequent major creations of life. Creations by the hand of God. Creations that were part of a plan whose goal was the creation of humans. God was creating the animal world one step at a time, each step rising higher toward perfection. For Agassiz every species was "a thought of God," a plan made manifest in bone and flesh. The fossil record was an Alps-size Sistine Chapel showing God's hand pointing to the crowning glory of creation.

Agassiz turned ice ages into God's curtain for clearing the world stage of imperfect acts and readying it for the next act of creation. (Noah's flood could account for only one round of cataclysm.) Agassiz called glaciers "God's great plough." Agassiz's equation, fossils + ices ages = God, dazzled much of the intellectual world, scientists and theologians alike, and made Agassiz a hero.

When Agassiz visited America in 1846 he found himself an even greater celebrity. Thousands of Bostonians flocked to hear his lecture "The Plan of Creation in the Animal Kingdom." American intellectual leaders like Emerson and Longfellow feted Agassiz. Emerson's own form of idealism, of seeing divinity in nature, had helped make America fertile ground for Agassiz. Longfellow wrote a poem in Agassiz's honor, hailing him for having gone "into regions yet untrod; / and read what is still unread / in the Manuscripts of God."[1] John Greenleaf Whittier wrote "The Prayer of Agassiz":

Said the Master to the Youth:
"We have come in search of truth,

Trying with uncertain key,
Door by door of mystery;
We are reaching through His laws,
To the garment-hem of Cause.[2]

Harvard University offered Agassiz a position, and he was happy to accept. In Europe Agassiz had many long-standing rivalries, but in America he became the giant in a very modest scientific world. Agassiz would remain in America for the rest of his life. His natural history expeditions to New England, the Great Lakes, the South, and the Rocky Mountains received wide attention. Americans gave his name to mountains in New Hampshire, California, and Arizona; to a famous giant tree in the Sierra Nevada; and to a glacier in Glacier National Park.

The patron who brought Agassiz to America was John Amory Lowell of the Lowell textile fortune, the same Lowell family that half a century later would send Percival Lowell to build his astronomical observatory near the base of Mount Agassiz. Thus, one Boston family littered the Flagstaff skyline with cosmic phantoms: Martians who never existed, a planet Pluto that was never entirely a planet, and a natural theology that was already dying by the time William Palmer named the volcano Mount Agassiz.

Louis Agassiz's towering reputation started declining with the 1859 publication of Charles Darwin's theory of biological evolution. In a few years Agassiz went from being an icon to being an anachronism. Darwinism struck at the heart of Agassiz's cosmos by eliminating any need for continuing acts of creation. The "before" and "after" species, the less perfect and more perfect, were united by a long series of natural changes.

At the Galapagos, atop a cluster of jagged volcanic mountain-islands thrust violently out of the sea and still racked by the sea, amid life forms undeniably weird, Darwin had seen that life too had erupted from undeniable underground plumes of chaos. The shell of Earth had cracked apart into the jigsaw mystery-shell game of tortoises. Raw, hot volcanic skin had died out and shriveled into rough dragon skin that craved the sun's warmth.

Agassiz took his stand against Darwin by insisting that the

fossil record showed no gradual changes, only abrupt discontinuities between species. The ice ages completely wiped out existing life forms; the successor life forms were distinctly new species. God created life forms for such highly specific survival modes that species could never adapt to new modes. Agassiz's stature gave anti-Darwinism a special credibility and momentum in America, and encouraged a creationist movement that wouldn't exist in Europe.

Yet as other scientists studied the fossil record they decided that it showed a great deal of gradual change. Even the young American scientists who had hero-worshipped Agassiz soon abandoned him. When Agassiz organized an 1866 expedition to Brazil to prove that even in the tropics ice ages had wiped out all life, even one of his crew members, William James, the future psychologist, considered Agassiz to be almost crazy: "Never did a man utter a greater amount of humbug."[3]

If Louis Agassiz went crazy fighting Darwin, it was for a sound reason. At risk was Christianity itself, and the concept that the world was created and ruled by a god both all-powerful and all-benevolent. Darwin threatened to banish the Creator and replace him with dumb matter and mere chance. The stakes were high enough that Agassiz could take comfort in images of glaciers inflicting on innocent animals coldness, hunger, bewilderment, despair, and death, none ever knowing why they had to be sacrificed. But perhaps Agassiz tried not to think about such images too much. Long before Darwin, the contradictions of monotheism had been making theologians crazy.

I reached the rim of the volcano. I stood there breath taking in both senses of the term. I looked down, more than two thousand feet down, into the pit of the volcano. I saw the source, the engine that had built the volcano. The volcano was full of powerful upward jagged shapes, full of surrealistic colors. I saw into an earth that had turned itself inside out.

As I'd approached the rim, I'd been walking into stronger winds, and on the rim the wind rushed past me with power and chill, blowing on my biological flame, stealing my tiny warmth. I got out a heavier jacket and buried my hands in its pockets. The wind blew my thoughts into an image of the continental air currents running into the mountain and being forced to rise. In winter this rising made the air condense into snow, and in summer it generated thunderstorms. As the wind topped the rim it accelerated and cascaded downward, an avalanche of air, a lava flow of air. The wind plunged into the volcano and then up and over the opposite rim and plunged down again, a long downward stroke that made that side of the volcano chronically windy, a stroke with which the wind painted with van Gogh energy an air portrait of the mountain. The wind painted my portrait and made me small and transient.

Cut into the opposite rim was a large gap where the volcano had collapsed long ago. I could see far into the distance, down another five thousand feet, dozens of miles into the Painted Desert, another landscape of surrealistic colors, painted by far more ancient volcanoes, which had also turned trees into stone.

The Painted Desert might be a hundred degrees today, but right below me were lingering stripes of snow. Once there had been glaciers. Agassiz Peak once held glaciers on both of its shoulders. Some two hundred thousand years ago glaciers 650 feet thick and four miles long had filled the volcano basin. An ice age came, and the snow falling atop Agassiz Peak never melted but built up year after year and turned into ice. From seven cirques the ice built up and began to merge and move downhill, carving into the lava, carving out the shape the inner volcano has today: its broad main basin, its sharp peaks and connecting ridges, its cirques, its moraines where the glaciers stopped and dumped their debris. Three times an ice age came and glaciers formed and flowed out of the volcano just as lava had once flowed out. The glaciers obliterated the life that had thrived inside the volcano.

Hallelujah, Louis Agassiz might have said. It was God's will; it was God's plan; it was God's plow for planting the crown of creation. Never mind if it wasn't clear how cleaning the San Francisco Peaks of life was necessary for human advent. Human minds are too imperfect to grasp Perfection itself. Never mind if for the first ten thousand years after the last ice age this land had been roamed, hunted, and planted by pagans thanking the wrong gods.

Standing on the volcano rim and looking down into the inner

basin was a bit like looking down into a kiva. This volcano didn't have the perfect, circular kiva-like rim of some volcanoes nearby, but it had the deepest chamber, a suitably grand kiva to be the home of the katsinas. I imagined the volcano chamber echoing with the chanting of the katsinas. I imagined that the katsinas went on singing and dancing even here, away from the Hopi villages, because it was in their nature to celebrate life always. I imagined the volcano echoing with drumbeats. I imagined the whole volcano as a drum for amplifying the steadfast, affirmative heartbeats and dance steps of the katsinas, amplifying them into the thunder of July storms that raise the corn and transfer katsina heartbeats and footsteps into Hopi heartbeats and footsteps. The katsinas never stopped because chaos was always sneaking up on the world, ready to assume any form: drought, disease, or *koyaanisqatsi*—moral and social decay. One time the katsinas created a volcano, Sunset Crater, to chastise and frighten the Hopis for their *koyaanisqatsi*, but the volcano itself got out of control, its lava burning the forests and grasslands and heading toward a Hopi village; the katsinas summoned the wind to blow onto the lava and cool it down and stop it.

A trail followed the rim and then dipped onto the back side of Agassiz Peak. I followed it, followed the contour of ancient violence, creativity, and collapse. I wasn't going to try to climb Agassiz Peak, for it was officially closed to protect a rare alpine wildflower that grew upon it, grew even here where there was little but rock and lichen. Ancient creativity. My boots crunched on the rocks rough and pocked from ancient violence, black rocks, a condensation of the night sky, a concentration of the ancient violence and creativity of the universe.

I doubt that Louis Agassiz would have approved of his peak being inhabited by pagan gods. Agassiz didn't have much respect for Native Americans. Agassiz was so averse to the possibility of evolution that he refused to accept that all the races of humans had descended from Adam and Eve, for this would mean that human types could change. Each race must have been created separately, and not equally. Agassiz's pronouncements about the inferiority of blacks made him especially popular in the American South. He saw Indians too as inferior, though their dead bodies made entertaining museum exhibits. Agassiz once wrote to Secretary of War Edwin Stanton asking to be sent "one or two handsome fellows entire and the heads of two or three more."[4]

Louis Agassiz might have preferred to see his volcano as a cathedral, a cathedral of arches soaring skyward, of heavy stone yielding to the ethereal, pointing away from Earth and earthly powers, toward a greater power that ruled the cosmos.

Monotheism was such a powerful idea that humans found it hard to resist, even when it came without conquistadores. Instead of humans being balls in a contest of hundreds of gods where even the best gods were limited and unreliable and where many were malicious, humans could have the complete protection of the power that created and moved every atom, every cell, every star in the universe, created them out of absolute love and moved them all for human benefit. Humans could know that their lives were part of a master plan of love that had existed before time and that beckoned them to a complete fulfillment in heaven. The monotheistic god was both far larger and far closer than nature gods, both infinite and very personal, knowing your every worry and wish and ready to translate needs into realities.

Monotheism gained momentum not just from personal needs but also from societal needs: as human societies became more complex, their needs were no longer answered by nature gods and tribal gods. In complex societies and in a world of conflicting empires, human survival was dependent less on nature and more on social relationships. The old nature gods had offered only limited moral codes, and the tribal gods had often encouraged humans to disregard and devour one another. Human survival now required universal and strong moral codes, enforceable by heaven and hell, requiring strangers to have moral duties to one another, requiring the strongest to respect the weakest.

The philosophical knot in monotheism was the problem of evil. If God was both all-powerful and all-good, it wasn't clear why evil should exist at all. In the pagan universe if a village or a child was obliterated by a volcano it only confirmed what you already knew about the universe: the volcano god was a treacherous rascal. The only question was whether humans had done something to offend the volcano god, and the answer was to make better offerings to the volcano god or to some antivolcano god. But in the monotheistic universe every innocent child and village obliterated was also a philosophical crisis. Why did God allow evil? Maybe God wasn't all-powerful after all, or maybe he wasn't really all-good, only capricious. To escape from the non sequiturs of monotheism, theologians have committed a few thousand years of philosophical contortions. The main escape route was to blame evil on humans, on Adam and Eve, who had ruined a perfect creation. But this raised all sorts of intractable problems, such as why an all-knowing God hadn't known that giving humans free will would bring ruin to his plans and misery to his beloved creation. Then there was the problem of how the hell that was required to regulate moral behavior could be reconciled with a loving God.

Then along came Darwin, who pulled the already shaky foundations out from under monotheism. If the creation didn't include the Garden of Eden, if chaos and predation and disease and volcanoes and death had existed long before humans appeared, then Adam and Eve couldn't take the blame and relieve God of creating an evil world.

Louis Agassiz became so obsessed with beating back Darwin that he too was ready to jettison the Garden of Eden and original sin, replacing them with multiple creations, creations of successive waves of life, creations of separate human races. Many theologians complained that Agassiz was missing the whole point: the moral logic of Christianity demanded Adam and Eve and original sin. Agassiz's vision of aeons of howling beasts and idiot dinosaurs was nearly as pointless and morally bankrupt as Darwin's vision. Yet Agassiz saw no escape. His system of ice ages and continuing creations was a tortured way of putting God back into command.

Theologians and scientists agreed on one thing, that Louis Agassiz had lost his head, or buried his head in the sand. The San Francisco earthquake of 1906, in which God destroyed a city and even churches named in honor of Saint Francis, provided a visual metaphor about Agassiz. Above the doorway of the Stanford University zoology building stood a statue of Agassiz. The earthquake knocked Agassiz off his pedestal and sent him flying headfirst into the concrete sidewalk, where he stood upside down, buried to his chest. People commented that Agassiz was trying to inspect the earthquake, or hide from it. The president of Stanford, David Starr Jordan, said that "Agassiz was great in the abstract but not in the concrete."[5] In truth, Agassiz had spent years hiding from the powers of the earth, the raw powers that moved tectonic plates and caused earthquakes and built volcanoes, powers that now shoved Agassiz from his pedestal as an authority on natural history.

As monotheism spread around the world it repeatedly contested with paganism for loyalties, and it offered new interpretations of natural forces. In 1892 Tennyson wrote a poem, "Kapiolani," about this clash of worldviews on Hawaii. Kapiolani, the wife of a Hawaiian chief, had converted to Christianity and was determined to prove that the native belief in Pele, the volcano goddess, was a foolish superstition. Kapiolani climbed to the rim of Kilauea, ignoring warnings that Pele would strike her dead. Kapiolani declared that she could not be killed by a nonexistent god, that the volcano had been created by her god, that her god gave her his protection. She broke another taboo by picking some sacred berries and eating them, when they were supposed to be offered to Pele. Then she threw stones into the volcano, another insult to Pele. Then she prayed and sang a Christian hymn. She walked down from the volcano unharmed and triumphant.

In Iceland the Vikings were strongly divided between their old religion and Christianity. At their annual assembly, the Althing, held in a volcanic amphitheater that amplified the voices of the speakers, the Vikings were debating if they should convert to Christianity. Then a messenger reported that a new volcanic eruption was threatening valuable farmlands. The pagan Vikings asserted that this was proof that the pagan gods were angry at being abandoned. But wise Snorri, the speaker of the Althing, pointed to the volcanic cliffs and plains all around them and asked what had angered the gods to make them create all this. Volcanism had always been here and always would be. Perhaps it was even a natural force. The Althing then voted to endorse Christianity.

Yet Christianity wouldn't stop volcanoes from erupting and threatening humans, and often people only switched from setting up pagan idols in the path of the lava to setting up iron crosses and statues of saints, which melted and burned up just as thoroughly.

The contest over the meanings of volcanoes goes on even today, even over the San Francisco Peaks. The Peaks remain sacred to the Hopis, who make ceremonial visits to longtime shrines there, to keep humans and nature in harmony. Yet whites have long been ready to impose their own meanings—or lack of meanings—onto the Peaks.

It started with the names. Saint Francis, with his respect for nature, was soon crowded by names honoring America's conquest of nature. The tallest peak was named for General A. A. Humphreys, chief of the Army Corps of Topographical Engineers, which made the maps for Manifest Destiny. Humphreys never even saw the peak named for him. The third-highest peak was named for John C. Frémont, "the Great Pathfinder of the West." Another peak was named for Allen Doyle, a local cattleman who got turned into a character in a Zane Grey novel.

Whites did their best to turn the Peaks into loot. Prospectors combed it but found little mineral wealth. Basque sheepherders roamed high and devastated the alpine vegetation and carved their names and love lives into thousands of aspen trees. Lumbermen would have scalped the peaks if not for the easier timber below. In the 1980s a teenager craze for stonewashed jeans fueled the rapid expansion of a pumice quarry on the side of the Peaks visible from the Hopi villages. In the 1930s locals started a ski area on the outer flank of Mount Agassiz. The Hopis didn't like it, but no one paid any attention to them. Decades later the ski area was expanded to near the top of Mount Agassiz, with an Agassiz Chairlift and an Agassiz Lodge. By 2000 a deepening drought was keeping the ski area closed for much of the winters, so the owners proposed snowmaking machinery, common enough elsewhere, but those elsewheres had ample water supplies; Arizona did not. Here the water would come from reclaimed sewage piped up the mountain. This was the white man's solution to global warming: pee on it. The Hopis compared it to their walking into a cathedral and urinating on the altar. The

Hopis had a thousand-year memory of what happens when drought strikes, but the skiers dismissed the Hopis as cranks.

In Glacier National Park, Agassiz Glacier was melting.

It was an inversion of global warming that gave rise to the most lasting symbol of technology run amok. Mary Shelley and Percy Bysshe Shelley and Lord Byron went to the Swiss Alps in 1816, the heyday of romanticism, to absorb the Alpine sublime. But 1816 was the year after Tambora erupted in Indonesia, the worst volcanic eruption in centuries. Tambora poured so much ash into the atmosphere that the whole Earth cooled down. In Europe there was no summer, only gloomy skies and rain, so Mary Shelley and her companions stayed indoors and tried to entertain themselves by inventing ghost stories. Mary Shelley created *Frankenstein*. Frankenstein's monster was congealed from angry volcanic ashes to warn Europeans about their notion that nature was controllable.

I stood right beneath Agassiz Peak, inside the volcano. I could have saved myself a lot of hiking effort by riding up the Agassiz Chairlift on the outside, which was open as a summer tourist attraction. Click-click, click-click, the gears and cables of the clockwork universe go. The click-clicks are powered by coal being burned, by carbon pouring into the sky, the carbon of ancient howling beasts and idiot plants, coal taken from the Hopi mesas, from under katsinas warning that nature might be beyond human control.

As Christianity spread, it often lightened perceptions of natural landscapes. It swept the evil spirits out of mountains, rivers, and clouds, and encouraged humans to see nature as a gift from God, a testament to God's power and generosity. It prepared the way for romantics to view the Alps not as a monstrous wilderness but as a realm of divinity. It gave Louis Agassiz permission to view Alpine glaciers as the helping hand of God. It encouraged romantics to view Native Americans like the Hopis as living harmoniously with harmonious nature. But there was one natural landscape that became more ominous: volcanoes.

In the Christian universe the moral drama became more central, punishment for moral failures became more urgent, and hell became more essential. Volcanoes were a perfect fit for hell. Christians pictured volcanoes as the chimneys of hell or the gateway to hell. Hell was a lake of lava-like fire, with choking, sulfurous fumes and black smoke. Mountains might be God's work, but volcanoes were the devil's lair. The hissings and roarings that came from volcanoes were the moans and screams of the damned. Preachers urged sinners to imagine their flesh burning in lava lakes for eternity. Dante made his inferno a deep pit reaching into the center of the earth, with many volcanic aspects. Milton had his devils build Pandemonium, the capital of hell, on the side of a volcano. In Iceland the Christians tried to de-demonize volcanoes like Hekla, but in the fourteenth century a German physician, Caspar Peucer, wrote: "Out of the bottomless abyss of Heklafell, or rather out of Hell itself, rise melancholy cries and loud wailings, so that these may be heard for many miles around. Coal-black ravens and vultures flutter about. There is to be found the Gate of Hell and whenever great battles are fought or there is bloody carnage somewhere on the globe, then there may be heard in the mountain fearful howlings, weeping and gnashing of teeth."[6]

I stared down into the pit of hell and listened for howlings. I heard only the howling of the wind. It was rather chilly too. This gate of hell had closed. Now it served a different vision of nature, served as the home of katsinas and rain clouds that brought life. Even within Christian cosmology, visions of hell were quite different from the vision of Saint Francis.

The Christian preoccupation with the moral drama, and the withdrawal of God from the natural world to a distant throne, seems to have left a void in the human heart. Humans still live in nature and respond to its seasons and weather and light and creatures; even the urban world is full of flowerpots and bird feeders. This void encouraged Christianized versions of old responses to nature. Mother Mary filled some of the role of the old Mother Earth goddesses. More than anyone, Saint Francis tried to repersonalize and respiritualize the human relationship with nature. He saw God everywhere in nature, a nature that was not an abstract symbol of divinity or a resource given for human exploitation, but a friendly fellowship of creatures. Saint Francis not only preached to people about birds, but also preached to the birds themselves about praising their creator. He didn't draw any borders at the inanimate world but saw the sun and moon—against which other Christians were wary due to long-standing pagan associations—as Brother Sun and Sister Moon. He took delight in everything and avoided harming anything; he couldn't even bear to blow out a candle flame, for it was Brother Fire: "beautiful, merry, robust, and strong."

Did Saint Francis even see erupting volcanoes as Brother Fire? Brother of Pompeii. Brother of Herculaneum. In Italy the volcanoes are fueled by the same tectonic plates that produced the 1997 earthquake that brought down the roof of the basilica of Saint Francis in Assisi, killing two Franciscan friars, cracking the frescoes showing Saint Francis communing with nature.

Was Saint Francis ever troubled by the contradictions of praising a creation that was cracked with flaws, with evil? Clearly, Saint Francis was obsessed with the inequities of the human world: he went to heroic lengths to live humbly and to help the poor.

Surely, a man of such conscience should be troubled by the inequities of the natural world, by sparrows being devoured by predators, by Franciscans being killed by geology. Perhaps he was troubled by inequities when he made his ascent of Mount La Verna, an ascent that would give rise to one of the most famous pilgrimages in Christendom. Francis was only two years away from dying, and his body was already failing. He was too weak to walk up Mount La Verna and had to ride on a donkey. He was going blind. The eyes that had given him glorious visions of natural beauty were being taken away from him. God's natural revelation would become only darkness. Francis was going up Mount La Verna to fast and pray in solitude for forty days.

Once in his youth Louis Agassiz nearly went blind. For weeks he was shut in a darkened room. He had to study his fossils by touch, and where his fingers weren't sensitive enough he started using his tongue. Agassiz tasted God's thoughts. God was speaking in tongues, speaking through the tongues of fishes and frogs, speaking a strange language that signified salvation.

Francis had become so close to God that miracles accompanied him everywhere. The previous Christmas, Francis was blessing a

nativity scene when the sleeping Christ doll opened his eyes. Now
on the hot trek up Mount La Verna one of his companions collapsed
from thirst, but Francis summoned the rocks to produce a spring.
When Francis sat under an oak tree to rest, birds came to welcome
him. During his forty-day vigil Francis's only companions were two
falcons, which awakened him each morning at the right time to
offer prayers. Francis believed that the strange boulders on Mount
La Verna were shaken loose by the same miraculous earthquake that
had accompanied the death of Christ.

Mount La Verna is an eerie landscape of peaks and chasms, caves
and cavities, columns and boulders. Mount La Verna is a volcanic
outcrop. It was a suitably strange landscape for the strangest miracle
of all. After praying and fasting and yearning, Francis reached such
intense spiritual ecstasy that at last he merged with God, merged
with Christ so thoroughly that Francis received Christ's marks of
Crucifixion: bleeding wounds in his palms, his feet, his side. It was
the first time that any believer had ever been given stigmata. Francis had long prayed to share in the suffering and humility of Christ,
and now he had been granted the ultimate blessing. Francis gazed at
his palms, at the raw, torn, raised craters where the nails had stabbed
out; he stared at the flesh volcanoes, volcanoes pouring out warm
blood. He reached out his hands in glory and thanks. He had been
granted a vision of the innermost secret workings of the universe.
The universe was a crucifixion. It had to be a crucifixion, for that was
the only way to solve the paradoxes of monotheism and to make the
universe a story of love and Brother Fire and birds singing praises
to the creator. Crucifixion was the only way to escape from Adam
and Eve creating evil, which in turn had been the only way to escape
from a benevolent God creating evil. There had to be a redemption,
a second chance to allow humans to escape the sin of Adam and Eve.
Evil might still be the fault of humans, but God would set things
right anyway because he loved humans so much he couldn't bear to
see them suffer. God would make a great sacrifice to set the universe
right, a sacrifice beyond the imaginings of the pagans who sacrificed
berries and goats and virgins by throwing them into volcanoes. God
would sacrifice himself; the God of the whole universe would nail

himself to a cross and bleed and suffer and die so that puny, unworthy humans could escape; God would leave humans in so much awe at his gift that they would forget all about the goddamned tortuous, hopeless illogic of creation, good and evil, imperfection and suffering, and they would rejoice.

Francis stared at the lava oozing from his palms, and he praised Brother Fire, by whom the Lord enlightened the night.

Brother of the crucified Pompeii. Brother of the crucified Herculaneum.

Volcanoes are like stigmata, the stigmata of the earth. An Earth that was covered with thousands of wounds, a leprosy of stigmata. Stigmata pouring out the planet's blood to congeal into bodies of rock and bodies of life, life whose every tree limb was a cross, whose every cactus was a crown of thorns, whose every crying eye socket and matter-rejecting anus was a wound, whose every death was an undeserved punishment. What crime had life committed to deserve its unceasing crucifixion? What original sin had the earth committed to require its unceasing volcanic sweat lodge of redemption? It was the crime and sin of primordial imperfection, which the earth had tried to heal by pouring from its volcanoes the more perfect bodies of life, then of humans, then of conscious answers to imperfection, answers like crucifixions and katsinas, elaborate story answers like *The Inferno* and *Paradise Lost*, geotheological answers like John Wesley saying that the earth was geoperfect until original sin caused earthquakes and volcanoes, or Louis Agassiz saying that glaciers plowed an ascension to perfection. But the imperfection went on and on; the suffering went on; the confusion went on; the cries of bewilderment went on; all the volcano stigmata of the earth went on pouring out blood but could never redeem creation. The volcanoes went on firing out red-hot lava bullets and ashes, firing them into the sky where at night they blended with the stars, burned with the stars, flew with the flying stars, stars that were the stigmata of a vast creation, a creation that remained wounded and bleeding and unredeemed by the crucifixion of the Big Bang.

I stared down into Saint Francis's volcano. The basin was like a giant palm, a palm being offered to the sky. I stared down into my own palms. Now I was holding out my hands as if I were making an offering. My hands were empty. Did this mean that I was offering nothing? Nothing to the nothing? No, this didn't seem correct. Hadn't I just climbed Saint Francis's mountain just like millions of pilgrims on Mount La Verna? Whatever I was seeking or bringing, I had made a major effort to bring it. I could have ridden up the Agassiz Chairlift: click-click, click-click. Instead, I had hiked for miles, hiked up thousands of feet, every step offered to the volcano. Just like a pilgrimage should, every step had helped wear down and sweat off the self of social presentation and pride and left me simply a body, not even just a human body anymore but a biological body, a body feeling the greater powers from which life arose. I stood there feeling tiny against the power of the volcano. I stood there staring at my outstretched palms. I was offering simply myself, not even myself but mycellf.

When you sweat off the varnish and the dirt and the differences of social roles and tribes and nations and races and history and geography, you are left with tiny human beings facing the enormous powers and mysteries of creation. You are left with the endless question of why the universe contained all the order to create life and humans yet never enough order to sustain and protect human lives—and ever enough chaos to inflict drought and disease and blindness and death. Humans tried every answer to chaos. They beat the drums in katsina ceremonies to try to beat the thunder into order and the rain into a stately procession. They raised crosses to serve as pillars to uphold the universe. They built Frankenstein monsters that only became servants of chaos. None of it worked. Chaos never answered. The offerings were ignored. Humans heard only the voice within themselves that insisted that life was urgently important and should not be extinguished by drought or blindness, fire or ice. If this was not after all the voice of God, then it was still a powerful voice. Perhaps it was the voice of the earth, containing the power of rain and volcanoes, of aeons of fish and forests. It was a voice that humans still honored even in the midst of being tiny bewildered creatures trying to kiva-amplify and cathedral-amplify it into the voice of God. It was honored by Louis Agassiz and his students climbing an

Alps peak to study glaciers and, upon reaching the top, breaking into dance out of sheer exuberance at the glacier-filled view. It was honored by the katsinas dancing upon and stirring up the dust of long-dead people and villages. It was honored by Saint Francis preaching to the birds in a language they spoke without knowing it.

It was honored by my standing on the rim of a volcano and seeing neither hell nor Alpine chasm divinity, but seeing, for cell-ebration, the only kiva or cathedral we would ever have.◦✦

NOTES

1. Quoted, without further reference, in Edwin Lurie, *Louis Agassiz: A Life in Science* (Chicago: University of Chicago Press, 1960), 203.

2. John Greenleaf Whittier, *The Complete Poetical Works of Whittier* (Boston: Houghton Mifflin, 1894), 450.

3. William James, letter to his father, quoted, without further reference, in Lurie, *Louis Agassiz*, 347.

4. Quoted, without further reference, in ibid., 338.

5. David Starr Jordan, *The Days of a Man: Being Memories of a Naturalist, Teacher, and Minor Prophet of Democracy* (Yonkers-on-Hudson, NY: World Book, 1922), 2:173.

6. Quoted, without further reference, in Haraldur Sigurdsson, *Melting the Earth: The History of Ideas on Volcanic Eruptions* (Oxford: Oxford University Press, 1999), 75.

SOURCES AND RESOURCES

This book has covered a lot of ground in both places and subject matters, and since it is not customary for literary nature writing to include extensive footnotes, readers may have some questions about some of these subjects and want to find books for exploring them further.

Geology is the bedrock—literally—of this region and this book, but it can seem an abstract and confusing subject. The book that best brings alive the geology of this region is *Ancient Landscapes of the Colorado Plateau* by Ron Blakey and Wayne Ranney (Grand Canyon: Grand Canyon Association, 2008). It includes dozens of ingenious photo-maps that make it easy to visualize landscapes as they changed over the aeons, with oceans and deserts and canyons coming and going, and it includes cross-sections of geological strata in different places. Another general geology book, but more oriented to travelers and hikers, is *Geology Underfoot in Northern Arizona* by Lon Abbott and Terri Cook (Missoula, MT: Mountain Press, 2007). Abbott and Cook include Meteor Crater, which at a mere fifty thousand years old did not qualify as an "ancient landscape" for the Blakey-Ranney book. The San Francisco volcanic field is the focus of the brief *Volcanoes of Northern Arizona* by Wendell A. Duffield (Grand Canyon: Grand Canyon Association, 1997), which includes an aerial photo of NASA's artificial moonscape where the Apollo astronauts did their geology training. That training was led by USGS geologist Dale Jackson, and his daughter Marie Jackson wrote a unique book, *Stone Landmarks: Flagstaff's Geology and Historic Building Stones* (Flagstaff, AZ: Piedra Azul Press, 1999) that includes the geological stories on display in downtown Flagstaff's old stone buildings.

The annular eclipse in the introduction happened in May 2012, not only at the Grand Canyon but across several southwestern states. The rangers at Grand Canyon National Park organized a large public event to honor the eclipse, including lectures and telescope viewings. By the start of the twenty-first century the National Park Service had discovered that many of its visitors, coming from urban areas, had never gotten a clear view of the night sky, never seen thousands of stars at once or the Milky Way. With their more remote locations, national parks offer brilliant skies, and the National Park Service has expanded its mission of introducing people to the wonders of nature to include telescope viewings of nature's largest dimension. The only book on this subject is *Stars Above, Earth Below: A Guide to Astronomy in the National Parks* by Tyler Nordgren (Chichester, UK: Springer, 2010). It makes many connections between sky and Earth, such as the geological common ground between red Mars and southwestern red rocks, and Ancestral Puebloan archaeoastronomy. It also contains a few pages on Meteor Crater, though the crater is not a national park. The best book about eclipses is *Totality: Eclipses of the Sun* by Mark Littmann, Ken Willcox, and Fred Espenak, 3rd ed. (New York: Oxford University Press, 2009).

Lowell Observatory, which "stars" in several of these chapters, offers one of the best public welcomes of any observatory in America, and you can even look through the 1895 Alvin Clark telescope that "discovered" the expanding universe. If you need to visit Lowell Observatory by book, a good introduction is *Lowell Observatory* by Kevin Schindler (Charleston, SC: Arcadia, 2016), part of the popular Images of America series that centers on historic photographs, with just enough text to explain the basics. A more in-depth book is Schindler's *The Far End of the Journey: Lowell Observatory's 24-Inch Clark Telescope* (Flagstaff, AZ: Lowell Observatory, 2016), a coffee-table book that covers all of Lowell Observatory history but focuses on the telescope itself and its recent renovation. Still more in-depth is *The Explorers of Mars Hill: More Than a Century of History at Lowell Observatory* by William Lowell Putnam and others (Flagstaff, AZ: Lowell Observatory, 2012). The best biography of founder Percival Lowell is *Percival Lowell: The Culture and Science of a Boston Brahmin* by David Strauss (Cambridge, MA: Harvard University Press, 2000). Lowell Observatory astronomer A. E. Douglass gave birth to the science of dendrochronology—tree-ring dating—and the book devoted to both is *Tree Rings and Telescopes: The Scientific Career of A. E. Douglass* (Tucson: University of Arizona Press, 1983).

Lowell Observatory provides one of this book's strongest connections between the ancient landscapes of the Southwest and the deep time and evolution of the scientific cosmos, for it was Lowell Observatory that discovered the most important evidence for the expanding universe: the redshifts of the galaxies. For decades science historians have given Edwin Hubble the credit for discovering the expanding universe, but lately a revisionist trend has spread the credit more broadly. The story of this discovery is best told by Marcia Bartusiak in *The Day We Found the Universe* (New York: Pantheon Books, 2009), which includes plenty of colorful background stories about the people involved, including Lowell Observatory's Vesto Slipher. With the best spectrograph of his time, Slipher began studying the motions of "spiral nebulae" and found that they showed fantastic motions, mostly outward, too fast for them to be mere gas clouds in our own galaxy, as had long been supposed. Yet Slipher hesitated, as did most astronomers, to draw the conclusion that the nebulae were other galaxies, for this required accepting two new and extraordinary ideas: the universe was vastly larger than we had ever imagined, and the galaxies were racing outward, as if the universe had had a beginning. Slipher probably also hesitated because Percival Lowell, in his obsession with Martians and their canals, had given Lowell Observatory a bad reputation, and Slipher was wary of endorsing far more outrageous ideas. Thus, it would be too generous to say that Slipher "discovered" the expanding universe and best to say that he discovered the primary evidence for it, which Edwin Hubble soon built upon to prove the idea. In 2012 Lowell Observatory hosted a scholarly conference on how the idea of the expanding universe took shape, and the proceedings can be found in *Origins of the Expanding Universe, 1912–1932* (San Francisco: Astronomical Society of the Pacific, 2013). Writing biographies of important astronomers is a neglected field, so there has been no biography of Slipher and only one major biography of Hubble: *Edwin Hubble: Mariner of the Nebulae* by Gale Christianson (New York: Farrar, Straus, and Giroux, 1995). Edwin Hubble's 1928 visit to Slipher and the Grand Canyon in search of a site for the world's greatest observatory is a long-lost story that I detailed in my own *Canyon of Dreams: Stories from Grand Canyon History* (Salt Lake City: University of Utah Press, 2014). The only previous mention of this story was by Donald E. Osterbrock in his *Pauper and Prince: Ritchey, Hale, and Big American Telescopes* (Tucson: University of Arizona Press, 1993), which offers the stories of the two other major astronomers in my "Storm Pattern" chapter, George Ritchey and George Hale. A more through biography of Hale is *Explorer of the Universe: A Biography of George Ellery Hale* by Helen Wright (New York: American Institute of Physics, 1994).

Mars was central to the history of Lowell Observatory and to my chapter "The Blood of the Martians." Percival Lowell's connection with Mars can be explored in William Graves Hoyt's *Lowell and Mars* (Tucson: University of Arizona Press, 1996). Available in various reprint editions are Percival Lowell's three books: *Mars* (1895), *Mars and Its Canals* (1906), and *Mars as the Abode of Life* (1908), in which Lowell spun elaborate theories about intelligent life on Mars. Two cultural histories that explore changing popular and fictional images of Mars are *Imagining Mars: A Literary History* by Robert Crossley (Middleton, CT: Wesleyan University Press, 2011) and *Dying Planet: Mars in Science and the Imagination* by Robert Markley (Durham, NC: Duke University Press, 2005). My science fiction visions of Mars come from Edgar Rice Burroughs, who published a dozen Mars novels beginning with *The Princess of Mars* (Chicago: A. C. McClurg, 1917), H. G. Wells's *The War of the Worlds* (New York: Penguin Viking, 2005), and Ray Bradbury's *The Martian Chronicles* (New York: Doubleday, 1950).

A good introduction to Meteor Crater is *Meteor Crater* by Neal F. Davis, part of the Images of America series (Charleston, SC: Arcadia, 2016), and a detailed look at its role in geological and astronomical history is *Coon Mountain Controversies: Meteor Crater and the Development of Impact Theory* by William Graves Hoyt (Tucson:

University of Arizona Press, 1987). It is surprising that right into the 1960s scientists were still debating whether Meteor Crater was indeed a meteor-impact crater, and the man who settled the question was Eugene Shoemaker, whose story can be found in *Shoemaker by Levy: The Man Who Made an Impact* by David Levy (Princeton, NJ: Princeton University Press, 2000). Shoemaker was also responsible for training the Apollo astronauts in geology, which included building the artificial moonscape in Flagstaff. Little has been written about this moonscape, but an in-depth book about the role of geology in the Apollo program is *To a Rocky Moon: A Geologist's History of Lunar Exploration* by Don E. Wilhelms (Tucson: University of Arizona Press, 1993). The most substantial and reliable biography of Neil Armstrong is *First Man: The Life of Neil A. Armstrong* by James R. Hansen (New York: Simon and Schuster, 2005). The story of the Apollo astronauts doing their geology training in and around the Grand Canyon is told in my own *Canyon of Dreams: Stories from Grand Canyon History*.

There is an abundance of books about the Grand Canyon, on every subject. For a history that offers something about everything, see my *Grand Canyon: A History of a Natural Wonder and National Park* (Reno: University of Nevada Press, 2015). The story of the Desert View Watchtower and Mary Colter is told, with many photos, in *Mary Colter: Architect of the Southwest* by Arnold Berke (New York: Princeton Architectural Press, 2002). Colter's own guidebook to the Desert View Watchtower, written in 1933 for the guides who would be giving tours of it, is now back in print: *Watchtower at Desert View* (Grand Canyon: Grand Canyon Association, 2015).

My Sedona chapter explores the way that humans see, or fail to see, the universe; it goes back and forth between the rock-real universe and humans aspirations for something more. The rock-real story is told (with many helpful illustrations) by Wayne Ranney in *Sedona Through Time: A Guide to Sedona's Geology* (Flagstaff, AZ: Zia Press, 2010). Psychologist Carl Jung was tempted by the idea of flying saucers and wise aliens, but he knew too much about the workings of the human mind not to see old human spiritual needs going to work on new material. His *Flying Saucers: A Modern Myth of Things Seen in the Sky* (Hove, UK: Psychology Press, 2002) was the first important book to treat UFOs as a psychological and cultural phenomenon. By the 1990s the Smithsonian Institution seemed to regard UFOs as a valid subject for cultural history, for in 1994 it published *Watch the Skies! A Chronicle of the Flying Saucer Myth* by Curtis Peebles, which traces the origin, personalities, and trends of the UFO phenomenon—though the trends have continued evolving since then. A more personal inquiry into UFO culture is *UFO Religion: Inside Flying Saucer Cults and Culture* (London: I. B. Tauris, 2007), and a scholarly collection is *UFO Religions*, edited by Christopher Partridge (Abingdon, UK: Rutledge, 2003). Anyone seeking books more sympathetic to UFOs or the New Age movement has plenty to choose from, but the ones mentioned here are Emanuel Swedenborg's *Life on Other Planets* (West Chester, PA: Swedenborg Foundation, 2006), Gary David's *The Orion Zone: Ancient Star Cities of the American Southwest* (Kempton, IL: Adventures Unlimited Press, 2015), *Lupo: Conversations with an E.T.* by Louise Rose Aveni (Sarasota, FL: Peppertree Press, 2007), and Jim Sparks's *The Keepers: An Alien Message for the Human Race*, 2nd ed. (Columbus, NC: Granite, 2008).

Most of the books about Monument Valley are basic introductions for tourists, but one that goes deeper into its lore is *Land of Room Enough and Time Enough* by Richard Klinck. First published by the University of New Mexico Press in 1953, it has gone in and out of print several times, from various publishers, but secondhand copies are not hard to find online.

The Hubbell Trading Post, now a National Historic Site, is a bit off the beaten path but offers a time-machine journey into the past, as it is maintained as a genuine 1900 Navajos trading post, its store with "bull pen" counters and an iron stove in the middle. You can still buy food there or high-quality Navajo rugs and other crafts. You can also take tours of the art-filled Hubbell home. The best book on the family and their business is *Hubbell Trading Post: Trade, Tourism, and the Navajo Southwest* by Erica Cottam (Norman: University of Oklahoma Press, 2015). A more biographical account of founder John Lorenzo Hubbell is *Indian Trader: The Life of J. L. Hubbell* by Martha Blue (Walnut, CA: Kiva, 2000). There are a number of memoirs written by trading-post owners, which often give excellent looks at Native American life. The two mentioned here are *Navajo Trading Days* by Elizabeth Compton Hegemann (Albuquerque: University of New Mexico Press, 1963) and *Navajo Trader* by Gladwell Richardson (Tucson: University of Arizona Press, 1986).

There are many books on Navajo weaving and rugs, but only some go into its history and meaning for Navajos. In the course of my research into the origins of the Storm Pattern design, I found that some authors take a dismissive attitude toward the Navajos, portraying them as merely following orders, merely weaving designs invented by and assigned to them by white trading-post owners, as if Navajos didn't have their own creativity, traditions, or spiritual life. This condescending attitude has been only reinforced by postmodernist trends in academia, which encourage historians to interpret virtually everything as a function of capitalist exploitation. But for the Storm Pattern design, at least, the truth is far richer, offering us a glimpse of ancient Navajo spirituality. Since its first publication in 1934, one of the most personal encounters with Navajo weaving is anthropologist Gladys A. Reichard's *Spider Woman: A Story of Navajo Weavers and Chanters* (Albuquerque: University of New Mexico Press, 1997), which looks not just at weaving but at Navajo religion and everyday life. Two books that focus more on the interaction between Navajo weavers and white traders are *Patterns of Exchange: Navajo Weavers and Traders* by Teresa J. Wilkins (Norman: University of Oklahoma Press, 2008) and *Rugs and Posts: The Story of Navajo Weaving and Indian Trading* by H. L. James (Atglen, PA: Schiffer Books, 2005).

Our understanding of Navajo creation stories and other spiritual traditions has often been garbled by Euro-American misunderstandings or impositions, Navajo reticence, blendings of Navajo ideas with Christianity or Puebloan ideas, or contradictory accounts. For anthropologists, one of the basic sources is Washington Matthews, who came to the Southwest in the 1880s as a US Army surgeon but was deeply fascinated by Navajo ceremonies and made extensive records of them, including *The Night Chant* and *The Mountain*

Chant, both kept in print by the University of Utah Press in 2002. A more recent and poetic rendering was given by Paul G. Zolbrod in *Diné Bahane': The Navajo Creation Story* (Albuquerque: University of New Mexico Press, 1984). My interpretation of the blendings of Navajo cosmology with Puebloan ideas owed much to Jerold E. Levy's *In the Beginning: The Navajo Genesis* (Berkeley: University of California Press, 1998).

For anyone intrigued to discover that the Navajos have their own constellations, based on lifeways and stories very different from Western traditions, the best book for pursuing this subject further is *Sharing the Skies: Navajo Astronomy* by Nancy C. Maryboy and David Begay (Tucson: Rio Nuevo Press, 2010). A more scholarly and detailed exploration of Navajo astronomy, especially as it manifests itself in sandpaintings, is *Earth Is My Mother, Sky Is My Father: Space, Time, and Astronomy in Navajo Sandpaintings* by Trudy Griffin-Pierce, a professor of anthropology at the University of Arizona (Albuquerque: University of New Mexico Press, 1992). A more basic introduction to sandpaintings is *Navajo Sandpaintings* by Mark Bahti and Eugene Baatsoslanni Joe (Tucson: Rio Nuevo Press, 2009). It includes many illustrations and a discussion of how sandpaintings have evolved—some Navajos would say "devolved"—from sacred ritual into commercial art. For readers ready for a Jungian interpretation of sandpaintings and Navajo spirituality, try *Navaho Symbols of Healing: A Jungian Exploration of Ritual, Image and Medicine* by Donald Sandner (Rochester, VT: Healing Arts Press, 1979).

For a more general introduction to Navajo life and culture, the best source may be *Navajo* by Susanne Page and Jake Page (Tucson: Rio Nuevo Press, 2010). A more thorough and politically minded history is *Diné: A History of the Navajos* by Peter Iverson (Albuquerque: University of New Mexico Press, 2002). For anyone wanting to explore Navajo and Hopi lands, a good travel guide, including a lot of background information, is *Native Roads: The Complete Motoring Guide to the Navajo and Hopi Nations* by Fran Kosik, 3rd ed. (Tucson: Rio Nuevo Press, 2013).

Even more than with the Navajos, ideas about the Hopis have been clouded by many impositions by whites, including academics, who have had their own agendas, whether political or spiritual. Unfortunately, the most widely read book about the Hopis, Frank Waters's *The Book of the Hopi* (New York: Viking Penguin, 1963), is also one of the least reliable. A more accurate introduction (and with beautiful photographs) is *Hopi* by Susanne Page and Jake Page (New York: Abrams, 1982). Also respected for its accuracy is Harold Courlander's *The Fourth World of the Hopis: The Epic Story of the Hopi Indians as Preserved in Their Legends and Traditions* (Albuquerque: University of New Mexico Press, 1971). For a Hopi-written introduction to katsinas and katsina dolls, see Alph H. Secakuku's *Hopi Kachina Traditions: Following the Sun and Moon* (Flagstaff, AZ: Northland, 1995). A scholarly study of evolving katsina practices is *Kachinas in the Pueblo World* edited by Polly Schaafsma (Salt Lake City: University of Utah Press, 2000), but as is often the case, the anthropological version of events does not entirely coincide with Native American traditions. The katsina-doll carver I mentioned, Ramson Lomatewama, is also a fine poet, and though his books are out of print they are easy to find online; the best start is *Going Through Ancestor Dreams: New and Selected Poems* (Flagstaff, AZ: Northland, 1993). The best book about cottonwood trees, including their mythology, is *The Cottonwood: An American Champion* by Kathleen Cain (Boulder, CO: Johnson Books, 2007).

From its first publication in 1960, Edward Lurie's biography *Louis Agassiz: A Life in Science* (Baltimore: Johns Hopkins University Press, 1988) remained the main biography of Agassiz, but it was joined, if not surpassed, by Christoph Irmscher's *Louis Agassiz: Creator of American Science* (Boston: Houghton Mifflin, 2013).•✦

ACKNOWLEDGMENTS

MY FIRST THANKS go to Judy LeFevre, a wonderful teacher who has mentored many students, but especially me. I have also appreciated the generous encouragement of Caroline Werkley and Terra Waters.

Literary astronomy essays are not a common form, but some creative editors have recognized their value and made room for my essays, starting with Richard Berry of the magazine *Astronomy*. Editors who published these chapters in their literary magazines were Ronald Spatz, Peter Stitt, Kim Groninga, Joanna Semeiks, Kwame Dawes, and Jessica Housand-Weaver. Other appreciated editors include Susan Bright, Ann Starr, Ruth Thompson, and Christine Cote. I am especially grateful to Justin Race of the University of Nevada Press for believing in this book, and Annette Wenda for her fine editing.

Thanks to the Stilley family for their friendship and for giving me such a great place to live.

Many friends have helped this book in various ways: Antoinette Beiser and Kevin Schindler of Lowell Observatory; Kim Besom, Mike Quinn, and Colleen Hyde of the Museum Collection at Grand Canyon National Park; Richard Quartaroli of Cline Library Special Collections at Northern Arizona University; and Jim Babbitt, Richard and Sherry Mangum, Stewart Aitchison, Wayne and Helen Ranney, Tom Martin, Hazel Clark, Tom Bean, Susan Lamb, Marie Jackson, Matt Goodwin, Ramson Lomatewama, Vernon Laban, and Jenny Blue.•✦

ABOUT THE AUTHOR

DON LAGO lives in a cabin in the pine forest outside Flagstaff, Arizona. For twenty-five years he has explored the Grand Canyon, kayaking it six times and doing backcountry research. He is the author of two Grand Canyon history books: *Grand Canyon: A History of a Natural Wonder and National Park* and *Canyon of Dreams: Stories from Grand Canyo–n History*. In the 1980s his personal nature and astronomy essays began appearing frequently in *Astronomy* and other magazines and literary reviews, winning several awards and a Pushcart Prize nomination; they were collected in *Starchild: The Human Meanings of the Big Bang Cosmos*. He is also the author of *On the Viking Trail: Travels in Scandinavian America.*▪✦